Growing Edges
in the
Psychology
of
Religion

Growing Edges
in the
Psychology
of
Religion

John R. Tisdale, Editor

Nelson-Hall nh Chicago

Library of Congress Cataloging in Publication Data
Main entry under title:

Growing Edges in the Psychology of Religion

Bibliography: p.
Includes index.
1. Psychology, Religious—Addresses, essays, lectures.
I. Tisdale, John R.
BL53.G784   200'.1'9   79-20116
ISBN 0-88229-338-9 (Cloth)
ISBN 0-88229-748-1 (Paper)

Manufactured in the United States of America

10   9   8   7   6   5   4   3   2   1

Contents

Preface

Why does one try to bring together a collection of materials such as this? In my own case it was precipitated by being asked to teach a class in the psychology of religion in the fall of 1974. I had been doing some research in a related area, and I had taught the course before, but I had not pursued the subject in detail for several years. An examination of the potential texts available and a review of my own experience deepened my conviction that there was an "aliveness" to the field that had not yet been well caught on paper. Out of that conviction came this book.

In order to reflect the current vitality of the psychology of religion, the articles to be included would have to be recent. Work concluded a generation ago might not be at all representative of today's interests. Therefore I had to decide on some point prior to which I would not go. The year 1964 turned out to be the somewhat arbitrary, but quite workable, *terminus a quo*. This is recent enough to be fresh, but far enough back for current trends to establish themselves. You will find nothing here, then, published before that date.

Further, the discovery that there are four rather clear areas of interest and activity is just that—a discovery. So far as I am aware, I had no a priori classification scheme into which I was going to fit the research. A clear sense of the growing edges emerged as I winnowed my way through the literature; it remained only for me to make them explicit. Perhaps this new ordering may provide some perspective that was not present before and some clearer foci for future research.

In their original form, journal articles and papers are not intended for either the general public or first- and second-year college students. Attempts to use them for this latter audience taught me clearly that, if this collection were to speak to more than just a narrow group of professionals, some modifications would be helpful. Accordingly, I set myself the task of "red-penciling" every article I hoped to use (including my own) with an eye toward helping each author to say what he intended as economically and simply as possible. In general, I have eliminated overlapping subject matter, quantitative details not necessary for our purposes here, and technical discussions not needed to understand an author's conclusions. All the articles in here have survived that process. If you sometimes feel that an author has not developed or illustrated a point as clearly as he might, it may be that my editing is at fault and that you should seek out the original version as a comparison. As further moves toward greater readability, I have imposed the same citation system upon every article (translating other systems into this when the original was different) and placed all references in a single list at the end of the book. An introduction to each group provides some background for the articles, and a section following each suggests some places you might wish to go if you are interested in further reading in that area.

A number of people, of course, have been helpful in bringing this to pass. Certainly it could not have happened without those who have been involved in these growing edges putting their work on paper, and copyright holders giving reprint permission. The hours of labor typing letters and drafts of the article revisions put in by Lorraine Cameron and Jill Jaros have been indispensable. A special kind of debt is also owed to Charles E. Peterson, the Dean who gave me the opportunity (and the necessity) to teach that course, and to the students in that 1974 class who reacted to my basic idea and the ways in which I first expressed it. Although the work was begun before we were married, Beverly created a very special atmosphere with her own warm encouragement and clear thinking.

Part One

Definition
and
Measurement

INTRODUCTION

One growing edge in the psychology of religion has to do with the nature of the concept being studied—religion itself. What is *religion*? How can it best be studied and measured? The answers to such questions are not separate from each other; they are intertwined. To a psychologist, how an individual's religion or religiousness is defined will certainly help to determine how it will be measured. Conversely, the methods used to measure a concept are operational definitions of the concept being measured. Though this kind of problem is probably not immediately exciting to most people, it is important, with implications for other areas of activity, and some history behind it.

The early psychologists of religion relied heavily on questionnaires to measure religion. They also relied upon individuals' own perceptions of what was religious for them. In his classic, William James (1902) analyzed some extreme literary reports of the religious phenomena he discussed, reasoning (in a manner not unlike an essential assumption of animal researchers) that, by examining cases in which behavior could be seen in purer, less complicated forms, one could better understand the mass of instances in which the behavior was not so readily observable. Leuba (1896 and 1912) made use of autobiographical questionnaires, as did Starbuck (1899) in a monumental study of conversion and religious (essentially Christian) growth. In 1916 Coe recognized these methods as well, but he added to them the necessity for laboratory experiments and the use of controls in field research. In this connection he specifically alluded to a method for ranking data but seems not to have used it himself. However, he had by that time already made use of temperament ratings and simple experiments on suggestibility (Coe, 1900).

Although most of these men did indeed have their own definitions of religion, they all insisted that, when carrying out empirical research, one must finally depend upon the subjects themselves to tell the investigators when their own actions or behaviors are religious or have religious significance. There were no really adequate external criteria for identifying individual religious behavior.

Nor are there today. Efforts to surmount this have been made, but not very successfully. As you read the articles selected for inclusion

3

here, you will notice that nearly all of them rely on verbal self-report. This will probably not soon change—if ever. Although King and Hunt's scales (see chapter 2) designed to measure institutional affiliations offer a potential objective criterion, even they are part of a questionnaire. I often wonder what would ensue, for instance, if financial gifts to religious institutions could be used as an indicator of one's religiousness, but the difficulty of getting access to such sensitive records seems insurmountable so far—and, perhaps, the results would be ambiguous anyway. The problem here seems ultimately to lie in the intensely personal nature of much religious experience and the often highly private meanings it has to those who profess it.

These problems are not unique to the psychology of religion. They are similar to those faced by investigators of other aspects of personality measurement. The paper by Gorsuch deals with some of these kinds of problems. Pointing out the need to conceive of religious commitment as a many-sided phenomenon, he goes on to indicate some considerations that must be faced in measuring different aspects of it. After looking at theoretical approaches, he examines the possibilities of more strictly empirical procedures. Throughout his discussion, the interaction between measurement procedures and construct definition is highlighted.

Not only is religion in many ways very private and difficult technically to measure, it is also exceedingly complex. Attempts to isolate its essential aspect have certainly been made frequently, but they often turn out to be too simplistic. The clearest recognition of its complexity is found in the assertion that religion is not unidimensional. That is, religion is not a single monolithic structure but a rather complicated piece of architecture whose various parts are often built differently from one another. Thus, asking you what you believe to be the nature of Ultimate Reality, observing (somehow) the number of times you meditate or contemplate this Reality, and checking your factual knowledge about the basic writings of your religion may all measure your religion, but they approach very different aspects of it.

The classification of Stark and Glock (1968) points this out clearly. Their five dimensions have been extremely influential as one of the clearest statements of multidimensionality. The aspects of religion that they believe to be potentially important include:

1. Belief. This has to do with the degree to which a person acknowledges the truthfulness of the creedal statements of his faith. Although organized religions have differing kinds of philosophical and theological statements, none are without them, and all expect some degree of adherence to them by their followers.
2. Knowledge. This has to do with how much factual information a follower has concerning his faith. Although knowledge is related to the dimension of belief, it is not the same, since one can have information about one's religious institution without necessarily believing that its claims are correct.
3. Experience. To some degree, every organized religion expects that its members will achieve some more-or-less particular kind of experience. All hold expectations that the individual will have a set of feelings, sensations, perceptions reflecting a sense of contact with ultimate reality, however that is defined.
4. Practice. This dimension has to do with the particular acts of meditation or devotion that the individual may use to express his religiousness. They are usually a blend of public and private, with the emphasis differing greatly from group to group.
5. Consequences. This has to do with the effects of the other four dimensions on one's behavior—the ways in which these are expressed in the person's "secular," or daily, living. Whether these are actually a part of the religious commitment or follow from it is left open, but it does seem to be a clearly identifiable dimension.

Morton King and Richard Hunt have also long been concerned with defining and measuring various aspects of religion. Relying largely on questionnaires and factor analysis, they have methodically developed a number of promising scales to do this. Their 1972 article is selected here because it gives a pretty comprehensive picture of the processes used in such scale construction, together with the dimensions and representative items that emerged from their work. A more recent extension of their subject group (King and Hunt, 1975) tends to confirm what they have found here.

An earlier study using interview and projective-test data attempted much the same thing. Cline and Richards subjected their data to factor analysis also, with some interesting results. Although there are some resemblances to King and Hunt's findings in the area of religious knowledge and behavior, there are no other correspondences that seem so clear. Perhaps this is a good example of the fact that the factors that emerge from the bottom end of the factor analysis "funnel" depend heavily on what data are poured in at the top.

One of the most influential attempts to specify particular aspects of religion was initiated by Gordon Allport (1960, 1966a, b) when he attempted to distinguish intrinsic from extrinsic religion. His concern arose from the discovery that, in a number of studies, prejudice was associated with religiousness. Allport's hypothesis that attempted to explain this was that two sorts of religion were being confused: intrinsic and extrinsic. Intrinsic religion was religion that was motivated without thought of external reward (functionally autonomous, really), while extrinsic religion was self-seeking and usually in the service of other motives.

In 1971 Hunt and King teamed to bring together a comprehensive review of nearly all that had then been done with the intrinsic-extrinsic concept. They provide us with a penetrating analysis of the material they examined and some suggestions for the future.

Some psychologists have made explicit attempts to suggest innovative approaches to measuring various dimensions of religion. Curiously, most of them have not been followed up in practice. Elkind discusses here an adaptation for religious purposes of the basic interview procedure used by Piaget. Ludwig and Blank report on their use of a projective technique to "get at" religiosity. In Strunk's paper involving reaction time as a measure, we find a refreshing alternative to simple self-report devices. Finally, I describe a way of analyzing open-ended and nonquantified data that was developed within the context of religious education and may have particular use in the area of religion.

1

Identifying the Religiously Committed Person*

Richard L. Gorsuch

Behavioral scientists find it necessary to utilize the concept of the religiously committed person whenever they wish to discuss man's total behavior. A significant segment of Western man often thinks in religious terminology and feels that his religious beliefs are an important influence on his behavior. Psychologists and sociologists have therefore felt a need to examine this aspect of behavior ever since the days of James (1902) and Freud (1928).

Since the concept of the religiously committed person has had a long history, it is apparent that its meaning has not been derived from its position in a theory developed from the study of man. Rather, it has been thrust upon psychology by the Western culture and by its prominent place in the lives of a significant minority of contemporary man. Thus, the investigator cannot just identify the religiously committed person as he sees fit. Behavioral scientists must look at broader frames of reference in order to define this concept and make

*The unedited version of this paper was presented originally at the annual meeting of the American Association for the Advancement of Science, Dallas, Texas, 1968. Reprinted by permission of the author.

it operational. The behavioral scientist begins with the culture's definitions and clarifies them through his research.

This author's orientation toward such a task is away from using simple categories, single traits, or solitary indicators. Rather than using any *one* score as an attempt to summarize completely the person's unique perspective, it emphasizes the need for a multivariate *set* of scores to define the individual's position. A person's religiosity is then defined, not by a single number, but by the intersection of his positions on numerous scales related to religion. Such an approach allows for a highly complex phenomenon to be described relatively well. Literally millions of unique profiles exist when only a dozen scales are used. The fact that this procedure also happens to use numbers is solely a convenience. The points along any continuum could be described by verbal labels just as well as by numbers. Numbers, however, offer the additional possibility of mathematical manipulation, without the excess connotations often found with words. The scores identifying the person's religious position can always be translated into verbal, qualitative descriptions if this be desired.

A multiple-dimension approach to identifying the religiously committed person implies a complex definition or definitions of the phenomena. This is seen as good, since any attempt to establish a single definition of the religiously committed person would assume that there is only one kind of religious commitment. By pursuing all of the aspects that might identify the religiously committed person, the behavioral scientist will retain a more objective role and provide data for the discussions of other disciplines.

A misunderstanding that might encourage a psychologist to prematurely define the religiously committed person stems from a misconception of the scientific process. One does not draw up a tight definition at the start of a research program and then make it operational in his research. Rather, the tight definition can only be drawn up after the research is virtually completed (Kaplan, 1964). While loose definitions and theoretical conceptions are a necessary starting point, the process of measurement will redefine the construct. And after a set of research studies is completed, the interaction of the theory and data should give rise to further refinements in both the theory and the measurement process itself. Specific definitions then are not part of the scientific process per se, but are rather a device for communicating one's hypothesis to a colleague or one's conclusions to an audience.

But if the behavioral scientist does not begin with drawing up an inflexible definition of the religious phenomena, how does he begin? Quite simply—with the obvious. He asks those questions that would be defined by almost anyone in the contemporary culture as measuring religiosity. Thus, a considerable amount of research has been done with one popular, obvious question: denominational membership. The research classically investigates the differences among Protestants, Catholics, and Jews. As with most cases involving the intuitively obvious approach, it usually oversimplifies the area. Stark and Glock (1968) have shown that the differences within Protestant groups are much wider than the differences between most Protestants and Catholics. To use such gross categories as Protestants and Catholics is probably to conceal more of religion's influence on behavior than it is to reveal it.

Lenski (1963), Stark and Glock (1968), and Whitam (1962) are among those taking a more sophisticated but still obvious approach. They attempt to range as broadly as possible and include in their operational definitions all the various facets of religiosity that are of apparent relevance for research. Lenski used measures of ritual participation, doctrinal orthodoxy, devotionalism, and associationism for his dimensions. Stark and Glock utilized five conceptual categories of religiosity—belief, practice, knowledge, experience, and consequences   to guide their data collection. While these constructs do not come from any highly developed sociological theory, they are attempts to develop operational distinctions specifically for behavioral science purposes.

Two approaches have been followed in attempting to improve the identification of the religiously committed person over that which comes from the obvious approach. The first places the emphasis upon theoretical considerations. It attempts to distinguish those aspects of the religious phenomena that would be of independent significance for sociological or psychological theory. These distinctions are then converted into an operational measuring tool that is used to test the theory. Since the measuring tools are never perfect, they are also examined in the light of the data collected to see if they really are testing the theory. At some points, the empirical results will lead to a recasting of the theory, whereas at other points the results will lead to a recasting of the measurement operation. Generally speaking, the theory is recast if there are data supporting the quality of the measurement but not the theory; the measurement is recast when there are data supporting the theoretical notion but not the measurement operation per se. It is, as can be easily seen, a bootstrap operation.

The other kind of approach puts chief emphasis on empirical considerations. Empirical approaches to identifying the religiously committed person reduce the biasing effect of the experimenter and his own personal concepts. These approaches rely on the cultural distinctions that people within the culture make and not on the experimenter's interpretation of them. One such approach (Fichtner, 1968) suggests that the degree of a person's religious commitment can be determined by measuring how far that individual is from the norms of the institution he himself professes to support. If he believes, feels, and acts the way that his particular faith says he should, then he would be considered to be religiously committed. This approach could provide an empirically based definition for our present purposes.

Another empirical approach is to follow the subjects themselves to generate the concepts. When Spilka, Armatas and Nussbaum (1964) were interested in making distinctions in the concept of God more operational, they asked individuals to report how they viewed the Deity. From this material they abstracted the adjectives that were used by the people themselves. They then gave these adjectives to groups of college students, who indicated how well each adjective described their own concept of God. Following this, they examined the interrelations of the adjectives for the constructs that people actually used. If people who, for example, described God as damning also described him as punishing and wrathful, while those who did not see him as damning also failed to use the terms punishing and wrathful, then these adjectives would establish a conceptual dimension.

While one can proceed by simply examining patterns of item responses to find the distinctions between different modes of conceptualization, there are more efficient procedures. One usually applies cluster and factor analytic techniques. These statistical procedures place together those variables that function to put in a group the people who belong there. The concepts derived are based upon the data and organize the data in the most economical way possible, i.e., in the fewest possible dimensions that will most adequately account for the individual variations that are present. Scales can many times, then, be used to measure the empirically found distinctions.

The dimensions that result from such statistical techniques point to distinctions for which the behavioral sciences must account. Any thorough psychology or sociology of religion must be able to point to those causative influences that lead to the development of a particular score on each dimension, as well as the reasons why these and only these dimensions are empirically distinct.

Even though the empirical approach does base its sampling upon open-ended questions to the people themselves, the questions asked will limit the range of response—although this limitation will be less serious than it is in the theoretical approach. As in any research study employing any technique, one cannot reach conclusions about dimensions that are excluded by the procedures.

Even if the people being studied do not generate the initial data, factor analytic procedures can still be used. They then become a cross between the obvious, theoretical approaches and the more explicitly empirical approach. The item pool would be based upon obvious and theoretical distinctions, but the resulting dimensions would be based upon the empirical data.

The results of the composite approach will vary with the quality of item sampling. Since factor analysis produces as many dimensions or distinctions as can be supported by the data, it produces more factors with more measurements. If one samples densely from a given item domain while sampling sparsely from another item domain, several factors will appear to represent the first item domain but only a single factor for the second item domain. Therefore the quality of such research is based primarily on the characteristics of the item sampling.

Scales from the composite theoretical-empirical approach and those derived from theoretical distinctions are usually overlapping but distinct. But the theoretical distinctions usually lead to more scales than the factor analytic approach, and these scales are more highly related to each other. The factor analytic approach generally covers the same area in essentially the same depth but with fewer scales. While the factor analytic scales have the advantage of parsimony, the theoretical scales are usually easier to understand and to integrate into present theory. Since both theoretical and factor analytical scales have their advantages, it does not seem that either is necessarily "better" than the other at the present time. The evaluations as to which scales are the best will need to be made in terms of the degree to which they aid in a specific scientific task.

The scales developed from any of the above approaches may draw relatively broad or narrow distinctions. Some investigators seek a few broad, general scales for identifying the religious person, and others seek numerous, specific ways by which to identify him. Dittes (1968) has supported the specific side by suggesting that the psychology of religion will see a continuing differentiation among the phenomena as the investigators become more expert in their area. He considers this a natural perceptual development; one distinguishes between more and more aspects of an object as he becomes better acquainted with it. This approach also implies that, as in the case of perceptual differentiation, one eventually learns which of the distinctions are worth noting and which can be ignored for any given purpose.

As normally used, factor analysis is not an answer to the problem of the breadth of the dimensions since, as noted above, the breadth of the factors is a function of the item sampling. If one has only a few relatively homogeneous religious items and places these in a broader context, he will come to establish religiosity as a single dimension. If, on the other hand, he uses numerous items from the area of religion itself, the result will be several dimensions. This is because the function of factor analysis is to distinguish among the variables themselves. If the analysis has more variables on which one can base distinctions in a given area, then finer distinctions are made. If however the data are relatively gross, then the distinctions will be gross. Factor analysis does the best it can with the data it is given.

Note that the question of generality vs. specificity need not involve an either-or issue. Usually one considers fine distinctions to be distinctions within a broader distinction. For example, the individual who sees his deity as being benevolent and eternal is different from the individual who sees his deity as being benevolent without stressing the eternal element. However, both viewpoints can be grouped together as positive and compared to the opinions of the individual who sees the concept of God from a completely negative perspective (Gorsuch, 1968). The total set of suggested distinctions among religious people may be grouped together in the area of the religiously committed person, just as one can consider a group of trees as a whole and call them a forest. While a person often finds it useful to examine the individual categories of trees—the elm, the walnut, the weeping willow, etc.—even specialists in horticulture find the broad concept of forest to be useful. Several levels of distinctions can be expected to be useful in the analysis of religious phenomena.

Factor analysis also can be used to organize the fine distinctions into broader ones. Assuming a sufficiently detailed sampling of items from the religious domain, the initial factors will give the fine distinctions. The relationships among these narrow factors can then be examined so that broader distinctions are developed from the empirical similarities among the finer distinctions. This is usually accomplished by factoring the correlations among the factors. The grouping of narrow distinctions into broader ones is continued as long as necessary, i.e., until the whole system of species, genus, family, order, class, and phylum is empirically determined for the domain of possible religious characteristics.

While the ultimate strategy is clear—drop any of the fine distinctions that do not prove their worth—the proximate strategy is not quite so simple. The finer distinction must be given a chance. This suggests that it is more efficient from a long-range view to collect data with the finest distinctions possible and then test these for their usefulness. And this needs to be repeated in each new area of research, since the fine distinctions may be quite valuable for limited areas. Only with such data in hand can the relative merits of fine vs. broad distinctions be evaluated.

With the exception of a few investigators, such as Tapp (1957), Cattell (1957) and Elkind (below in this section), researchers have used a fairly standard answer to the question of how to define operationally the distinctions they are interested in. They ask people. Questionnaires or structured interviews may be used, but the data depend on verbal self-report. While psychologists have been hesitant to use self-report as a standard tool of investigation, it has been noted that it is often more useful than other approaches (Peterson, 1965). Part of the success of this approach in the area of measuring religion comes from the fact that the Western religious tradition includes a strong verbal orientation.

A second fact encouraging verbal report is that being religious is commonly accepted as involving institutionalized, public behavior. Therefore people can be asked how often they have been going to church, how many friends they have in religious organizations, etc. Here the verbal report procedure is somewhat more doubtful, since it is not as accurate as actually observing the behavior. Unfortunately, a systematic checking of the verbal reports of behavior with actual institutional records and observations has not yet been done.

One basic problem with questionnaires on religiosity is the numerous ways in which the answers may be distorted. Some individuals are quite likely to report religious attitudes and behaviors so as to appear more religious than they actually are because these answers are valued in their particular subculture: they respond in the socially desirable direction. Questions are often misunderstood because of ambiguous language. And the individual may respond as much in terms of what he wishes as in terms of what he is.

The questions may also be distorted by the context in which they are asked. If a minister asks a group to report what their highest value is, one would expect different results than if a sociologist asked the same question. The problem here is not one of deliberate distortion, but one of suggestion. The role of the minister suggests religious elements to the subjects, and the question is perceived as coming from an interest in religious phenomena. However, the interpretation is probably broader and the direct suggestive element is different when the sociologist asks the question. And this shift in set will produce different responses.

Many items concerned with religiosity are probably unidirectional indicators of the religious commitment of the individual. That is, if a person answers in one direction, one knows something about him, but an answer in the opposite direction could be from so many different causes that one can say very little indeed about the person's religious commitment. For example, the person who tells the Gallup Poll interviewer that he believes in God is probably not communicating a great deal. As Stark and Glock (1968) point out, agreement with this statement is from, first, a variety of reasons (e.g., a strong religious commitment, a desire to appear acceptable to the culture, etc.) and, second, a degree of ambiguity in the phrase "believe in God" (e.g., ranging from a fundamentalist, orthodox interpretation of a theistic deity to a unitarian, liberal interpretation of "God" as the impersonal basic force and creative power of the universe). But when the person says that he does not believe in God—and very few state this—it is probably a definite indication that the individual is not religiously committed in the traditional sense. Thus this item discriminates in the negative direction but not in the positive. The results could be quite different if one used a positive unidirectional indicator instead.

The result of a multiple item scale is almost always assumed to have at least an *ordinal* metric—that is, a person with a higher score on the scale would have more of what the scale is measuring than a person with a lower score. Although psychologists were concerned about the accuracy of this assumption some ten years ago, it is now usually considered to have demonstrable utility. The results from the statistics are sufficiently accurate so as to improve prediction when this assumption is made over when it is not made (Nunnally, 1967).

While an investigator need not hesitate to argue for the utility of this, the fact that this is an assumption should not be forgotten. The ordered metric in any scale is the result of our imposition on the data; someone else could take the same data and set up another order if he so desired. While Stark and Glock (1968) arranged their data to place the denominations on a scale ranging from liberal to conservative, it would be equally correct to order these denominations along a continuum according to their degree of structure (Brown, 1962) or their liturgy. The fact that Stark and Glock did not do so is a function of their interests in other data; they were not examining liturgy but they were examining conservative versus liberal beliefs.

The argument for assuming that a scale is at the equal *interval* level is that it appears to work as such; this assumption would be dropped whenever it is not warranted. If numerous skewed distributions or curvilinear relationships are found, other methods of conceptualizing that particular dimension need to be considered.

It may be that distinguishing the religiously committed individual from the nonreligious individual is best conceptualized along a partially ordered scale instead of a completely ordered scale. This appears to be what Dittes (1967) was suggesting when he argued that religious research should be conducted with individuals who show some degree of religious involvement. While one may be able to draw legitimate distinctions between different kinds of religiously committed individuals, the extension of these distinctions to the nonreligious person may not be possible.

The various facets that have been discussed interact in producing the final definition by which the religiously committed person is identified. Initial attempts at operationalization assume at least a tentative definition of the area of interest and some theoretical sophistication. The initial empirical (or operational) definition never quite matches the theoretical definition. The extent, direction, and value of its departure are unknown until empirical data are collected. But by the time sufficient data are collected adequately to evaluate this attempt, the theory will probably have developed beyond the initial definition. Therefore a new operational definition needs to build upon both the theoretical and measurement developments. But will this definition be perfect? No, it will only begin the next stage of the repetitive process (Kaplan, 1964). One would suspect that the measurement will become more and more stabilized as the area develops, but that it will never be perfected.

No matter what the quality of the theory's definition of the religiously committed person, the definition is only as good as its measurement. The quality of the research instrument that embodies the definition can only be partially determined by examining the item content and measurement procedures. The actual definition of the religiously committed person is known when research using the projected definitions has been extensive. Fortunately, the psychology and sociology of religion do not lack scales of possible value. So the next stage is to encourage sufficient use of the same scales so that their scientific utility can be determined.

2

Measuring the Religious Variable: Replication*

*Morton B. King and
Richard A. Hunt*

INTRODUCTION

Need for better measures of the religious variable has been recognized since at least 1950. Simple, often single-item, measures were proving inadequate tools for discovering the correlates of religious behavior.

The idea that religion has many dimensions was quickly accepted as a potential solution. Much useful research was thereby spawned. Lacking, however, were (1) an empirical test of the multidimensional hypothesis itself, and (2) a systematic empirical search for usable dimensions using correlational techniques.

King (1967) and King and Hunt (1969) reported a 1965 pilot study with those objectives, with encouraging results. In 1968, the study was repeated on a larger and more diverse population of subjects, with a modified universe of items, and using similar but not identical analytical procedures.

*The unedited version of this article appeared originally in *The Journal for the Scientific Study of Religion*, 1972, *11*: 240-51. Copyright 1972 by the Society for the Scientific Study of Religion. Reprinted by permission.

METHODS AND PROCEDURES

The questionnaire contained 132 items. Of these, 91 related to religious belief, knowledge, and practice; 27 to cognitive style variables; and 14 to a variety of personal information ranging from conditions of first joining the church (conversion, confirmation training, etc.) to such demographic data as age, sex, education, and income.

The total universe of items differed from that in 1965. Sixty-eight out of the 120 "religious" items were retained: 37 in identical form; 14 reworded in major ways; and 17 slightly modified in wording or answer format. There were 23 completely new religious items, selected to strengthen one of the dimensions or to represent a dimension not found in 1965. The 27 cognitive-style items comprised nine that were identical and 18 that were completely new. Therefore, of the 118 items factor analyzed, 46 were identical to ones in 1965, 17 were modified slightly, 14 were changed in major ways, and 41 were brand new. That is, we were "sampling" from a rather different universe of items.

Subjects were members of four Protestant denominations in the Dallas-Fort Worth metropolitan area. As in 1965, inner city and suburban congregations were purposively selected to include different socioeconomic levels and varied theological and liturgical styles. A systematic sample was drawn in each congregation of all members sixteen and over who were local residents. Questionnaires were mailed out with a covering letter from each pastor, to be returned directly to the research director. Confidentiality was promised both respondents and congregations. Code numbers were used which made possible telephone follow-up of nonrespondents.

The 1,356 usable returns represented a 44 percent response rate, rather equally divided among the denominations: Disciples; Lutheran, Missouri Synod; Presbyterian, U.S.; and United Methodist; there were also thirteen questionnaires with denominations unknown. The subjects were homogeneous: white, mainline Protestants in urban north Texas who could read and write well enough to complete questionnaires and were motivated to do so. They differed, among other ways, in denominational affiliation, degree of congregational activity, age, sex, education, and income—although on the latter two indices the lowest quartile of the total population was largely missing.

A factor analysis was applied to the data for all cases combined. Nineteen factors were produced. The content of high-loading items on each factor was examined subjectively, and fifteen sets were judged to "make sense" as an aspect of religious behavior. These were subjected to an item-scale analysis (Hunt, 1970) based on the covariance matrix. The program uses predetermined criteria to search the matrix, adding to the set highly correlated items and dropping items with low correlation. By this process, some sets "grow" into a more homogeneous form; others "wilt" as a result of low homogeneity or of instability. The information thus obtained aids selection of item sets whose internal consistency, as well as item content, indicates possible usefulness. Using this and two other criteria, ten scales were selected.

FINDINGS

The Appendix lists the items for the ten religious scales believed to be of greatest potential interest to social scientists and church officials. Each will be discussed briefly in relation to the work of Allport, Glock, Lenski, and others, and to our 1965 findings. Of the eleven 1965 scales (King and Hunt, 1969; or 1972: chapter IV), all but two were also derived from the 1968 data. One new scale (VI-B, Salience: Cognition) was developed. Two scales were given different labels, as noted below.

The first six scales shown are similar to dimensions discussed by Glock (1962) and Lenski (1963).

1. "Creedal assent" (seven items) is similar to Glock's "ideological" and Lenski's "doctrinal orthodoxy." One difference is that our items attempted to avoid a literal-fundamentalist bias. They were worded to encourage assent from a broad spectrum of believing Christians. The 1965 and 1968 scales both have seven items, six of which are identical. "I know that I need God's continual love and care" was dropped. "I believe honestly and

wholeheartedly in the doctrines and teaching of the Church"
was added as the last (lowest item-scale correlation) to be
included.

2. "Devotionalism" (five items) bears some similarity to Glock's
definition of "experiential," but is most like Lenski's "devotionalism." The items deal with personal prayer, closeness to
and communication with God. The 1965 scale (then called
"Personal Religious Experience") had seven items. The 1968
scale is composed of five of them. The two dropped as less
useful are: "I know that God answers my prayers" and "To
what extent has God influenced *your* life?"

3. Three "congregational involvement" scales are shown. These
sets of items, while interrelated, are separable aspects of
Glock's "ritualistic" and Lenski's "associational" dimensions.
As in 1965, items related to attending worship services are
associated with organizational activities. Although several new
items were written, in consultation with a professor of worship,
no homogeneous cluster of items could be developed for a
"liturgical" or worship dimension.

   a. "Church attendance" has three items compared to four in
   1965. One is identical, one slightly reworded, and one
   similar. The item dropped was "How would you rate your
   activity in this congregation?"

   b. "Organizational activity" consists of six items in both
   studies. Four are identical and one slightly revised. "How
   many times during the last month have you attended Sunday School or some equivalent educational activity?" was
   dropped. "How would you rate your activity in this congregation?" was added.

   c. "Financial support" has five items in both years. Three
   are identical and two slightly reworded. A "financial factor" or factors appeared in the analyses of both 1965 and
   1968 data.

4. "Religious knowledge" (eight items) provides a way of measuring Glock's "intellectual" dimension. It contains all five 1965
items in identical form, plus three new ones prepared for the
restudy.

The preceding six scales are considered indicators of religious dimensions, different aspects of religious behavior. They are clear-cut, having no overlapping items with each other. The following four are different in two ways. First, three are "composite" scales, having one or more items present in one or more other scales. The items that overlap are indicated in the Appendix. Scale V-A has two items in common with VI-B, and one each with II and VI-A. In addition, VI-B shares one item with II. Correlation coefficients among these scales, especially between V-A and VI-B, should be interpreted with caution. Despite this overlapping, the overall "meaning" of each set of items seems to be different. Secondly, they measure orientations to religion, at least in its institutionalized congregational form, rather than dimensions of religious behavior.

5. "Orientation." Two sets of items, similar to ones derived in 1965, indicate orientations to religion.

    a. "Growth and striving" (six items) includes two items from a similar 1965 scale, but in substantially reworded form. It has four items that are on other scales. Therefore, its use and interpretation in relation to those dimensions should be especially cautious. However, it has adequate homogeneity, and it reflects an orientation to religion that is both theologically and ecclesiastically important. It appears to measure the opposite of an "I've-got-it-made" attitude. Rather, the high scorer expresses dissatisfaction with his current religious state and a feeling of need to learn, change, and grow.

    b. "Extrinsic" (seven items). This scale is one of the two derived from the 1968 data. It presents all five of the Allport-Feagin extrinsic items included in the questionnaire with two others. Its homogeneity is low, but higher than that of the Allport-Feagin items considered alone. The other five-item scale contains none of the Allport-Feagin items. The meaning of the item content is similar in both: an instrumental, selfish attitude toward religion (see Feagin, 1964).

6. "Salience." Two sets of items seem to indicate two types of salience that religion has in the lives of these individuals.

a.   "Behavior" (seven items). "Salience: Behavior" is quite similar to the six-item 1965 scale called "Talking and Reading About Religion." The four identical, one very slightly modified, and two new items relate to the relevance of religion for certain kinds of out-of-church personal activities.

b.   "Cognition" (five items). "Salience: Cognition" is the new scale, developed around three of the seven Allport-Feagin intrinsic items (Feagin, 1964; Allport and Ross, 1967) included in the 1968 questionnaire. Total item content suggests the salience of religion for thought and feeling, more than Allport's (1960, 1966a) definitions of "intrinsic."

DISCUSSION

The conclusions of the 1965 pilot study were, in general, supported. The methods enabled multiple dimensions of religious belief and practice to be identified by reasonably homogeneous scales. The scales, when correlated with each other and with measures of cognitive style variables, exhibited enough explanatory power to indicate potential usefulness. Of the eleven scales derived from the 1965 data, nine were rederived in similar form. Seven of the ten 1968 scales (I; II; III-A, B, and C; IV; and V-B) are similar to dimensions in the Allport (1960), Glock (1962), and Lenski (1963) typologies. We believe that the possibility and usefulness of multidimensional measures of religion have been confirmed.

The study has a number of limitations that must be considered in evaluating its findings and our conclusions. We are aware of six main ones.

The study is culture-bound. It emphasizes, and is largely confined to, congregationally related aspects of institutional, mainline Protestant Christianity. The project was called a Church Involvement Study. It is an excellent example of work that Luckmann (1967) has properly criticized as reducing the sociology of religion to a "sociology of the church." The scales by no means tap the whole spectrum of behaviors that can be considered "religious," Christian, or even mainline Protestant. Glock's typology (1954, 1959, 1962), as modified after Fukuyama (1960), was the principal inspiration of our work. It was presented as universal, applying to all religions. Our research strategy was, first, to search for dimensions and scales within homogeneous populations of subjects and of items, and second—provided useful scales were developed—to test them on gradually expanding and more diverse populations. The present study is a small beginning on the second step.

The subjects are not a "sample" of any population. The availability of four denominations, purposive selection of congregations, and low response rate make the returns studied unrepresentative even of mainline Protestants in metropolitan north Texas. Luckily, the purposes of the study were not to estimate parameters for any universe. We sought a number of subjects sufficient for correlation analyses and with a balance between homogeneity and heterogeneity. The number and mix obtained proved acceptable for the exploratory aims of the research. The product is a set of scales to be tested on other populations, not a description of the four denominations.

Questionnaire data of the kind used present problems of reliability and validity. If the item stimuli were presented at another time or in another context, we do not know how the subjects would respond. Nor do we know (one rarely does in such studies) the relation of the paper-and-pencil responses obtained to the "real" thoughts, feelings, and actions of the subjects. Therefore, for this reason also, our data would be inadequate to describe the religious life even of the subjects who responded. That, however, is not necessarily the only important use of scales. A scale is useful if it can be so correlated with another variable that the latter is predicted more efficiently or "understood" more thoroughly, within tolerable margins of error. The ten scales show an informative pattern of correlations with measures of ethnic prejudice and of intolerance of ambiguity.

Correlation methods are not inductive statistics. They do not usually test hypotheses. Decisions regarding the "existence" of dimensions and the utility of scales are personal judgments of the researchers. Such judgments are influenced by subjective considerations, by knowledge of the data and subjects, and by results of the quantitative analysis. The mathematical procedures used only put the data in forms that instruct the human judgments and partially objectify them.

Dimensions and scales are not "things" that we discover. They should not be reified. They are constructs, relative to and dependent upon the population of subjects, the universe of items, and the analytical procedures (both mathematical and subjective). Change any of the research procedures or the conditions surrounding them, and our "findings" might change or even disappear. It is paradoxical, but true, that appropriate replication requires both similarity and variation in subjects, items, and tools of analysis. The present restudy introduced changes in all three. Under these conditions, the 1965 findings and conclusions were supported.

The scales are simple, additive, unweighted. As noted above, methodologists are coming to view the more complicated procedures as "almost never worth the trouble" (Nunnally, 1967). An important test is whether scales correlate in meaningful ways with measures of other variables. Ours do.

Therefore, we offer for use ten scales measuring selected aspects of religious behavior. They are not finished products with established reliability, validity, and norms for different populations. They are only ready for testing in use on a variety of populations and in questionnaires with other items. We are pretty confident they are useful for research (both theoretically relevant and ecclesiastically useful) with mainline Protestants throughout the United States and in similar societies such as Canada and the Netherlands. Use with Roman Catholics or Protestant Pentecostals, for example, is problematical. With substantial changes in most items, the scales might be tried on Jewish and Muslim subjects. Beyond that, they are probably not applicable at all (see, for example, Keene's work on Bahais in the United States, 1967).

The proof will be in repeated cautious use.

APPENDIX

ITEMS FOR TEN RELIGIOUS SCALES[1]

I.   Creedal Assent

1. All items have four alternative answers, except the knowledge items (E1-E8), which have six. Most items are answered on a four-point scale from "Strongly Agree" to "Strongly Disagree." Sixteen "how often" items have "Regularly," "Fairly Frequently," "Occasionally," and "Seldom or Never" as alternatives. The alternatives for other items are indicated in parentheses.

1. I believe that the word of God is revealed in the Scriptures
2. I believe in God as a Heavenly Father who watches over me and to whom I am accountable
3. I believe that God revealed himself to man in Jesus Christ
4. I believe that Christ is a living reality
5. I believe in eternal life
6. I believe in salvation as release from sin and freedom for new life with God
7. I believe honestly and wholeheartedly in the doctrines and teachings of the Church

II. Devotionalism
1. How often do you pray privately in places other than at church?
2. How often do you ask God to forgive your sin?
3. Private prayer is one of the most important and satisfying aspects of my religious experience
4. When you have decisions to make in your everyday life, how often do you try to find out what God wants you to do?[2]
5. I frequently feel very close to God in prayer, during public worship, or at important moments in my daily life[2]

III. Congregational Involvement
A. Church Attendance
1. How often have you taken Holy Communion (The Lord's Supper, The Eucharist) during the past year?
2. During the last year, how many Sundays per month on the average have you gone to a worship service? (None—Three or more)
3. If not prevented by unavoidable circumstances, I attend Church: (More than once a week—Less than once a month)
B. Organizational Activity

---

2. Items that also appear on another scale.

1. How would you rate your activity in this congregation? (Very active—Inactive)
2. How often do you spend evenings at church meetings or in church work?
3. I enjoy working in the activities of the Church
4. Church activities (meetings, committee work, etc.) are a major source of satisfaction in my life
5. I keep pretty well informed about my congregation and have some influence on its decisions
6. List the church offices, committees, or jobs of any kind in which you served during the past 12 months

C. Financial Support

1. Last year, approximately what percent of your income was contributed to the Church?
2. I make financial contributions to church: (In regular, planned amounts—Seldom or never)
3. During the last year, what was the average monthly contribution of your family to your local congregation? (Under $5—$50 and up)
4. In proportion to your income, do you consider that your contributions to the Church are? (Generous—Small)
5. During the last year, how often have you made contributions to the Church in addition to the general budget and Sunday School? (Regularly—Never)

IV. Religious Knowledge

1. Which of the following were Old Testament prophets? (Deuteronomy; Ecclesiastes; Elijah; Isaiah; Jeremiah; Leviticus)
2. Which of the following books are included in the Four Gospels? (James; John; Mark; Matthew; Peter; Thomas)
3. Which of the following were among the Twelve Disciples of Christ? (Daniel; John; Judas; Paul; Peter; Samuel)
4. Which of the following acts were performed by Jesus Christ during his earthly ministry? (Resisting the temptations of Satan; Healing ten lepers; Leading His people against the priests of Baal; Parting the waters to cross the

Red Sea; Overcoming Goliath; Turning water into wine)
5.   Which of the following men were leaders of the Protestant Reformation? (Aquinas; Augustine; Calvin; Cranmer; Hegel; Luther)
6.   Which of the following principles are supported by most Protestant denominations? (Bible as the Word of God; Separation of Church and State; Power to clergy to forgive sins; Final authority of the Church; Justification by faith; Justification by good works)
7.   Which of the following books are in the Old Testament? (Acts; James; Galatians; Hebrews; Hosea; Psalms)
8.   Which of the following denominations in the United States have bishops? (Disciples; Episcopal; Lutheran; Methodist; Presbyterian; Roman Catholic)

V.   Orientation to Religion
   A.   Growth and Striving
   1.   How often do you read literature about your faith (or church)? (Frequently—Never)
   2.   How often do you read the Bible?
   3.   I try hard to grow in understanding of what it means to live as a child of God
   4.   When you have decisions to make in your everyday life, how often do you try to find out what God wants you to do?[2]
   5.   The amount of time I spend trying to grow in understanding of my faith is (Very much—Little or none)
   6.   I try hard to carry my religion over into all my other dealings in life[2,3]
   B.   Extrinsic
   1.   It is part of one's patriotic duty to worship in the church of his choice
   2.   The Church is most important as a place to formulate good social relationships
   3.   The purpose of prayer is to secure a happy and peaceful life[3]

---

3. Allport-Feagin items (See Feagin, 1964).

4. Church membership has helped me to meet the right kind of people

5. What religion offers me most is comfort when sorrows and misfortune strike[3]

6. One reason for my being a church member is that such membership helps to establish a person in the community[3]

7. Religion helps to keep my life balanced and steady in exactly the same way as my citizenship, friendships, and other memberships do[3]

VI. Salience
   A. Behavior
1. How often in the last year have you shared with another church member the problems and joys of trying to live a life of faith in God?

2. How often have you personally tried to convert someone to faith in God?

3. How often do you talk about religion with your friends, neighbors, or fellow workers?

4. When faced by decisions regarding social problems, how often do you seek guidance from statements and publications provided by the Church?

5. How often do you read the Bible?

6. How often do you talk with the pastor (or some other official) about some part of the worship service: for example, the sermon, Scripture, choice of hymns, etc.?

7. During the last year, how often have you visited someone in need, besides your own relatives?

   B. Cognition
1. My religious beliefs are what really lie behind my whole approach to life[3]

2. I try hard to grow in understanding of what it means to live as a child of God[2]

3. Religion is especially important to me because it answers many questions about the meaning of life[3]

4. I try hard to carry my religion over into all my other dealings in life[2,3]

5. I frequently feel very close to God in prayer, during public worship, or at important moments in my daily life[2]

3

A Factor Analytic Study of Religious Belief and Behavior*

*Victor B. Cline and
James M. Richards, Jr.*

The authors of the study presented in this paper have been interested in studying the impact of religion and religious belief on behavior, but they have been concerned about the looseness and lack of rigor of most of the "research" in this area. In an effort to make greater use of the tools of empiricism and scientific methodology, the researchers proceeded with variable success to study a most complex phenomenon as developed below.

METHOD

SELECTION OF SAMPLE

A random sample of 155 adult males and females was drawn from the City Directory listing every adult residing in the greater metro-

*The unedited version of this article appeared originally in *The Journal of Personality and Social Psychology*, 1965, *1*: 569-78. Copyright 1965 by the American Psychological Association. Reprinted by permission.

politan Salt Lake area. The only individuals not included were non-resident transients and tourists staying briefly in motels or hotels. Ten percent of the sample drawn did not participate in this study. In such cases, the researchers used as substitutes another adult of the appropriate sex who lived in or adjacent to the apartment or residence in question.

METHOD OF DATA COLLECTION

A single trained interviewer collected all of the test data and other information in the following manner. First, individuals selected for the study were sent a letter indicating that the University of Utah was conducting a research project. They were told that the researchers would like to survey their opinions and attitudes about a number of questions. No hint or information was given as to the nature of the questions or the purpose of the study. Later, a phone call or personal visit was made in order to secure a specific appointment time with the individual. When the interviewer arrived for the appointment, he asked permission to record the interview, which was granted by the participants without exception. Later, stenographers made type-scripts of each of the 155 interviews. During the session with the subject, three types of procedures were administered: a modified TAT-type test, a depth interview, and a sixty-seven-item Religious Belief-Behavior Questionnaire.

INSTRUMENTS USED

Modified TAT. After securing permission to record the inter-view, the interviewer without any further explanation presented, serially, a set of seven TAT-type projective pictures. The instruc-tions required that the respondent look at each picture and tell what was happening, what the people were thinking and feeling, and what would be the outcome. After the initial response to each picture, the interviewer probed considerably as to the full implications of the response and inquired about features in the card that might have escaped comment. In doing this, great care was taken not to suggest the focus of the study. The pictures, described below, were presented in this order:

1. A man is putting fishing tackle in his car, while across the street people are entering a church or synagogue.
2. A man is speaking in front of a group of people inside a building. This could be a clergyman in a church, but the cues are somewhat ambiguous.
3. A man is placing some money in what appears to be a collection plate, but again the scene is somewhat ambiguous and could be interpreted variously.
4. A young boy is kneeling at his bedside in a posture suggesting prayer.
5. A physician tells a woman sitting at the bedside of a man who is apparently very ill, "There is nothing more I can do."
6. The scene is a graveside funeral. A casket is being lowered into the grave.
7. A group of shrouded figures is gathered together in a depressing and dismal scene. Hovering above is a "Satanic and evil looking" figure faintly seen.

Responses to the TAT type pictures were converted to scores in the following way. Three trained raters reviewed each subject's protocol and made six summary ratings using a scale of one to five. These six ratings were: overall religious commitment, feelings of guilt, religious conflict, defensiveness about religion, sheer number of religious themes, and number of themes suggesting hostility toward religion. In making these ratings, the raters considered the entire set of responses a subject gave to all seven pictures rather than considering or scoring each picture separately. The score each subject received on each of the six variables was the average of the three raters' ratings.

Depth interview.   Following the administration of the modified TAT, the researcher proceeded to conduct a depth interview aimed at searching out the quality, nature, and intensity of the subjects' beliefs about deity and church and what impact, if any, these had upon his life and his relationship with parents, spouse, associates, etc. Typescripts of these interviews were read, studied, and rated by five graduate psychologists and sociologists, including the original interviewer. They made thirty-eight ratings on each subject, using for the most part a scale of one to five. Ratings were based on a total analysis of the interview material. A subject's final score for a particular variable was the mean of these ratings. These raters were selected so that their own attitudes and orientation toward religion were heterogeneous.

Religious Belief-Behavior Questionnaire.   Following the interview, the subject was given a questionnaire, developed by the authors, consisting of eight scales and sixty-seven Likert-type items. This questionnaire assessed both religious belief and behavior. The names of the eight scales suggest something of the content of the items: Public Religious Behavior, Personal Religious "Experience," Beliefs about God, Beliefs about Good versus Evil, Beliefs about Organized Religion, Beliefs about Immortality, and Beliefs about the Scriptures.

It proved difficult to avoid the common error of previous studies of religiosity, which typically have used questionnaires that measured primarily "orthodoxy" or "conventionality" of belief, and therefore penalized members of the more liberal religious groups or persons having a less orthodox kind of religious orientation. For example, a question about the existence of Satan would, perhaps, unduly discriminate against some Protestants who view Satan as a symbolic or mythical figure but who in other ways could be considered deeply religious.

Similarly, a belief in immortality is an important part of the faith of most Christians, but not of the faith of many liberal Jews. On the other hand, a questionnaire devoid of any items dealing with specific dogma would tap nothing more than vague, unspecified attitudes toward religion. As a compromise, the researchers attempted to solve these problems by grouping items into eight subareas, so that, for example, if a person disclaimed belief in the personal existence of Satan, this would not necessarily be combined or lumped together numerically with his beliefs about the personal existence of God. In order to permit comparisons with other studies, however, scores on the eight subscales were also combined into a total score.

Thus, in summary, this study included fifty-eight separate measures relevant to the religious beliefs and practices of the subjects: six ratings of responses to the TAT-type pictures, thirty-nine ratings based upon the depth interview, nine subscale scores as well as a total score from the Religious Belief-Behavior Questionnaire, and four demographic variables (age, religious and political preference, and sex). All of the variables were intercorrelated and factor analyzed.

RESULTS

INFORMATION ABOUT AND CHARACTERISTICS OF THE SAMPLE

The sample was exactly divided between male and female subjects, as was provided for in the original research design. Politically, 33 percent listed Democrat and 28 percent Republican as their choice—while another 39 percent listed themselves as Independent, or "I vote for the man—not the party." With regard to age range, 14 percent were in the twenty to twenty-nine category, 39 percent were thirty to forty-five, another 27 percent were forty-six to sixty, and 20 percent were sixty-one or over. With regard to religious preference, 72 percent listed themselves as LDS (Mormon), 11 percent gave no preference, 9 percent were Protestant, 4 percent Catholic, and 4 percent other (Jewish, Christian Science, etc.).

RELATIONSHIP AMONG THE THREE MEASURES OF RELIGIOSITY

A most important question to be answered involves the relationship of the overall religiosity or religious commitment index from the projective tests, interview data, and questionnaire procedure. Their average intercorrelation was .66 with a range of from .50 to .84, which is remarkably high, especially for the projective TAT-like device. Many previous studies using fantasy materials have found them monotonously disappointing in their yield and of questionable validity. It may be that projective tests in some cases need to be custom-made (as was done in this study) to tap specific dimensions germane to the research. The relatively high correlations among the three quite different procedures assessing overall religious commitment amount to a kind of cross-method validity.

Intercorrelational and Factor Analysis

In analyzing these data, the next step was to intercorrelate the fifty-eight test and rating variables for the sexes separately. The results reveal considerable complexity within the religiosity domain, a finding contrasting with most theoretical formulations which imply a single global factor or at most two or three factors. In the present study, twelve factors were found for men and eleven factors for women. The factors obtained are named and/or described below.

Female factors.　　Factor I is entitled "Religious Belief and Behavior," with high loadings on all questionnaire scale variables, the religious-commitment variable from the projective test, and interview variables reflecting belief in God, importance of religion, and participation in organized religion. It thus is highly similar to the common meaning of *religiosity.*

Factor II involves having a spouse who had good relations with religious parents, as measured by the interview.

Factor III might most appropriately be termed the "Compassionate Samaritan" factor. It has high loadings on the interview ratings of "love and compassion," "being a Good Samaritan," and being liked by the raters of the interview protocol, and a high negative loading on being self-centered. The most significant thing about this factor is undoubtedly its relative independence of acceptance of conventional religious dogma.

Factor IV involves "Projected Guilt," since its highest loading is on the projective test guilt variable. Secondary loadings suggest that persons scoring high on this variable tend to believe in God but do not live up to the teachings of their church, nor are they particularly moral in their personal life. The projected guilt almost certainly results from the "cognitive dissonance" arising from this beliefs-actions inconsistency.

Factor V involves having good relations with a religious father as reported in the interview.

Factor VI involves primarily "Projective Test Religiosity," with high positive loadings on the projective test variables of "number of religious themes" and "religious commitment," and negative loadings on "hostile themes," "defensiveness about religion," and "religious conflict."

Factor VII has high loadings on age, tragedy, and suffering, as revealed in the interview. The high loading on marital status, because of the peculiarities of the scoring system for this variable, indicates that persons scoring high on this variable tend to be widows. Thus this factor involves tragedy and suffering in later life alone. The tendency toward rated "neuroticism" of persons scoring high appears to be a result of this tragedy and suffering, and an understandable reaction to their life situation.

Factor VIII involves having good relations with a religious mother, and a tendency not to change one's own religious views, whatever those views might be.

Factor IX involves "Religious Hypocrisy" with high loadings on interview ratings as being a religious "phony," as exploiting religion, as having conflict and doubts about religion, and on projective measures of defensiveness and religious conflict.

Factor X has a high loading on "Political Preference" which, due to the scoring of this variable, indicates a tendency to conservative political beliefs. It is interesting to note that, contrary to common opinion, this is not necessarily accompanied by religious conservatism.

Factor XI appears to be "Dogmatic Authoritarianism," with high loadings on the interview variables of authoritarian and dogmatic. Again it should be noted that, contrary to some current theories of authoritarianism, this factor does not involve any tendency toward conventional or conservative religious belief. These results suggest, therefore, that an unbeliever is just as likely to be authoritarian about his unbelief as a believer is to be authoritarian about the dogmas of his faith, which is entirely consistent with Rokeach's (1960) reformulation of the problem of authoritarianism.

Male factors. Factor I appears to involve "Religious Behavior," with its highest loadings on the church attendance, prayer life, and religious activity scales from the interview, and the public and private religious behavior from the questionnaire scales. There is a tendency for men scoring high on this scale to have spouses who view religion as important and who are active in church activities. It should be noted that there is a fairly strong tendency for high scorers on this factor to be rated as "exploiting" their religion.

Factor II is most appropriately called the "Compassionate Samaritan" factor, with high loadings on the interview scales of being a Good Samaritan, being loving and compassionate, leading a good moral life, and being liked by the raters. This factor, of course, is virtually identical with Factor III in the female sample.

Factor III is similar to Female Factor XI and involves a tendency toward "Dogmatic Authoritarianism." High positive loadings were obtained on the interview scales of authoritarian and dogmatic and a high negative loading on humbleness.

Factor IV involves having a spouse who had good relations with religious parents.

Factor V involves having good relations with a spouse who is herself religious.

Factor VI, like Female Factor VI, involves "Projective Test Religiosity." If reflected, it has high positive loadings on the number of religious themes given in response to the projective material and the estimate of religious commitment based on these themes, and a moderate negative loading on the degree of defensiveness about religion aroused by the pictures.

High scorers on Factor VII are men who had good relations with their own religious parents.

Factor VIII has some similarities to Female Factor VII and thus might be termed "Tragedy and Suffering in Later Life," since its highest loadings are on age and the amount of tragedy and suffering revealed in the interview. In contrast to the corresponding female sample, however, there was no strong tendency in the male sample for high scorers to have survived their spouse nor for them to display neurotic symptoms.

Factor IX appears to be "Loss of Faith," since its two highest loadings indicate that high scorers have changed their religious beliefs toward a less religious position. Secondary loadings indicate that high scorers are more pragmatic and theological, less dogmatic and less literal in their religious views, and have more knowledge about religion.

Factor X appears to involve "Religious Belief," since its highest loadings are on the questionnaire belief scales and the interview scale concerning belief in God. This factor is sharply different from Male

Factor I, which emphasizes religious behavior with a minimum of religious belief.

Factor XI involves "Neuroticism." High scorers tend to be viewed by the interview raters as being neurotic and "religious phonies," as exploiting their religion, as lacking humbleness, and as being disliked by the raters themselves.

Factor XII might be termed "Projective Test Religious Conflict," with high loadings on the projective test scales involving religious conflict, defensiveness about religion, and number of hostile themes given. High scorers on this factor also reveal more than average conflict and doubt about religion in the interview and tend to reject, in the questionnaire, conventional beliefs about God, good versus evil, and the church.

Factor XIII is similar to Female Factor X, involving "Political Preference." Again, due to the scoring of this variable, this factor involves primarily a tendency toward conservative political views.

DISCUSSION

The results described above provide considerable evidence of important sex differences in patterns of religiosity. For example, the first factors that emerged for both men and women (and that accounted for the lion's share of variance in both factor solutions) were religious in content but with some very interesting differences. In the case of the females, we would call Factor I "Religious Belief and Behavior" because it rather neatly integrates belief variables from the questionnaire, the projective test, and the interview with behavior variables from both questionnaire and interview. Thus, with our female, the deeper and more intense her religious beliefs and convictions are, the more apt she is to behave and do things in her everyday life consistent with these beliefs. And, likewise, the more she participates behaviorally in religious activities, the greater the likelihood that her beliefs and convictions will be strengthened.

However, with our males the picture is somewhat different. The most accurate title or description we can give to their primary Factor I is "Religious Behavior." High scorers in this category are characterized by intense "activity" (high attendance, holding a church job, frequent prayer, etc.) but, in comparison with women, have a greater degree of doubt, fuzziness, and ambiguity about the nature of God, the validity and accuracy of the Scriptures, immortality, etc. In fact, for men we find another somewhat distant and independent Factor X, which we would title "Religious Belief." What this means, apparently, is that some men can be very high in their religious activity, yet at the same time come close to "failing" a belief test. On the other hand, some men can be relatively inactive yet, at the belief level, be deeply "religious" (for example, have a completely committed belief in God's existence, in a life after death, and/or in the validity and accuracy of the Scriptures, etc.). Of course there are many men high in religious activity as well as belief, or low in both—but, overall, in comparison with the females, belief and behavior for men in the religious area are not inextricably linked, or at least not to the same degree.

Religious commitment factors emerge from the projective test material for both men and women. Since these factors are relatively unrelated to each other, this could mean that this test is tapping an "unconscious" kind of religious variable. However, further research will be required before one can conjecture more on the exact nature of this factor.

With the males one finds another interesting factor, Factor IX, "Loss of Faith," which is not present in the female sample. This suggests that, with at least some of the males, there exists a certain pattern of becoming "unconverted" or rejecting the religion of one's youth. This is characterized by a tendency to view one's religion from a "theoretical or philosophical point of view" rather than by "faith." It coincides with doubt and inner conflict, considerable guilt, and an increasingly rejecting attitude toward a "literal interpretation" of the Scriptures. Finally there is a pragmatic demand for tangible absolute proof for the religionists' claims, which when not met leads to further estrangement and loss of faith but not without some inner turmoil.

However, while a "loss of faith" factor is absent in the female sample, one finds for them two very interesting other factors not present with the males. The first is Factor IX, "The Religious Hypocrite.'' And while this is not a major religious dimension among women, it does suggest that there are a small cluster who apparently are insincere and "two-faced" about their religiousness and who, to some extent, exploit religion for their own purposes. We might infer that possibly men do not have to be hypocrites (at least consciously)—if they do not like their religion they just become inactive or leave it. The other female factor is Factor IV, "Projected Guilt." This may suggest that "guilt" has a greater psychic impact with women than with men, or that women tend to internalize the values and conscience of their religious culture with greater effectiveness. Associated with feelings of guilt for women are tendencies to accept the Scriptures literally and by faith, and to be rejecting of a philosophical, theoretical, or pragmatic view of religion that might allow one to rationalize her "sins." There are also some evidences that this "Factor IV woman" views herself as not living up to the tenets of her religion as she should.

For both men and women, there are factors related to "political preference" (roughly along a liberalism-conservatism continuum) that appear not to be related to religiosity. There are also factors for both that might be called "dogmatic authoritarianism" which, again, are not related to whether one is religious or not.

In both samples, we find that the factors in the middle group (IV, V, and VII for men and II, V, and VIII for women) have in common something to do with family relationships and the religiosity of other family members. These factors for the most part are unrelated to the person's own religiousness in any of its senses. An analysis of their content and relationships suggests the following: (1) The degree of religiousness in one's parents is significantly related to the quality of family relationships. This is particularly true if the father is religious. The relationship most benefited by his being religious is with his daughter, though his sons also benefit to a lesser degree. The father's religiousness is also related to better husband-wife relationships. (2) It was found that the religiousness of the mother has a greater influence in another area (though it also contributes to better relationships with the offspring), and that is in increasing the likelihood that her children (especially her son) will also be religious. However, while the relationship between the religiousness of the parents and that of their offspring is positive and significant, it is still not very great—and, in fact, considering the potential influence parents have on their children, it is remarkably low. The relationship between the "religiosity" of husbands and wives produced correlations in the fifties, suggesting a moderate correspondence as might be expected.

Thus, when the two primarily "religious" factors for men (for example, I: "Religious Behavior," and X: "Religious Belief") are correlated with such variables as "being a Good Samaritan," "having love and compassion for one's fellow man," and being "humble"—certainly cardinal virtues in the Christian ethic (to which at least 85 percent of the sample subscribe)—we find almost no relationship. In the case of our female sample, the relationship is very slight between these variables and the main female religiosity factor. What this means essentially is that the "irreligious" in our sample are nearly as frequently rated as being a Good Samaritan, having love and compassion for their fellow man, and being humble as the most devout and religious of our group studied. Or to put it another way, there are a lot of devout, religious, churchgoing "non-Christians" in the sample studied if the Sermon on the Mount and the Four Gospels are considered relevant to Christian belief and practice. Thus it would appear that the churches (primarily the Christian denominations), while being able to have considerable impact on their membership, seem limited to inducing frequent prayer, high attendance, the giving of money, and concern about personal salvation—but somehow have apparently failed to induce much sense of responsibility toward one's fellow man. However, one might argue that the behavior of the irreligious (i.e., nonattenders, noncontributors, nonbelievers) may in many indirect and subtle ways still be influenced far more than one realizes by the Judeo-Christian "folk culture" in America.

The question should be raised as to what extent one might generalize these findings, since the Salt Lake population with its many Mormons is not representative of the country as a whole with respect to religious preference. While Mormon theology has some relatively unique aspects, it is believed that Mormon values correspond fairly closely to the "Protestant ethic" that is still predominant in the United States. As another approach to this problem, a separate factor analysis of all variables was run for the non-Mormon sample, with factor structure emerging that was strikingly similar to the total sample for ten mutual factors and had fair similarity for four other pairs (not only on which variables loaded on which factor, but on the actual size of the loadings). However, the non-Mormon group produced one extra factor (VIII) that did not show up in the total sample: this had to do with being a tolerant, open-minded female who lives a good moral life (this was *not* related to being religious in the conventional sense). In a secondary way, these findings also suggest that these factors may have a certain universality across religions, even possibly including persons without specific religious preference.

In conclusion, it would be important for the reader not to overgeneralize these findings, since the Salt Lake population is not completely representative of the country as a whole with respect to religion. However, one should not undergeneralize these results either because, as noted, these findings, if anything, come through with even sharper clarity and consistency for the non-Mormon sample, thus making it difficult to conclude that they were only due to sample peculiarities or bias.

With the sample limitation noted, this study has suggested that religiosity or religious commitment is no simple, single dimension, but is factorially extremely complex; or, more simply, there are many ways to be religious and to express this behaviorally. The differences in the ways men and women approach religion and integrate it in their lives are marked. These sex differences, it should be noted, are much more than mean differences in variables, but involve quite divergent patterning of correlations and factors. Some commonly held stereotypes, such as "religious people are more authoritarian than nonreligious," did not hold up. Additionally it was found that the three quite different assessments of overall religious commitment measures (i.e., projective test, coded depth interview, and questionnaire) had intercorrelations averaging .66, suggesting stability and a kind of cross-method validity.

4

The Intrinsic-Extrinsic Concept: A Review and Evaluation*

*Richard A. Hunt and
Morton B. King*

Allport's concept of Intrinsic (I) and Extrinsic (E) orientations to religion was a major contribution to the empirical study of religion (1950, 1954, 1959, 1960, 1966a; Allport and Ross, 1967). His ideas have stimulated both empirical data collection and theoretical analyses that have proved fruitful. Preliminary stock-taking of these results is now appropriate. This paper will review selected research reports and other papers in an attempt to bring their findings and conclusions to bear on four questions:

1. Is there an I-E dimension? Can it be identified operationally as a one-dimensional, two-pole variable?
2. What components, in theory and in research practice, does the I-E concept contain? Can separate dimensions be made operational?

*The unedited version of this article appeared originally in *The Journal for the Scientific Study of Religion*, 1971, *10*: 339-56. Copyright 1971 by the Society for the Scientific Study of Religion. Reprinted by permission.

3. To what kind or kinds of phenomena does the concept refer: a kind of religion or a way of responding to or orienting to religion? Religious behavior or motive for behavior? A religious or a personality variable?
4. What is the present and possible future utility of the concept and of measures associated with it?

The sources reviewed will be presented in chronological order, with no attempt to give a general summary of each or to describe the research methodology of each. Only those aspects that seem germane to the above questions will be treated. A concluding section will attempt to derive answers to each question from the survey summary.

EARLY HISTORY AND DEFINITIONS

The germ of the I-E concept appeared undefined and unnamed in *The Individual and His Religion* (Allport, 1950). In *The Nature of Prejudice*, Allport (1954) discussed "two kinds of religion" related to ethnic prejudice. The terms *interiorized* and *institutionalized* were used for I and E, respectively, but no formal definition was given. He first introduced I and E as labels in the Tufts lecture published as "Religion and Prejudice" (Allport, 1959). The first of his two succinct, formal definitions appeared in a preface written for a reprinting of that article (Allport, 1960). His most complete, and unfortunately his last, discussions of the concept were in "The Religious Context of Prejudice" (Allport, 1966a) and "Personal Religious Orientation and Prejudice" (Allport and Ross, 1967). In the former, he used two sets of labels; in the latter, I-E alone.

NATURE OF I-E

What light do Allport's conceptual formulations throw on our questions? First, what is the bearing of his general discussions on the nature of the phenomena (Q.3) and how they are viewed (Q.1)? Before the 1960 preface, emphasis was on E as the kind of religion associated with ethnic prejudice. The opposite, I, was partially and poorly defined. Those early statements referred variously to kinds of "religion," "religious sentiments," or "religious outlook." Eventually, a bipolar continuum was clearly conceptualized: I and E are "two polar types of religious affiliation" (1966 a); "most people, if they profess religion at all, fall upon a continuum between these poles" (1967). There was also a clear progression toward viewing the phenomena as a type of motivation. What was being studied came to be seen as, not "religion" or behaviors considered "religious," but the motives associated with religious belief and practice.

COMPONENTS

Secondly, what do the definitions indicate about the components (Q.2) of the I-E concept? In 1960, Allport published (p. 257) the first formal definitions of both I and E.

> *Extrinsic* religion is a self-serving, utilitarian, self-protective form of religious outlook, which provides the believer with comfort and salvation at the expense of outgroups. *Intrinsic* religion marks the life that has interiorized the total creed of his faith without reservation, including the commandment to love one's neighbor. A person of this sort is more intent on serving his religion than on making it serve him.

Seven years later, Allport and Ross (1967, p. 434) gave the most extended formal definition:

> *Extrinsic Orientation.* Persons with this orientation are disposed to use religion for their own ends. The term is borrowed from axiology, to designate an interest that is held because it serves other, more ultimate interests. Extrinsic values are always instrumental and utilitarian. Persons with this orientation may find religion useful in a variety of ways—to provide security and solace, sociability and distraction, status and self justification. The embraced creed is lightly held or else selectively shaped to fit more primary needs. In theological terms, the extrinsic type turns to God, but without turning away from self.

> *Intrinsic Orientation.* Persons with this orientation find their master motive in religion. Other needs, strong as they may be, are regarded as of less ultimate significance, and they are, so far as possible, brought into harmony with the religious beliefs and prescriptions. Having embraced a creed the individual endeavors to internalize it and follow it fully. It is in this sense that he *lives* his religion.

In sum: ". . . the extrinsically motivated person *uses* his religion, whereas the intrinsically motivated *lives* his religion.''

The definitions do not describe a single idea. Rather, Allport has introduced a number of variables. While they may be interrelated, conceptually they are separable, thus suggesting that I-E is not one relatively simple continuum. In order to explore these separate components, Chart A was developed from Allport's definitions. Words and phrases used to refer to I or E were assigned to categories. Each category was assigned a number and descriptive label. The Roman numerals indicate, roughly, the time sequence in which the ideas appeared, first by date of publication and then within each source. The number(s) after a word or phrase give(s) the date(s) of the work(s) in which it appeared.

Chart A
Components of I-E Definitions

	Intrinsic	Extrinsic
I.	Reflective vs. Uncritical	
	reflective (1950)	unreflective, uncritical (1950)
II.	Differentiated vs. Undifferentiated	
	highly differentiated (1950)	undifferentiated (1950)
III.	Personal vs. Institutional	
	?	institutional (1950, 1954)
	"interiorized" (1954, 1960)	"institutionalized" (1954)
	vital, deeper level (1967)	external (1954)
	devout, internalized (1967)	
IV.	Universal vs. Parochial	
	universalistic (1954)	exclusionist (1950, 59)
	infused with the character of ethics (1954)	ethnocentric, exclusive, in-group (1954)

creed, ideals of brotherhood (1954, 66a)	at expense of out-groups (1960)
conditioned to love one's neighbor (1960)	favors provincialism (1966a)
compassion (1967)	

V. Unselfish vs. Selfish

not self-centered (1959)	self-centered (1950)
strives to transcend self-centered needs (1966a)	self-interest (1959); self-serving, self-protective (1960); useful to self (1966a); uses for own ends (1967)

VI. Relevance for All of Life

distilled into thought and conduct (1954)	single segment (1959)
floods whole life with motivation and meaning (1959, 1966a)	not integrated into their way of life (1966a)
not limited to single segments (1966a)	favors compartmentalization (1966a)
other needs brought into harmony with religious beliefs and prescriptions (1967)	
follows creed fully (1967)	

VII. Salience

faith really matters (1954)	full creed and teaching not adopted (1959)
sincerely believing (1954)	
accepts total creed (1960)	faith, beliefs lightly held (1967)

Chart A—Continued
Components of I-E Definitions

without reservations (1960)

follows creed fully (1967)

VIII. Ultimate vs. Instrumental

an end in itself (1954, 66a)	utilitarian, means to ends (1954)
"intrinsic" (1959, 1960, 1966a, 1967)	"extrinsic" (1959, 1960, 1966a, 1967)
intent on serving his religion (1960)	not master motive (1959) instrumental (1959, 1966a, 1967)
a final good (1966a)	supports and serves nonreligious ends (1966a)
faith is supreme value; the master motive (1967)	uses religion (1967)
ultimate significance (1967)	serves other than . . . ultimate interests (1967)

IX. Associational vs. Communal

?	political and social aspects
"associational" (1966a, 1967)	"communal" (1966a, 1967)
seeking deeper values (1967)	sociocultural (1966a)
involved for religious fellowship (1967)	affiliates for communal identification, need to belong (1966a)
	no true association with the religious function of the

church (1966a)

involved for sociability and status (1967)

X. Humility vs. Dogmatism

humility (1959, 1967)   dogmatic (?1959, 1966a)

XI. Regularity of Church Attendance

constant (1967)   casual and peripheral churchgoers (1966a)

feel no need to attend regularly (1966a)

The eleven categories chosen are, of course, arbitrary. There could have been more. Numbers VI and VII, and perhaps VIII and IX, might be combined to give fewer categories.

Five of the components dominated the definitions. Others were mentioned, but none seemed as central as these:

IV. Universal-Parochial: brotherhood and love of neighbor vs. ethnocentrism and exclusion of those unlike oneself.

V. Unselfish-Selfish: effort to transcend self-centered needs vs. self-serving protective use for own ends.

VI. Relevance for All of Life: floods whole life with motivation and meaning vs. compartmentalized, not integrated into one's way of life.

VII. Ultimate-Instrumental: end vs. means; master motive vs. utilitarian uses; intrinsic vs. extrinsic in the axiological sense.

IX. Associational-Communal: involved for religious fellowship and deeper values vs. affiliation for sociability and status.

SUMMARY

Allport attempted to describe two orientations to religion as poles of a continuum. However, in his own definitions, we discovered an expanding bundle of component variables. To deal with these complications, we now examine the content of items used to make the I-E concept operational.

OPERATIONAL DEFINITIONS

WILSON

Wilson (1960) made the first report of empirical research based on the I-E concept. With Allport's help, he developed an "Extrinsic Religious Values Scale" (ERV) consisting of fifteen items of two kinds, corresponding to categories III and VIII, institutional and instrumental. All items, however, were treated as one scale with one pole as the "extrinsic religious value." The other pole was "not positively defined, but simply reflects the absence" of E.

Implications. Wilson's study shed some light on all four questions. Q1. Rather than being clearly unidimensional, ERV had at least two components and only one pole. Q2. It seemed to be an index of E alone; with I undefined and unmeasured. Q3. Wilson (1960) stated that ERV did not measure "the content of religious beliefs," but "attempts to measure . . . the motivations for affiliating with a religious institution." Thus, he established early the view that what was being measured was motivation for religion, not a kind of religion or a dimension of religion. Q4. That ERV had some validity and research utility was shown by the fact that it was significantly correlated with a measure of anti-Semitism in all ten subject groups (.41 to .72).

FEAGIN

Feagin (1964) made a major forward step in making the I-E concept operational. He used an "Intrinsic/Extrinsic Scale" of twenty-one items, developed by Allport's seminar. It included only two items from Wilson's ERV. According to Feagin, twelve were "extrinsically stated," six "intrinsically stated," while three belonged to an unnamed residual category. The I items seem only reverse statements of E, but were a first, small attempt to define another end of the continuum.

These items (hereafter identified as *Allport-Feagin*) were the basis of subsequent research and deserve careful attention. Chart B was prepared to aid the analysis. Examined in terms of the components in Chart A, six of the E items can be classified as both VIII and V, instrumental and selfish. Most of the other E items are hard to classify. One each is considered III (institutional), VI (nonrelevant), VII (nonsalient), and IX (communal). The other two are unclassifiable. Three of the I items are considered III (personal); two, VI (relevant); and one, VII (salient). The three unlabeled items are classified as XI (church attendance), IX (associational/communal), and unclassifiable. Thus, the total item content places primary emphasis on instrumental/selfish. Three items each were devoted to the personal-institutional and the relevance components; two items each, to salience and associational-communal; and one, to church attendance. Three items were left unclassified.

Chart B
Items to Measure I-E

Intrinsic:
2. *I try hard to carry my religion over into all my other dealings in life. (A&R, K&H) [VI]
7. Quite often I have been keenly aware of the presence of God or of the Divine Being. (A&R) [III]
8. *My religious beliefs are what really lie behind my whole approach to life. (A&R, K&H) [VI]
9. *The prayers I say when I am alone carry as much meaning and personal emotion as those said by me during services. (A&R, K&H) [III]
16. Religion is especially important to me because it answers many questions about the meaning of life. (A&R, K&H) [VII]
20. *It is important to me to spend periods of time in private religious thought and meditation. (A&R, K&H) [III]

Unlabeled by Feagin, but called I by Allport and Ross:
13. *If not prevented by unavoidable circumstances, I attend Church at least once a week or oftener, two or three times a month, once every month or two, rarely. (A&R, K&H) [XI]

Chart B—Continued
Items to Measure I-E

14. If I were to join a church group I would prefer to join (A) a Bible Study group or, (B) a social fellowship. (A&R) [IX]
18. *I read literature about my faith (or church) frequently, occasionally, rarely, never. (A&R, K&H) [?]

Extrinsic:

1. *What religion offers most is comfort when sorrow and misfortune strike. (A&R, K&H) [V, VIII]
3. *Religion helps to keep my life balanced and steady in exactly the same way as my citizenship, friendships, and other memberships do. (W, K&H) [V, VIII]
4. *One reason for my being a church member is that such membership helps to establish a person in the community. (W, A&R, K&H) [V, VIII]
5. *The purpose of prayer is to secure a happy and peaceful life. (A&R, K&H) [V, VIII]
6. It doesn't matter so much what I believe as long as I lead a moral life. (A&R) [?]
10. Although I am a religious person, I refuse to let religious considerations influence my everyday affairs. (A&R) [?VI]
11. *The Church is most important as a place to formulate good social relationships. (A&R, K&H) [V, VIII]
12. Although I believe in my religion, I feel there are many more important things in life. (A&R) [VII]
15. I pray chiefly because I have been taught to pray. (A&R) [III]
17. A primary reason for my interest in religion is that my church is a congenial social activity. (A&R) [IX]
19. Occasionally I find it necessary to compromise my religious beliefs in order to protect my social and economic well-being. (A&R) [?]
21. *The primary purpose of prayer is to gain relief and protection. (A&R) [V, VIII]

*Items selected by Feagin for factorially-derived I and E scales.

NOTE: The items are identified by their numbers in Feagin (1964).

The letters after each item indicate other studies in which it was used: W, Wilson (1960); A&R, Allport and Ross (1967); K&H, King and Hunt (unpublished). Roman numerals in brackets after each item indicate the conceptual component (Chart A) to which it is assigned.

Feagin's factor analysis produced separate I and E factors. From these, he selected two scales composed of six items each. All E items combined both instrumental and selfish components. The I scale was mixed, having two items indicating relevance; two, personal; and two, religious practices: church attendance and reading religious literature. The last had the highest factor loading and item-scale correlation.

Implications.   Feagin's findings bear directly on the questions. Q1. He demonstrated that the twenty-one items were "not unidimensional." His separate factors pointed toward separate I and E dimensions. Q2. His items illustrated several components. His factorially derived E scale clearly defined "extrinsic" as instrumental and selfish. The I scale, with three components, provided a less useful definition of "intrinsic." He was uncertain "whether any of the items are measuring 'intrinsic-devout' religiosity." The findings indicate that Q1. I and E scales do in fact measure different things; Q2. they are more useful separately than the twenty-one items combined; and Q4. they have some validity and research utility.

ALLPORT AND ROSS

Allport and Ross (1967) reported a study using twenty of the same items, divided into two subscales (E, 11; I, 9) based apparently on subjective evaluation of item content. (See Chart B.) Neither factor nor item-scale analyses are reported beyond item correlations with the combined I-E scale. Two findings led them to question the utility of I and E items combined into one scale. The E items alone were more highly correlated with prejudice. There was "only a very low correlation between the I and E items scored separately." It was, they said, "apparent . . . that subjects who endorse extrinsically worded items do not necessarily reject those worded intrinsically, or vice versa." Many subjects "persist in endorsing any or all items that to them seem favorable to religion in any sense." Such subjects were called "indiscriminately proreligious."

Allport and Ross (1967) used the I and E items, scored as separate scales, to divide the subjects into three groups: "intrinsic," those who were above the median on I and below on E; "extrinsic," those in reverse categories; "indiscriminately proreligious," those who gave "approximately 50% more intrinsic responses on the intrinsic subscale than we should expect from (their) extrinsic responses on the extrinsic subscale." Comparing mean scores of the three groups on five measures of prejudice, they found that intrinsic subjects were least prejudiced and the indiscriminately proreligious were most prejudiced. Those who were "extremely indiscriminate" were more prejudiced than those moderately so.

Implications. This study led to several tentative conclusions: Q1. I-E is not one unidimensional variable. Q2. The items can be used to measure the "indiscriminately proreligious" as well as I and E. The authors considered this category a third dimension or orientation and presented a separate psychodynamic explanation to account for its high correlation with prejudice. The same multiple components found in Feagin's twenty-one items are present in their twenty, of course. Q3. Allport and Ross made clear that they were measuring "motivation" for or "orientation" to religion, not its types or forms. I-E was discussed as if it were a personality variable. Q4. Correlations of I and E with prejudice and other variables to form explanatory patterns of theoretical interest indicate some validity and research utility for the measures.

King and Hunt

King and Hunt (1969) reported results of factor and item-scale analyses on a large number of items indicating varied aspects of religious belief and practice. The questionnaire contained about fifteen I-E items. A six-item scale composed of E-type items was developed. Nothing that could be called an "intrinsic" factor or scale appeared. The I-type items were scattered among several factors, including a quite general first factor.

In 1968 items from that study, together with many new items, were included in a questionnaire returned by 1,356 members of four Protestant denominations. Seven I and five E items were included from the Allport-Feagin list shown in Chart B. Two E-type scales were derived. One with seven items had six belonging to the instrumental/selfish component, five of which were Allport-Feagin items. Another five-item scale contained no Allport-Feagin items but had three that were instrumental-selfish. The other two were unclassified.

The seven Allport-Feagin I items did not form a stable, homogeneous cluster. They were scattered among several factors, including a first, general factor. Two of the scales derived contained some Allport-Feagin I items but were given names to represent the total item content. "Orientation to Growth and Striving" and "Salience: Cognition," parallel to "Salience: Behavior."

Implications. What are the implications for our questions? Q1. No I-E continuum is apparent. I and E were clearly not opposites, but rather two somewhat related but separable variables. Q2. Our findings, like Feagin's, indicate that E can be isolated and specified as instrumental/selfish. Neither the Allport-Feagin I items nor any subset of them were successfully isolated by factor analysis. Our findings, like Feagin's, fail to define I with any clarity or homogeneity. Q3. In our study the I and E items appear to indicate orientation to, or the way a person relates to, religion. Q4. Our E scale is not useful in relation to the tolerance/prejudice variable. However, its correlation with other variables indicated some analytical power. The I-type scales, while conceptually fuzzy, have some use through a positive relation to tolerance.

OTHER RELATED STUDIES

USING ALLPORT ITEMS

Three other studies used the twenty Allport and Ross items in empirical studies. Hood (1970) used them, as Allport and Ross (1967) suggested, to divide his subjects into four categories: I, E, and indiscriminately proreligious or antireligious. He found that the I and E subscales were not significantly correlated. I was significantly correlated with his "religious experience episodes measure" (REEM); E was not. Hood reported difficulty in distinguishing "intrinsically oriented" from "indiscriminately proreligious" persons, because of the "methodological problem of distinguishing a genuine report . . . from a response set." Relating his findings to our questions: Q1. Hood did not treat, and had no basis for treating, I-E as a single continuum. He did not find I and E related, as bipoles or otherwise. Q2. His REEM seemed to measure the I aspect of the Personal-Institutional component (III), and he treated both indiscriminately proreligious and antireligious as useful dimensions. Q3. He considered I and E to be orientations to religion. Q4. Despite careful attention to the reliability and validity of REEM, Hood presented no such evidence for the I and E subscales.

McConahay and Hough (1969) used the twenty items in a study with forty-eight original items. The latter were designed to indicate perspectives based on love, guilt, and forgiveness themes in Christian theology, plus a "culture-oriented" or "conventional" orientation. Several of their findings bear on our questions: Q1. "The third factor was . . . clearly the Allport and Ross factor with Extrinsic items loading high positively and the Intrinsic low negatively." However, they used the I and E items separately as subscales and reported a statistically significant correlation of −.25 between them. Q2. Their "conventional" scale contained five original items, all of which have E-like content. Two can be classified as instrumental/selfish (V and VII) and one as communal (IX). The other two were unclassified. This scale had a significant correlation of +.35 with the Allport and Ross E items. Items on their "Love Oriented−Other Centered" scale had content similar to definitions of I. Three of the five items could be classified as IV, universal (brotherhood of all men). However, neither the I nor the E subscales were significantly correlated with it. Items were not shown for their "Church Involvement in Social Action" scale. However, the description of it sounds like component VI, relevance for all of life. Surprisingly, its correlation with the I items was −.38. Q3. McConahay and Hough considered that the I-E items measured "motivation for religious practices," in contrast to the "theological content" of their love-guilt scales. However, all their scales seemed to be of the "orientation to" or "perspective on" type. Q4. The pattern of correlation between their scales led to theoretically interesting interpretations. Therefore, the I, E, conventional, love oriented−other centered indices had enough utility to encourage their testing through further use.

Strickland and Shaffer (1971) used the twenty items in a study with "Adorno's Fascism scale" and Rotter's scale measuring "belief in internal as opposed to external control of reinforcement." Q1. In a small pilot study, I and E were found to have a negative correlation of .54. The authors were persuaded that I and E were poles of a continuum and the "two subscales were combined into one overall extrinsic score." Q3. I and E, like the other variables, are considered "belief systems." Q4. The I-E scale was significantly correlated with control of reinforcement, I being related to belief that "behavior will have an impact on . . . life situations." It was not related to an authoritarian belief system.

USING THE I-E CONCEPT

Brown (1964), Tisdale (1966), and Vanecko (1966) conducted empirical studies using the I E concept but not the Allport-Feagin items. In the first of several studies, Tisdale used Wilson's ERV and the others used original items and methods. Some light was thrown on our questions. Q1. Brown (1964) and his judges were unable to classify sentence-completion data as either I or E. Instead, seven categories were proposed. However, no obvious continuum emerged. Q2. He treated I and E as separate, mutually exclusive categories. Two of his categories were "self-serving extrinsic" and "extrinsic through conventional acceptance." These correspond to the instrumental-selfish (V, VIII) and institutional (III) components. VII, salience, was also implicit in his discussion. Q3. Brown proposed that disbelief, as well as belief, had its intrinsic and extrinsic orientations. His proposal that "more research is needed to show whether the origins and functions of extreme belief and disbelief are in fact the same" suggested that I-E refers to a pervasive personality process.

Tisdale (1966), in answer to Q1, thought that ERV measured one variable, an "extrinsic orientation." Q3 and Q4. The ERV correlation with personality variables led to the conclusion that this religious orientation was related to certain "manifest needs in normal individuals," supporting Allport and Adorno theories of the relation of religion, personality dynamics, and prejudice.

Vanecko (1966) used original measures of several religious dimensions to study their relation to prejudice. While his items and scales were not given, some variables, as described, sound like components of I and E. "Acceptance of ethical norms," "acceptance of social teachings," and "devotional practices" could be considered I-aspects of the "relevance" (VI) and "personal" (III) components. His "instrumental" was E, and it may be interpreted as "instrumental/selfish" (VIII, V). Q1. Vanecko presented his scales as measures of separate variables. Q2. They were similar to several I-E components. Q3. Vanecko thought of his variables as forms of "religious behavior." Q4. "Acceptance of ethical norms" was negatively associated with prejudice and "instrumental" was positively associated, thereby supporting Allport's theory.

OTHER FACTOR STUDIES

Studies by Keene (1967) and Monaghan (1967) used factor analysis on item pools quite different from Feagin's (1964). Both developed typologies that overlap with the I-E concept and with its components. Keene (1967) sought to identify "the basic dimensions of religious behavior" in studying Bahais, Jews, Christians, and unaffiliated subjects. He distinguished four dimensions: (1) Salient/Irrelevant, (2) Spiritual/Secular, (3) Skeptical/Approving, and (4) Orthodox/Personal. Examination of his item content allows conclusions regarding Q2: Some items in his "salient" were similar to our "salience" (VII), but his also had a "church attendance" item (XI) and other measures of participation. "Spiritual" items were partly creedal and partly the "personal" or I aspect of component III. "Orthodox" was primarily the "institutional" or E aspect of III.

Monaghan (1967) attempted to discover "motivations" for church membership and attendance. He distinguished three "hypothetical type(s) of person(s)": the "authority-seeker," "comfort-seeker," and "social participator." Q2. The latter two were similar to the E aspects of several components. "Comfort-seeking" had much in common with instrumental/selfish (VIII, V), nonrelevant (VI), and nonsalient (VII). "Social participation" contained inner conflicts. Some items pointed toward the E and others toward the I aspects of IX and thus did not distinguish communal and associational motives for participation.

Finally, reference should be made to Allen and Spilka's (1967) careful attempt to measure orientations to religion in relation to prejudice. Their committed/consensual (Cm/Cs) dimension had some relationship to I-E (see Dittes, 1969). In relation to Q2: three of the five Cm/Cs categories were similar to I-E components: "Clarity" and "reflective-unreflective" (I); "Complexity" and "differentiated-undifferentiated" (II); "Importance" and "relevance" (VI). None of these components was covered by the Allport-Feagin items. The first two were not mentioned by Allport after 1950. In Allport and Ross (1967) "unreflective" was explicitly, and "undifferentiated" was implicitly, assigned to the new "indiscriminately proreligious" orientation. Cm/Cs did not correlate with Wilson's (1960) ERV. As conceptualized and especially as made operational, I-E and Cm/Cs are largely different variables. Q3. In one way, however, they are similar. I and E are most usefully viewed as orientations to or motivations behind religion. Allen and Spilka conceived of Cm/Cs as a composite of five "cognitive dimensions." That is, both I/E and Cm/Cs seem to be pointing to pervasive personality characteristics. Q4. Cm was associated with prejudice and Cs with tolerance, which parallels the prediction of I-E theory.

CONCLUSION

Allport's I-E concept has generated fruitful scholarly activity, both theoretical and empirical, among sociologists as well as psychologists. Their work has added to an understanding of the relationship between religion and ethnic prejudice. (See Allport and Ross, 1967, and Dittes, 1969, in particular.) Some contribution may have been made to the psychology of personality itself. On the other hand, we believe the time has come to abandon the early generalized definitions and rough measures in favor of more specific definitions and a complex set of measuring tools. To justify those conclusions, what can we conclude regarding the four questions proposed?

1. Is there a single I-E dimension? Can it be identified operationally as a unidimensional, bipolar variable?

The preponderance of evidence says No. Feagin (1964) found two factors, and our own data produce several. Feagin (1964) and Allport and Ross (1967) found that I and E used separately were better predictors of prejudice than the two combined. Brown (1964) concluded that two and perhaps three dimensions were involved. Factor analysis (Keene, 1967; Monaghan, 1967; King and Hunt, 1969 and unpublished data) revealed a complex structure. Examination of item content indicated several components, even in the Wilson (1960) ERV scale. Evidence in favor of unidimensionality is slight. Strickland and Shaffer (1971) combined I and E items into one scale, based on a correlation of .54 in a pilot study. McConahay and Hough (1969) obtained what they call the "Allport and Ross factor." From their description (the items are not shown), it is dominated by E items, the I items having low loadings.

The evidence indicates, secondly, that I and E are separate dimensions, not bipoles of one. Feagin (1964) stated that his I and E factors were "orthogonal" to each other. The Strickland and Shaffer (1971) finding that r=.54 seems to support the idea of a bipolar continuum. However, there were only twenty-four pilot subjects, and Strickland and Shaffer report no test based on their study data. The other studies reported no correlation or low correlations between I and E, with both plus and minus signs.

I-E, we conclude, has not been successfully operationalized as one dimension with I and E as its poles.

2.   What components, in theory and in research practice, does the I-E concept comprise? Can separate dimensions be made operational?

Examination of Allport's definitions revealed a number of conceptually separable components. The eleven displayed in Chart A might be expanded or combined. Other minds would produce different lists, but, we believe, they would discern several components. Our list proved useful for the classification of the content of items prepared in the Allport tradition. It was much less useful in classifying other items. The main components seen in the items were: III, Personal-Institutional; V, Unselfish-Selfish; VI, Relevance for All of Life; VIII, Ultimate-Instrumental; and IX, Associational-Communal. In addition to those, IV, Universal-Parochial, was prominent in the later definitions.

Which components have received separate operational definition by a useful or potentially useful scale? Only one, the instrumental/selfish combination, is clearly established. Since Feagin (1964), "extrinsic" has had no other useful definition, and his six items are still its best measure. Support for this definition of E was found in Brown (1964), Vanecko (1966), Monaghan (1967), and King and Hunt (1969 and unpublished data). In general, two kinds of item matrices have been factored or otherwise analyzed. When a small number of items was selected to meet Allport's definitions, an E factor composed primarily of instrumental/selfish items appeared. Most of the remaining items appeared as a first or general factor which, in that limited context, seemed to be a relatively homogeneous definition of I. However, in a larger, more heterogeneous matrix, the structure was different. An E factor or factors appeared, dominated by selfish/instrumental items. The I items, however, were scattered among several factors. Operational definition of I is still lacking; no one satisfactory scale has been developed.

The studies reviewed have indicated several other variables of potential utility, including both I and E components. All these warrant further study to test their research utility. Indicators of VI, Relevance for All of Life, were found in Feagin (1964), Monaghan (1967), in McConahay and Hough's (1969) "Church Involvement in Social Action," and perhaps in their "Love Oriented-Other Centered" dimension. The latter, however, also has the "brotherhood" aspects of IV, Universal-Parochial. Indicators of VII, Salience, were present in Feagin (1964), Keene (1967), Monaghan (1967), and King and Hunt (unpublished data). The Personal (not institutional) aspect of III appeared in Feagin (1964), Keene (1967), and Hood's (1970) REEM; and the "Personal Religious Experience" scale of King and Hunt (1969 and unpublished data) had items or scales measuring one or more aspects of congregational participation. However, none seem to measure the motivation for such behavior, which is what makes the idea of IX, Associational-Communal, interesting. Brown (1964) and McConahay and Hough (1969) identified a "conventional" dimension that is related to the E aspect of III, Personal-Institutional. Allport and Ross (1967) introduced and Hood (1970) supported the idea of two "indiscriminately pro- and anti-religious" dimensions.

3.   To what kind(s) of phenomena does the I-E concept refer?

As early as Wilson (1960), emphasis was placed on I-E as orientation to or motivation for religion, rather than as a kind of religion or of religious behavior. That emphasis was clearer in definitions, and in the discussion of research findings, than in item content. However, it was in Allport and Ross (1967) and the parallel work of Allen and Spilka (1967) that the I-E phenomena began to look more like a personality variable and less like "religion." Allport and Ross (1967) referred to both I-E and prejudice as "states of mind," "enmeshed with" each other, "deeply embedded in personality structure." Prejudice, explicitly, and I-E, implicitly, were considered "a consistent cognitive style." Allen and Spilka (1967), engaged in the same search for the relation of religion to prejudice, arrived at a similar terminus: five categories of cognitive style. Brown (1964) proposed that I-E is a variable that cuts across disbelief as well as belief. His discussion suggests a pervasive personality process.

What social scientists have tried to measure under the label of "real," "internalized," "intrinsic" religion and its extrinsic opposite may prove to be basic, pervasive personality variables. If so, it would help to understand and predict all behavior, and not just "religious" behavior. Read the items in Feagin's instrumental/selfish scale. Could these not be rewritten to apply just as well to any area of institutional behavior: work relationships, education, even the family? Is it only the church and religious behavior that one uses for selfish purposes? Indeed, in some theological perspectives *all* behavior is religious, since by implication it expresses one's faith perspective, his orientation to the ultimate meanings of life.

4.   What is the present and possible future utility of the I-E concept and of measures associated with it?

How does one evaluate utility? We have used as our criteria conceptual clarity and, especially, ability to explain the variance in other variables. On both grounds, we found I-E lacking as a single variable. The label, certainly, and probably the gross idea should be abandoned. Both have served a useful purpose. Now attention should be focused on labels, ideas, and scales of greater specificity. The supporting evidence includes: the variety of conceptual components identified in definitions, item content, and empirical findings; general failure to find one homogeneous set of items; the fact that Feagin (1964), Allport and Ross (1967), and others found that the E items alone were more closely related to prejudice than all items combined.

As noted above, however, "extrinsic" as measured by Feagin's

(1964) instrumental/selfish scale is definitely useful. No other definition of E has proved so useful. The McConahay and Hough (1971) "conventional" scale may be refined as a measure of another E component.

We conclude that I as a single religious dimension should be abandoned, as a label and as an idea. First, its conceptual complexity is supported by the fact that items chosen to measure it turn up on several separate factors. Some such dimensions may be interpreted in the I-E context (e.g., relevance, devotionalism); others may not (e.g., congregational participation). Second, I is hard to distinguish from "indiscriminately proreligious." (See Hood, 1970.) Third, serious problems of reliability and validity are involved. The root meanings of I have been "inner," and "real," and "ultimate." All require inferences made from observed and reported behaviors that are believed to be symbols, indicators of something beyond themselves. Deciding what is "real" is a metaphysical, not empirical, operation. Deciding what is "ultimate" is even harder. Who has the perspective from which to decide what is in fact ultimate, even in the psychic economy of one person? What indices should be used? Will they be consistent when comparing persons?

As noted above, separate I components were identified or measured in Allport and Ross (1967), McConahay and Hough (1971), Strickland and Shaffer (1971), and King and Hunt (unpublished data). Efforts to refine them should continue.

The idea of indiscriminately proreligious and antireligious dimensions deserves careful theoretical and empirical attention. Allport and Ross (1967) and Hood (1970) derived measures from their I and E scales. What they measured may be only a proreligious response set encouraged by church-oriented research procedures. Our data share the same problem, and most of our scales developed for different religious dimensions have low positive correlations, even I and E. Future research reports should attempt to report correlations corrected for this bias. The phenomenon may be an expression of general yea- or nay-saying, as Allport and Ross suggest. Couch and Keniston (1960) report that nay-sayers have good internal controls and high ego strength. Yea-sayers are impulsive and low in ego strength, with their "behavior determined more by external factors in the immediate situation." Is this a personality syndrome that explains differences in both prejudiced and religious behavior? Here, again, "religious" scales may be pointing us to those basic personality variables related to perception, cognition, and patterns of response that should be the central focus of "religious" research.

Evaluation of research related to the I-E concept and other religious dimensions points to a paradox. Some scholars try to identify and measure the kind of religion that does, can, or should provide a master motive for all of life. Others aim at discovery of the motive(s) behind kinds of behavior called "religious." They, and personality psychologists, find that motivation that explains "religious" behavior is a pervasive variable that explains "secular" behavior also.

There seems little doubt that what deserves to be called "religious" behavior is involved in the personality structure at its deepest levels, and probably in multiple ways. That view is consistent with the thought of those who seek to define religion by its function in life, rather than by historical and/or institutionalized substance. For example, Luckmann (1967) states that the "social processes that lead to the formation of the self are fundamentally religious."

Starting at any of several points on the research circumference, we are led to a common center for the social psychological study of the person and his relations with all other persons, things, and events. Work on the I-E concept, started by Allport, now points empirical students of religion to these research opportunities and to the need to join with other social scientists in common tasks.

5

Contributions to Research Method: 1. Piaget's Semiclinical Interview and the Study of Spontaneous Religion*

David Elkind

For research purposes it is convenient to distinguish between the spontaneous and the acquired religion of the child. The child's spontaneous religion consists of all those ideas and beliets that he has constructed in his attempts to interpret religious terms and practices that are beyond his level of comprehension. In contrast to these spontaneous mental constructions, there are many religious ideas and beliefs that the child acquires directly from adults either through imitation or through instruction. A child's recitation of the standard

*The unedited version of this article appeared originally in *The Journal for the Scientific Study of Religion*, 1964, 4: 40-47. Copyright 1964 by the Society for the Scientific Study of Religion. Reprinted by permission.

definition of theological terms or of particular prayers would thus reflect acquired rather than spontaneous religion.

It is fair to say that by far the majority of research on religious development has concerned itself with acquired rather than with spontaneous religion. While such studies of acquired religion are of value for assessing the degree to which children profit from religious education, they do not reveal the full nature of religious development. Indeed, they can be misleading!

This is not to say that results from the traditional questionnaire studies of religious development are wrong, but only that the acquired religion revealed by these results does not follow the same developmental course as spontaneous religion. Since even the young child can memorize definitions of religious terms, it is not surprising that when children are tested on these definitions the young children do about as well as the older children. If, on the other hand, the *understanding* of these definitions were to be evaluated, it is likely that significant age differences would be found because the understandings would reflect the child's spontaneous and not his acquired ideas. Only the child's spontaneous ideas follow the sequence from the concrete to the abstract that we have come to expect in developmental studies of concept formation.

As yet, however, we have little information about the spontaneous religion of the child, and the purpose of the present paper is to describe a method for exploring the child's own interpretations of religious terms and practices. The method is the semiclinical interview devised by the Swiss psychologist Jean Piaget.

THE SEMICLINICAL INTERVIEW

Piaget was one of the first investigators to realize that the child's spontaneous remarks were more than amusing errors and that they reflected forms of thought that were different from those used by adults. In order to investigate children's spontaneous thought, Piaget was forced to devise his own method. The specifications for such a method, however, were exceedingly stringent and apparently contradictory. For what Piaget required was a method with sufficient flexibility to enable him to follow the meandering stream of any particular child's thought and yet with enough standardization to enable him to reach the same destination with many different children at different age levels.

The only method that met the first of these specifications was the psychiatric interview, while the only method that met the second specification was the mental test. This being the case, Piaget combined the standard questions of the mental test with the free inquiry of the psychiatric interview and labeled the result the semiclinical interview. The union of standard question and free inquiry was a happy one.

Despite the proven fruitfulness of the semiclinical interview, however, it has seldom been employed by American psychologists and, with one exception (Elkind, 1961, 1962, 1963), has never been brought to bear on the study of religious development. The reasons for this neglect of Piaget's method are several, including the amount of time and skill required of the examiner and the difficulty involved in interpreting the obtained data. While those objections are well taken, they do not outweigh the potential value of the method for exploring spontaneous religion.

In the first place, although the interview is more time consuming than the questionnaire, the obtained data will be much more complete and therefore more revealing than those obtained by more rapid group testing procedures. In the second place, while skill in conversing with children is required, most investigators dealing with children have the basic requirements for a good interviewer: a liking for children, a respect for their individuality, and patience. As for the difficulty in interpreting responses, this is present no matter what method is used, and, in fact, Piaget has given particular attention to this problem and has worked out techniques and criteria for discriminating between the significant and the trivial in children's verbalizations. So on this point the Piaget method is actually superior to the questionnaire wherein no such discriminations can be made. There are, then, no really good reasons for not using the interview techniques in studying religious growth.

CONSTRUCTION OF INTERVIEW QUESTIONS

Since the construction of appropriate questions is one of the most difficult features of the semiclinical interview, an illustration of how the author proceeds in formulating such questions might be helpful to prospective investigators. In general, one begins with a remark that suggests the presence of a spontaneous conceptualization. For example, after the tragic death of President Kennedy, the author heard a child say, "Are they going to shoot God too?" This remark suggested that the child identified God with famous persons in high offices and opened up a whole new path of inquiry. If we desire to follow this lead, we might begin formulating some questions about God and high offices. For example we might ask, "Can God be president of the United States? Why or why not?" Furthermore, we might ask about how God obtained his position. For example one might ask, "Who chooses the president? Who chooses God, or how did God become God?"

If this line of inquiry proved unfruitful, we might go back to the original remark and note that it also suggests that God is conceived as a person. This notion leads to quite another line of questioning ("Can God dance? Talk French?" etc.). Should this line of inquiry prove barren, we might approach the problem from the fact that the term *God* is a name and ask such things as "How did God get his name? Does God have a first name?" etc. The only requirement in formulating questions is that they be so absurd, to the adult way of thought, that one can be reasonably certain children have not been trained one way or the other regarding them. Trial and error with various questions proposed to one's own or to neighbor children will soon reveal which questions are the most productive of unstereotyped, spontaneous replies.

Interview Technique

Once a group of related questions about a given topic has been gathered, the actual interviewing can begin. The child should be seen in a quiet place where there are few distractions and at a time when he does not desire to be somewhere else. As soon as the examiner has won rapport with the child—most easily accomplished by asking the youngster a few questions about himself—he can begin putting his interview questions. After the child has replied, it is usually necessary to ask additional questions to clarify the meaning of the response. It is in this free-inquiry part of the interview that the most skill is required, because the examiner must direct the child's thought without, at the same time, suggesting an appropriate answer.

INTERPRETATION OF RESULTS: VALIDITY

Both during the examination and afterwards, in analyzing the data, the most important question is to what extent the child's response truly reflects his own mental constructions. To this end, Piaget has described five types of response that need to be distinguished in any examination of the child. When the child is not at all interested in the question and is bored or tired, he may simply answer with anything that comes into his head just to be relieved of the burden of having to answer. Piaget speaks of such responses as *answers at random*. When a child fabricates or invents an answer, without really reflecting about the question, Piaget speaks of *romancing*. On the other hand, when the child does attend to the question but his answer is determined by a desire to please the examiner or is suggested by the question, Piaget speaks of *suggested conviction*.

In contrast to the three foregoing types of reply, which are of little value to the investigator, the following two types are of very great significance. When the child reflects about a question that is new to him and answers it from the reservoirs of his own thought, Piaget calls this a *liberated conviction*. And when the child answers quickly, without reflection, because he has already formulated the solution or because it was latently formulated, it is called by Piaget a *spontaneous conviction*.

Since the investigator is primarily interested in the liberated and the spontaneous conviction, it is important to have ways of separating them from random, romancing, and suggested convictions. This can be done at two points in the investigation, one during and the other following the interview. If, during the interview itself, the examiner suspects that a reply is other than a spontaneous or a liberated conviction, he can check this in several ways. First, he can offer countersuggestions to determine how firmly rooted the idea is in the child's thought. A true liberated or spontaneous conviction will withstand countersuggestion, whereas romancing, suggested convictions, and answers at random are easily changed by countersuggestions. Secondly, he can ask about related issues. If the idea is truly a conviction of the child's, it will fit a pattern or system of ideas that follows a general principle or rule that Piaget calls a *schema*. If the child's response fits the general trend or schema of his thought, this is a good indication that it is either a spontaneous or a liberated conviction.

The second point at which one can determine whether or not replies obtained in the interview represent genuine convictions occurs after the data have been collected and age trends can be examined. First of all, if the majority of children at the same age level give similar replies, this is evidence that the responses reflect a form of thought characteristic of that age. Secondly, if the responses show a gradual evolution with age in the direction of a closer approximation to the adult conception, this is another piece of evidence that the replies reflect a true developmental trend. Finally, a valid developmental sequence must give signs of continuity in the sense that traces of concrete ideas held at early age levels (adherences) are present among the abstract conceptions of older children and in the sense that foreshadowings of abstract ideas typical of older children (anticipations) are present among the concrete expressions of the young children.

INTERPRETATION OF RESULTS: RELIABILITY

Although Piaget has always been concerned about the validity of his observations, he has almost ignored the question of their reliability, i.e., their repeatability. Two such measures are needed. One is a measure of the consistency with which individual children respond to interview questions at different times. This measure can be obtained by retesting each of the subjects, preferably not before a month and not later than six months after the original examination. The correlation of initial and retest responses will provide an index of response reliability.

The second index of reliability that should be obtained relates to the categorization of responses into stages or sequences of development. That is to say, it is necessary to determine whether the responses are sufficiently distinctive that independent workers will classify them in similar ways. If several persons independently categorize the responses and a measure of their agreement is determined, this measure will serve as an index of the reliability of the categorization. These steps to ensure the reliability of response, together with the fulfillment of Piaget's criteria for determining validity, should suffice to guarantee that investigations employing the semiclinical interview will be acceptable to even the most hardheaded experimentalist.

POTENTIAL APPLICATIONS

The foregoing sections have described a method for exploring the spontaneous religion of children. Among the problems to which the semiclinical interview could be appropriately applied are the traditional ones of the developmental psychology of religion. Conceptions of God, of belief, of prayer, of sin, of morality, and many others all deserve to be looked at from the point of view of spontaneous religion. It would be fascinating, too, if someone were to undertake a study of children's theologies and cosmologies, of children's confusions between magic and ritual, and of children's attempts at integrating moral and religious ideas. For the study of these issues and of many more like them, the semiclinical interview is a necessary starting point.

6

Contributions to Research Method: 2. Measurement of Religion as Perceptual Set*

*David J. Ludwig and
Thomas Blank*

Although the multidimensionality of religious behavior has been well supported, typical studies have measured religiosity by questionnaire (cognitive response). The present study extends this exploration by adding another dimension: perceptual set as measured by projective techniques.

*The unedited version of this article appeared originally in *The Journal for the Scientific Study of Religion*, 1969, 8: 319-21. Copyright 1969 by the Society for the Scientific Study of Religion. Reprinted by permission.

METHOD

QUESTIONNAIRE MEASURES

Three well-known, standardized questionnaires were used as the cognitive measures. The first of these was the "Belief Pattern Scale: Attitude of Religiosity" developed by Kirkpatrick. A high score on this scale reflects approval of the organized church and of its dogma.

The second measure was a combination of two scales developed by Chave and Thurstone, called the "Reality of God Scale" and the "Attitude of God: Influence in Conduct Scale." These scales measure the influence of religion on the person's life and were combined because they intercorrelate highly and show similar correlation with the other scales.

The third scale used was also a questionnaire, but it asked the person to report his actual religious behavior (e.g., how often he prays, goes to church, etc.). This scale is a modified, but representative, form of the one developed by Cline and Richards (see chapter 3). All of these are available in Shaw and Wright (1967).

PERCEPTION MEASURES

The fourth scale was an attempt to measure religious perception by presenting the person with ambiguous pictures taken from the Thematic Apperception Test (TAT) (Murray, 1943) and incomplete sentences.

In scoring, two points were given for direct reference to God and to a living relationship to him (e.g., the sentence completion, "My strength lies *in my God,*" or the response, "These are men gathered around the cross of Christ," to a TAT ambiguous picture of a crowd of people).

One point was given for an indirect or impersonal reference to God or religion (e.g., the response to the picture of a woman at the bedside of a man, "I will have to look for help outside human hands," or the sentence completion, "Life *is influenced by the spiritual*").

If no reference was made to God, no points were given.

These two measures were combined because of a fairly high intercorrelation and because they also show similar correlation with the other measures.

SUBJECTS

The subjects used for this study were 76 preministerial students selected at random from approximately 250 juniors at Concordia Senior College, Fort Wayne, Indiana. All of the subjects were members of the Lutheran Church—Missouri Synod, and all intended to enter a theological seminary at the conclusion of their liberal arts training.

PROCEDURE

The subjects were brought to a classroom with the statement that they were going to help with the development of some measures. At the beginning of the testing situation, the subjects were given a sheet of paper and were instructed to write down their first impression of what the central character was thinking as a TAT picture was flashed on a screen for twenty seconds (with twenty seconds between pictures). Following this, they were given eight minutes to complete fifteen sentences. Then the questionnaires were handed out, and the subjects spent the rest of the testing hour filling out the Belief Scale, the two Reality of God Scales, and the Practice Scale, in that order.

RESULTS

Table 1 shows that all correlations among the measures are positive and significant.

The results, in a meager way, support the assumption that religious faith pervades many dimensions or levels of behavior: the cognitive level, the practice level, and the level of perception. Thus one can interpret faith as a set to respond in terms of religious attitudes, religious practice, and religious perception. It is not only a cognitive expression, nor even limited to a set of practices, but it also is a way of looking at things—a perceptual set.

Methodological limitations may have enhanced or attenuated the intercorrelations. Some of the correlation may be accounted for by response set, since the subjects filled all the scales at the same sitting. The correlations may have been constricted by the use of a very homogeneous group of subjects. If subjects other than preministerial males were used, one would expect the correlations to increase in magnitude.

Table 1
Correlations Among the Four Scales

	Reality of God in One's Life	Report of Religious Practice	Reference to God in Response to Ambiguous Stimuli
Acceptance of Orthodox Statements	.34**	.23*	.22*
Reality of God in One's Life		.54**	.37**
Report of Religious Practice			.27*

*significant at .05 level of confidence
**significant at .01 level of confidence

7

Contributions to Research Method: 3. Timed Cross-Examination: A Methodological Innovation in the Study of Religious Beliefs and Attitudes*

Orlo Strunk, Jr.

Since the very beginning, a lack of methodological sophistication has plagued the psychology of religion. In the early days when behaviorism was on the psychological throne, the psychology of religion became a near impossibility. With the liberalization of methodology in the present century, the psychological study of religion began to pick up momentum. Greater acceptance of clinical methods

---

*The unedited version of this article appeared originally in *The Review of Religious Research*, 1966, 7: 121-23. Copyright 1966 by the Religious Research Association. Reprinted by permission.

and the use of personal documents permitted the psychologist of religion more freedom in which to conduct his research.

Unfortunately, methodological liberalization brought with it a greater use of paper-and-pencil tests, especially questionnaires. Despite the fact that every behavioral scientist knows the severe limitations of paper-and-pencil instruments, they continue to be the dominant method employed in the psychological study of religious phenomena. Probably, it is not an exaggeration to say that most of our generalizations about religious behavior are based wholly, or mostly, on results obtained from various pencil-and-paper tests.

Certainly it is apparent to all that a degree of self-deceit and desire for social approval permeates most of our studies based on self-reports. Even thoroughly reliable and validated paper-and-pencil tests suffer from the unavoidable shortcomings of subjects lacking self-insight, having self-delusions, or—especially in our day—wishing to say the personally and socially desirable thing. What is needed is some technique that can subject the "yes" and "no" unqualified scores of such tests to a critical examination at the moment of their being obtained.

Thanks to the research of A. R. Gilbert (1946, 1958, 1961, 1963), such a technique is now available. It is called *timed cross-examination.*

The timed cross-examination approach is actually two instruments rolled into one. One instrument is the personality test or attitude scale already validated and reliable; the other instrument is the timed cross-examination device, superimposed on the former.

When taking a timed cross-examination test, the subject seemingly takes a traditional paper-and-pencil test. However, he takes it in a modified form: instead of reading the items in a test booklet, he is exposed to reading them in succession in the window of a presentation unit; and instead of marking his answer with pencil on paper, he moves a lever to the "agree" or "disagree" position.

The ordinary self-report of the subject is double-checked by the timed cross-examination innovation: first, by measuring automatically the time interval from the moment of exposure of the stimulus item to the moment of the subject's motor response, the lever action, indicating his judgment of the item; second, by exposing the subject later, interrupted by unrelated items, to the polar opposite of the same item, and taking the same measures as before.

Not only, then, is the subject's consistency of choice regarding the particular dimension ascertained, but the speed of the simple response is also automatically noted. From these scores or patterns of responses, the investigator can identify differences between self-report scores and the timed cross-examination scores. These differences are in reality discrepancies between the conscious-voluntary and the subconscious-automatic reaction time (RT) responses.

To illustrate the technique, let us turn to a time-honored instrument in the measuring of attitudes toward the church: "The Thurstone Attitude Toward the Church Scale" (1929).

This particular scale consists of forty-five statements designed to express subjects' sentiments toward the church. To use the scale for timed cross-examination purposes, it is first necessary to write polar-opposite statements for each statement appearing in the original. For example, the statement "I do not have contempt for the church" needs the polar-opposite statement "I have nothing but contempt for the church." The original statements and their polar opposites are then randomized and presented to the subject by the window-lever technique; his agree-disagree responses are automatically recorded with his reaction times.

The actual analysis of a subject's responses may be plotted so that a self-report profile and a timed cross-examination profile may be compared. Purely for illustrative purposes, let us look at one pattern of a preministerial student whose general profile may be considered unwholesome:

On the statement "I don't regard the church as a monument to human ignorance," the subject agreed with a RT of 4.99 seconds. Though he disagreed with the polar opposite statement, he did so in 3.15 seconds, a discrepancy suggestive of an emotional block not detected in the traditional scale.

Perhaps more dramatic is the subject's response to the item "I do not have contempt for the church"; though he agreed with the statement, he also agreed with the polar opposite, "I have nothing but contempt for the church.'' Thus, he reveals here an ambiguous, nonpolar response.

Of course, the actual patterns are more numerous and more subtle than the brief illustration given here. Actually, Gilbert has identified four major interpretive patterns that he calls (1) polar regular pattern, (2) polar irregular pattern, (3) nonpolar pattern, and (4) reversed polar pattern. Adding the identification of inordinately lengthened RT's to these patterns gives the researcher ample opportunity to identify anxiety loadings or emotional blocks, possible underlying specific personality dimensions on which the cross-examinative stimulus items are patterned.

The following two areas of research especially can profit from the timed cross-examination techniques:

1. Study of religious beliefs and attitudes. As was indicated early in this paper, practically all of our generalizations about religious beliefs and attitudes are based on paper-and-pencil instruments. Of course, self-report studies are exceedingly important, but such studies need penetration in depth, recognition and appreciation of the double system of motivation characteristic of most psychological phenomena. The timed cross-examination method, coupled with the traditional self-report, will go a long way in adding caution and integrity to the generalizations we make about religious behavior.

2. The study of the motivational systems of religious practitioners. As we all know, theological schools throughout the United States are concerned about the growing number of ministerial candidates seemingly lacking existential commitments to their calling. Perhaps, if we can identify some of these deeper areas of doubt and other psychological schemata, we can better give guidance and counsel to these young men and women.

8

Contributions to Research Method: 4. Assessing Qualitative Differences between Sets of Data*

John R. Tisdale

INTRODUCTION

Some years ago, a research method called "characteristic differences" was described briefly in connection with its demonstration at a research section meeting of a national religious group (Ligon and O'Brien, 1954). Since then, it has been developed to a point at which an additional description and evaluation seem both possible and desirable.

Basically, the approach makes use of a consensus of individual judgments concerning two (or more) sets of data. It is thus related, though distantly, to the use of judgments in clinical diagnosis, psy-

*The unedited version of this article appeared originally in *The Journal of Psychology*, 1967, 66, 175-79. Reprinted by permission of The Journal Press.

chophysics, and attitude scaling. One of its chief differences, however, lies in its appropriateness for constructed-response or open-ended data.

Usually a group of judges is given two sets of data, which they are asked to examine for any differences between the two sets that they might observe. Only those differences are accepted that are agreed upon by some specified fraction of the judging group. The data might consist of such things as self-descriptive statements from two different subjects, critical incidents reported by observers of some process under study, responses to different forms of a test or examination, or the like.

STRENGTHS

The strengths of this method lie in its simplicity, its flexibility and potentially diverse applicability, and its appropriateness for dealing with qualitative differences among samples. It requires no data-processing equipment nor elaborate instructions. The basic data on which it is carried out need not be ordered, but may be separated only in terms of some single criterion that may be external to the data. The educational level and technical competence of the judges need not necessarily be high, depending on the complexity of the discriminations that the experimenter might wish to have made.

It is this simplicity itself that makes this method such a flexible tool with a wide variety of possible applications. A sociologist might use it in preliminary studies of differences in leadership expectations between various types of work groups. An anthropologist might search for tentative value differences between two different cultural groups. A pastor might use it to search for things that distinguish "successful" from "unsuccessful" sermons.

The search for characteristic differences might also prove helpful as a partial check on the validity of some separation criterion itself. Assume, for instance, that one wishes to develop a rationally constructed test of some personality trait, such as extrinsic religion. After making up a pool of items that, in the test author's judgment, would seem to indicate the presence or absence of this trait, one administers the test to a group of subjects presumed to vary on the trait in question. An item analysis might then be taken to discover items discriminating between high and low quartiles. The items characteristically endorsed by the high scorers are then compared with those endorsed by the low scorers. The differences between the groups, as reported by the judges, should reflect substantially the same differences that the author initially set out to measure. This can provide a helpful early step in the construct validation of a personality test.

Too, this basic method can be used to arrive at a consensus concerning similarities between groups as well as differences, often concurrently. It may be used with three or four groups instead of two, although such use may involve complication. Use with more than three or four groups, however, becomes impractical.

In all of these instances, this approach was used with data that could not easily be quantified or for which quantification would be undesirable. In many cases, particularly in exploratory stages of research in an area, strictly quantitative methods may overlook valuable insights or even be quite inappropriate. In a study of a pilot project designed to teach scientific decision-making skills to a college sample, for instance, no significant differences could be found between participants and nonparticipants on nearly all of the quantitative measures used. The characteristic differences procedure, however, indicated some specific qualitative differences that opened up a new area for further investigation (Tisdale, 1967b).

As described here, then, this approach is best suited for exploratory research with open-ended data designed to generate promising leads to be followed up more closely later. It is not per se a method of hypothesis testing. Thus, the results one finds with it must always be accepted tentatively, subject to further verification by more precise techniques.

LIMITATIONS

As with any research device, of course, there are certain limitations that should be observed. In describing areas of usefulness above, potential areas of misapplication have been suggested. Another caution has to do with the background of the judges used. When it was stated that the method did not necessarily require highly trained judges for its use, it was not meant to imply that the judges' training and skill were irrelevant to the results. For the use of the characteristic-differences method, the nature of the data and the level of discrimination potentially sought will dictate the necessary technical competence demanded of the judges. It would (presumably, at least) be inappropriate to use college sophomores in looking for differences among Thematic Apperception Test (TAT) protocols, where the possibility of rather subtle distinctions might exist. On the other hand, if one is interested only in large and very obvious differences, the judges' level of training and ability may be much less important. The decision as to what kind of judges to use with any given sets of data must ultimately lie with the experimenter himself.

A basic implied assumption is that the reliability of the method is best measured by interjudge agreement. This is defensible since, from a hardheaded operational point of view, one cannot meaningfully speak of differences being "there" that someone does not judge to be there; and consensual validation ultimately is the usual scientific basis for deciding on what is "really" there.

On the other hand, the desire to obtain agreement should not blind one to certain values inherent in the fact of divergent reports of differences. A variety of judgments may signal lack of agreement, but it also yields a variety of hypotheses for possible future testing. Thus, the divergent perceptions produced by a minority of the judges in an exploratory research situation may in the long run prove more fruitful than the things upon which all or most of the judges can agree.

Fortunately, a validation technique exists that may be used to check both divergent and agreed-upon reports of differences. Using a "sortback" approach, one can validate the observed characteristic difference in a way similar to cross-validation of psychological test construction. The items (in this instance) from the two groups of data are put into a common pool and given to a new set of judges with instructions to sort the items into groups according to the characteristic difference being tested. If the new judges are able to place the items accurately into the two original classes, the reported difference may be accepted.

Another potential problem may lie in the tendency of judges to be overzealous in searching for differences. The fact that they have been given material to judge may well imply to them that the experimenter expects differences to be found and will be disappointed if they are not. If the data allow it, one can check on this possibility by asking judges to examine at least two different paired sets of data, one of which (a control) consists of material drawn from a single homogeneous parent population and randomly assigned to two groups (Tisdale, 1967a).

In examining the kinds of differences that judges report, one should note too whether certain individual items in the data seem to be influencing judgments unnecessarily. It is possible, certainly, for one negative statement in a group of neutral ones to lead one to characterize the whole group as negative in tone. Here a set of instructions that are explicit about the degree of halo effect regarded as desirable can be helpful. Nevertheless, the precise influence here of the nature and homogeneity of the data upon the type of differences observed has not yet been investigated.

It is, finally, absolutely necessary to observe stringent safeguards concerning contamination of judgments from the judges' knowledge of the makeup of the groups. No judge should know the nature of the source of the data, nor should there be any indication in advance of whether the experimenter is looking for or expecting particular types of differences. If necessary, some editing of the data may have to be done in order to obscure sex or educational differences between the groups where such knowledge might unnecessarily influence the differences found. Placing the data uniformly typed on plain pages with only enough description to make them comprehensible would seem best.

For Further Reading

Several of the books mentioned in the Introduction to this section might provide take-off points for you if you are interested in some historical perspective on the psychological study of religion. James's *Varieties of Religious Experience* (available in several reprint editions: Collier, Mentor, Modern Library) is the single most important volume, while the books by Coe, Lueba, and Starbuck provide other earlier perspectives. Modern treatments of the subject organized around traditional topics have been done by Paul Johnson (*Psychology of Religion*, rev. ed. [Nashville: Abingdon, 1970]), and Walter Houston Clark (*The Psychology of Religion* [New York: Macmillan, 1958]). Paul Pruyser orders the material differently, using psychological categories in his *A Dynamic Psychology of Religion* (New York: Harper and Row, 1968), while Wayne Oates added some new topics from a slightly different perspective in his *The Psychology of Religion* (Waco, Tex.: Word Books, 1973).

There haven't been any books written and published on research methods in the psychology of religion, as such, although Samuel Southard's *Religious Inquiry* (Nashville: Abingdon, 1976) is a relevant and clearly written work. Two brief introductory volumes of a more general nature might also be helpful: Theodore R. Sarbin and William C. Coe's *The Student Psychologist's Handbook* (Cambridge, Mass.: Schenkman, 1969) or Barry Anderson's *The Psychology Experiment* (Belmont, Cal.: Brooks/Cole, 1966). Several parts, if not all, of Irvin Child's *Humanistic Psychology and the Research Tradition* (New York: Wiley, 1973) may catch your interest if you are at a bit more advanced level.

Historically, there have been some other approaches to the definition of religion that provide different perspectives from the multidimensional ones highlighted in the readings; Oates summarizes some of them. In addition, Freud emphasized the wish-fulfilling and unprovable nature of religious belief in his *Future of an Illusion* (1927; included in *Standard Edition of the Complete Psychological Works,* vol. 21 [London: Hogarth, 1961]). Jung, on the other hand, saw religion as expressing symbolically some basic truths about the nature of man. I haven't found as yet a single place in which he does this succinctly, but perhaps volume 11 of his *Collected Works*

(Princeton: Princeton University Press, 1969) has the best collection of material.

Some newer understandings see religion functioning to provide man with meaning in life. Erwin R. Goodenough's *The Psychology of Religious Experience* (New York: Basic Books, 1965) and Viktor Frankl's *Man's Search for Meaning* (Boston: Beacon, 1962) are in this spirit.

Part Two

Religious Development

INTRODUCTION

Interest in the place of religion in the developing personality has long been a concern of psychologists investigating religion. It continues as a growing edge. Further, so complex is this area of personality development that no single theoretical perspective has emerged with which to tie together what has been done. To be sure, Elkind (in the first article in this section) speaks from a Piagetian perspective as he describes how religion may meet four cognitive needs as they develop in the preadult personality. However, Piaget alone is not enough. Perhaps a kind of rudimentary summary of personality development drawing on other theorists as well (Maslow, Erikson, Freud, Keniston, Kohlberg) might provide a step in that direction and (to mix metaphors) a place from which to view the next group of articles.

From birth until walking is mastered, the child lives completely in his present experience, largely out of touch with both his own past and his future. He is dominated by needs for the maintenance of his own organism. Most of his world, particularly during the first part of this period, is experienced tactually—through tasting and touch. His thinking and knowing are probably limited to the direct bodily sensations he has and externals that are perceptually immediate for him. He seems to learn the working difference between inside and outside, the "me" and the "not-me." The discovery that his percepts refer to objects that are relatively permanent is one of the usual outcomes of this period. The regular succession of events and his own preverbal conviction that the world is predictable lead to a sense of safety or confidence in the orderliness of that which he experiences. If circumstances are good, he also senses his world as benevolent. He does not have separate religious or moral categories as such, but in all likelihood his capacity for what religions often call a faith relationship—a relationship of trust and confidence—will be largely determined by his experiences at this age. Responses to such instruments as King and Hunt's "Orientation" and "Devotionalism" scales (see chapter 2) may well have their genesis during this period, when the child shapes his basic worldview.

During early childhood, the period in our society until the youngster enters school, the child is still very much a creature of the

95

moment, but with some expanding horizons. With his survival no longer in question, he feels more acutely the need to be part of a family or another primary group. He is now able to discriminate a sign from the item or concept to which it refers, and he is making his first efforts to use symbols (or "representations") correctly. With the advent of walking as a means instead of an end, he faces the question of whether or not it is safe to explore his world, to "intrude" into new places, to manipulate, to test, to discover, to use his initiative. As toilet training and socialization proceed successfully, he discovers the ability to exercise control over his own body— preparation for controlling aspects of the external world that lie ahead. Here, too, he forms important impressions of himself and his own value. He knows love and the threat of its withdrawal if he is not "good." The human experiences expressed in the Protestant doctrines of original sin and salvation by faith, not works, may be related to the ways in which the tasks of this period are completed. It is difficult to say whether he is truly moral or not, but such morality as he possesses is either a matter of simple acquiescence to authority or a kind of eye-for-an-eye justice. Questions related to Hunt and King's "Creedal Assent" and "Religious Knowledge" factors begin here, not exclusively in terms of content, but in terms of orientation. Too literal interpretations of reality that begin in this stage may have to be corrected later.

Formal education begins next, bringing with it an increase and expansion of the child's dealings with the larger world while his physical growth rate slows. His conceptions become organized as functional parts of larger wholes; he achieves an understanding of the relations among the specifics to which he is exposed inside and outside of school. His movement into this "real" world of institutionalized education provides the child with the opportunity to have "real" effects on things, instead of just playing games (important as these are). Successes bring a sense of accomplishment and self-esteem as he tests himself against the activities of his peers. During this stage, he is also learning about the moral expectations of the larger society of which he is a part. Toward the end of this period, his standards for judging morality begin to shift from an emphasis on particular acts to a sense that values consist in maintaining one's expected role and the larger social fabric of which it is a part. His understandings of and knowledge about his religious affiliations expand as he gathers himself for the changes that puberty will bring.

Adolescence brings with it the second high of the diphasic human growth curve. Physical proportions change for both boys and girls as sexual needs focus and mature. Having learned to relate facts and probabilities, teenagers move into a period in which the ability to manipulate abstractions and to consider the world of pure possibility is developed. They come to ask the profound existential question, Who am I? the answer to which will require many years to work out fully. Morality may become less a matter of supporting and maintaining conventional obligations and more a matter of defining principles that have validity apart from the individual's membership in any particular group or even from the existence of the group itself. The question of identity and one's place in the universe in this period brings with it some renewed interest in religious beliefs and the relevance of religion to daily living as an expression of one's self, although not necessarily of one's group membership. The assertion of individual responsibility found in the book of Ezekiel might be relevant to what teenagers experience during these years. In the part of a longer article that is reprinted in this section, Hepburn examines what seems to be known about religious attitudes during these years. He also points out the problems involved in defining religion that we saw in the first section of this volume.

For some individuals in our society, there is a stage of development yet to be lived through before adulthood is reached. Those who are in this probable minority have completed the individual development tasks of adolescence but have not yet made a firm commitment to (or against) "the System." Their personal identity is well on the way to being worked out, but the ways in which they will relate to the structures of society need to be examined more fully. Many of them can be found in colleges and universities, which in a number of ways prolong adolescence while seeming to prepare for adulthood. Without explicitly recognizing this stage of development, Feldman takes a very careful look at the many factors that might affect the religious values of college students. Although there may be a general trend toward decreasing orthodoxy of belief over the college years, the different institutional factors and differences among students make it difficult to generalize very fully. The achievement of this period is an individual life style in some kind of relation to (as opposed to alienation from) social institutions. Moral development continues, as abstract principles are examined and tested in specific contexts. Religious institutional allegiances are also probed, so that questions of congregational involvement are important. Those who pass through this stage are those who are likely to work out idiosyncratic sets of religious beliefs and to experience discomfort in participating in many of the conventional churches and/or synagogues. They are beginning to explore new ways of experiencing and describing reality.

Development does not end with the beginning of adulthood. Heenan recognizes this, but as he looks specifically at later adulthood he finds very little research available. This is true of the earlier adult years as well. Although new cognitive structures may not develop, knowledge is extended and specific intellectual abilities are sharpened throughout the changing circumstances of adult living. Questions of religious knowledge, of the relevance and nature of institutional affiliations, and of the importance of religious practices continue to be asked. For some, the changes of midlife, as energy turns from dealing with the external world to the world within, renew unsolved problems of identity and one's relation to ultimate reality. It is in midlife that self-actualization is most likely to be dominant. Concerns with intimacy that were acute during the early years of adulthood may expand into concerns beyond one's immediate circle, perhaps as a reflection of the "compassionate Samaritan" factor in Cline and Richards's paper. These in turn may resolve into attempts to face death as a personal experience instead of an impersonal event in some distant future. Not everyone will wrestle with the meaning of his own death and thus of his own life. To each who does, however, and who does so successfully, may come the paradoxical sense both of being part of a process and yet of being fully responsible for life as it was lived. With this sense of fully developed selfhood, death can be met with dignity and integrity.

Given such a context, we still note the curious fact that empirical work on religious development as such seems to be at a temporary standstill. The publication of Strommen's monumental volume in 1971 apparently marked a kind of growth plateau. Elkind, in the Strommen book, seems to have sensed this when he stated that "we are . . . at the threshold of an exciting new period of research on religious growth and understanding" (p. 683). Perhaps those interested in this area, like the proverbial and now anachronistic fearful bride, are waiting for a lover to carry them over the threshold and consummate the promise.

Our own group of articles here closes with two that show some renewed interest in conversion, long viewed as a developmental phenomenon and clearly treated that way by Allison. Stanley's is a tightly knit hypothesis-testing study, with variables clearly defined and conclusions explicitly drawn. It illustrates as well an interest in viewing conversion from the standpoint of its relation to mental health. Allison turns the methodological clock back to an earlier period in the study of conversion by reporting on a case study. But it is a very skillfully done individual study, and it provides some significant hypotheses for future testing and an excellent insight into the psychological dynamics of such an experience in one man's life. Whether similar dynamics would hold for women is yet to be determined.

9

The Origins of Religion
in the Child*

David Elkind

Every social institution, whether it be science, art, or religion, can
be regarded as an externalized adaptation that serves both the individual and society. From the point of view of the group, social
institutions provide the ground rules and regulations that make society and social progress possible. Looked at from the standpoint of the
individual, social institutions afford ready-made solutions to the
inevitable conflicts with social and physical reality that the individual
encounters in his march through life. Social institutions, therefore,
originate from and evolve out of the adaptive efforts of both society
and the individual. It follows that any complete account of the origins
of religion must deal with both individual and social processes of
adaptation.

In the present paper, I propose to treat the origins of religion solely
from the perspective of the individual and not from that of society. It
is not my intent, therefore, to give a comprehensive account of the
origins of religion in general or in any way to negate the central
importance of social factors in the origination and historical evolu-

*The unedited version of this article appeared originally in *The Review of Religious Research*, 1970,
12: 35-42. Copyright 1970 by the Religious Research Association. Reprinted by permission.

tion of religion. All that I hope to demonstrate is that religion has an individual as well as a social lineage and that this individual lineage can be traced to certain cognitive need capacities that emerge in the course of mental growth. To whatever extent religion derives from society's efforts to resolve the conflicts engendered by these individual need capacities, we are justified in speaking of the origins of religion in the child.

Briefly stated, the paper will describe four need capacities with respect to the age at which they first make their appearance, the problems of adaptation that they engender, and corresponding resolutions that may be offered by religion. A concluding section will take up the question of the uniqueness of religious adaptations from the point of view of the individual.

INFANCY AND THE SEARCH FOR CONSERVATION

During the first two years of life, the human infant makes truly remarkable progress. From an uncoordinated, primarily reflex organism, he is within the course of a short two-year period transformed into an upright, talking, semisocialized being, more advanced intellectually than the most mature animal of any species. Of the many accomplishments during this period, none is perhaps as significant nor of such general importance as the discovery that objects exist when they are no longer present to the senses, that is to say, the discovery that objects are conserved.

For the adult, with whom the world and the self are clearly demarcated, it is hard to envision the infant's situation. The closest we can come to it is in a state of reverie or semiconsciousness when the boundaries of awareness waver and we are embedded in the very pictures we are sensing. This is the perpetual state of the infant, for whom all awareness can hardly be more than a series of blurred pictures following one another in an unpredictable sequence. Only gradually does the child begin to separate his own actions from things and to discriminate among different things, such as the human face. Even when the response to the human face occurs, usually in the second and third months of life, there is still no awareness that the face exists when it is no longer present.

Only toward the end of the second year does the infant give evidence that for him objects now exist and have a permanence of their own quite independent of his immediate sensory experience. This awareness of the permanence or conservation of objects comes about when the progressive coordinations of behavior give rise to internal representations or images of absent objects. It is the two year old's capacity to represent absent objects mentally that results in knowledge of their conservation.

The construction of permanent objects is important because it is a prerequisite for all later mental activity. All of our concepts start from or involve objects in one way or another, so the recognition of their permanence is a necessary starting point for intellectual growth in general. Object permanence, however, is just the first of many such permanences or conservations that the child must construct. As his mental capacities expand, he encounters new situations that parallel, though at a higher level of abstraction, the disappearance of objects. Illusions are a case in point. A spoon in water looks bent or even broken, the moon appears to follow us when we walk, just as the sun appears to revolve around the earth. Similar problems present themselves on the social plane. The child must learn to distinguish, for example, a true invitation to stay at a friend's home from an invitation that is, in fact, a polite dismissal. In all of these cases, the child has to distinguish between appearance and reality, between how things look and how they really are. Infancy thus bears witness to a new mental ability, the capacity to deal with absent objects, and to a corresponding need, the search for conservation, a lifelong quest for permanence amidst a world of change.

One of the problems of conservation that all children eventually encounter, and to which they must all adapt, is the discovery that they and their loved ones must ultimately die. In contrast to the conservation of the object, which is first transient and only later permanent, the child begins by assuming that life is everlasting and is shocked when he finds out that it is transient. After the initial recognition, often accompanied by intense emotional outbursts, the child seeks means whereby life can be conserved, a quest that continues throughout his existence.

In many cases, the conflict between the search for conservation and the inevitability of death does not arise with its full impact until adolescence. Religion, to which the young person has already been exposed, offers a ready solution. This solution lies in the concept of God or Spirit which appears to be religion's universal answer to the problem of the conservation of life. God is the ultimate conservation since "he" transcends the bounds of space, time, and corporality. By accepting God, the young person participates in his immortality and hence resolves the problem of the conservation of life. Obviously, whether in any particular case the young person will accept this religious solution will be determined by a host of personal and sociocultural factors. All that I wish to emphasize here is that religion offers an immediate solution to the seemingly universal human problem posed by the search for conservation of life and the reality of death.

EARLY CHILDHOOD AND THE
SEARCH FOR REPRESENTATION

As was true for the period of infancy, the preschool period is one of rapid mental growth and of wide-ranging intellectual accomplishments. Foremost among these is the mastery of language. With the conquest of language, the child goes far beyond the representation of things by mental images. Language is a series of conventional signs that bear no physical resemblance to that which they represent. The child must now painstakingly learn to represent all of those objects that were so laboriously constructed during the first years of life. The child is not, however, limited to representing things by language; he can now also employ symbols that bear some resemblance to the objects they represent. It is at this stage, too, that the child dons adult clothes and plays house, store, and school. All of these behaviors, the mastery of language and engagement in symbolic play activities, bear witness to a new cognitive capacity, the ability to use signs and symbols, and to a new cognitive need, the search for representation.

The search for representation, which makes its appearance in early childhood, like the search for conservation, continues throughout life. At each point in his development, the young person seeks to represent both the contents of his own thought and those of his physical and social environment. As his knowledge of himself and his world grows more exact, he seeks more exacting forms of representation. Not only does his vocabulary increase at an extraordinary rate, but he also begins to acquire new tools of representation, such as mathematics and the graphic arts. Yet, the more exacting the child becomes in his search for representation, the more dissatisfied he becomes with the results. One reason, to illustrate, why children usually give up drawing in about the fourth or fifth grade is their disgust with the discrepancy between what they wish to portray and what they have actually drawn. In the same way, as the child matures he gradually realizes that language is a lumbering means at best for conveying his thoughts and is hopelessly inadequate for expressing his feelings.

For the young person who has accepted God, the search for representation poses special problems. If religion provided only a concept of God and nothing else, he would be at a loss to represent the transcendent. How, after all, does one signify that which is neither spatial, temporal, nor corporeal? Religion, however, affords more than a simple God concept; it also provides representations of the transcendent. In primitive religions the representations were totems or idols, whereas in modern "revealed" religions the transcendent may find its representation in some kind of scripture. Here again, however, as in the case of the concept of God, the individual's acceptance of this religious solution is multidetermined and difficult to predict in the particular case. What must be stressed is that, once the individual accepts the concept of God, the question of his representation is an inevitable outcome of the search for representation in general.

CHILDHOOD AND THE SEARCH
FOR RELATIONS

The school age period is one of less rapid intellectual growth than was true for the preceding two periods. During this epoch in the child's life, he is, for the first time, exposed to formal instruction and must acquire a prescribed body of knowledge and special skills such as reading and writing. The acquisition of a prescribed body of knowledge, however, presupposes a mental system that is, in part at least, comparable to the mental systems of adults who transmit the knowledge. Such a system does come into being at around the sixth or seventh year, the traditional "age of reason."

One general feature of this new ability to reason in a logical manner is that the child now tries to relate phenomena in the world about him in a systematic manner. The youngster at this stage wants to know how things work, how they are put together, where they come from, and out of what they are made. Moreover, his concepts of time and space have broadened, and he can now grasp historical time and conceive of such distant places as foreign countries. It seems appropriate, therefore, to speak of the new ability that surfaces at school age as the capacity for practical reason and of the corresponding need as the search for relations.

The search for relations, which makes its appearance in childhood proper, continues throughout life. As the young person matures, he seeks to relate himself to his social and physical milieu and to relate the things and events in his world to one another. While his search for relations is often gratifying, it is also on occasion disheartening. There are many events in life that cannot be related to one another in any simple rational way. The quirks of fate and accident are of this kind and defy man's rational efforts. There is often no simple rational answer to the question, Why did this happen to me? So, while the quest for relations helps man to understand himself and his world better, it also makes him aware of how much he cannot know and understand.

Within the religious sphere, the young person who has accepted the concept of God and his scriptural representation is confronted with the problem of putting himself in relation to the Transcendent. Here again, in the absence of a ready-made solution, the young person might flounder and his resolution of the problem would be makeshift at best. Religion, however, affords a means whereby the individual can relate himself to the Deity, for it offers the sacrament of worship. By participating in worship, the young person can relate himself to the Transcendent in a direct and personal way. To be sure, the young person's acceptance of religion's answer to the problem will again be determined by a variety of factors. Indeed, some of our research (Elkind and Elkind, 1962; Long, Elkind, and Spilka, 1967) suggests that many young people reject the formal worship service but nonetheless engage in individual worship in the privacy of their rooms. In any case, for the adolescent who has accepted God and his scriptural representation, the question of relating himself to God is an inevitable one, no matter how it is resolved.

ADOLESCENCE AND THE SEARCH
FOR COMPREHENSION

The physical and physiological transformations so prominent in adolescence frequently obscure the equally momentous changes undergone by intelligence during the same period. As a consequence of both maturation and experience, a new mental system emerges in adolescence which enables the young person to accomplish feats of thought that far surpass the elementary reasonings of the child. One feat that makes its appearance is the capacity to introspect, to take one's thought and feeling as if they were external objects and to examine and reason about them. Still another feat is the capacity to construct ideal or contrary-to-fact situations, to conceive of utopian societies, ideal mates, and preeminent careers. Finally, in problem-solving situations, the adolescent, in contrast to the child, can take all of the possible factors into account and test their possibilities in a systematic fashion.

Implicit in all of these new mental accomplishments is the capacity to construct and think in terms of overriding theories that enable the young person not only to grasp relations but also to grasp the underlying reasons for them. To use a biological analogy, the child is concerned with "phenotypes," whereas the adolescent focuses his attention upon the "genotypes," the underlying laws and principles that relate a variety of apparently diverse phenomena. It seems reasonable, therefore, to characterize the mental ability that emerges in adolescence as the capacity for theory construction, and the corresponding need as the search for comprehension.

As in the case of the other need capacities we have considered, the search for comprehension persists throughout life, although it takes different forms at different stages in the life cycle. The search for comprehension is also like the other need capacities in the sense that it never meets with complete success. Whether it be in the field of science, art, history, or government, each new effort at comprehension uncovers new puzzles for the understanding. The same holds true for the personal place. Although the adolescent, to illustrate, now has a conception of personality that enables him to understand people in some depth, he still encounters human foibles and eccentricities that defy his generalizations. And, though his newfound capacity for comprehension enables him to hold a mirror to his mind, he still frequently fails to understand himself.

In the domain of religion, the problem of comprehension arises naturally to those who have accepted God, his scriptural representation, and the sacrament of worship. Many young people often seek such comprehension on their own, with the result that they become bewildered and disheartened by the failure of their efforts. Religion again provides a solution. Every religion has a body of myth, legend, and history that provides a means for comprehending God in various aspects.

In modern religions, the resolution to the problem of comprehension is provided by theology. It may be, however, that the ferment within present-day theological discussions makes it more difficult than heretofore for the young person to accept the religious solution to the problem of comprehension. Be that as it may, for the individual who has accepted God, his representation, and his worship, the problem of comprehension must be faced regardless of how it may be resolved.

CONCLUSION

I am aware that the foregoing discussion probably raises many more questions than it has answered. All that I have tried to do is to present a scheme to illustrate the extraordinary fit between certain basic cognitive need capacities and the major elements of institutional religion. It is probable that this fit is not accidental and that religion has, in part at least, evolved to provide solutions to the problems of adaptation posed by these need capacities. To the extent that this is true, then to that extent are we justified in speaking of the origins of religion in the child.

Psychologists who have concerned themselves with religious phenomena (e.g., Allport, 1950; Dunlap, 1956; James, 1902) are in general agreement with respect to one point, namely, that there are no uniquely religious psychic elements. Insofar as anyone has been able to determine, there are no drives, sentiments, emotions, or mental categories that are inherently religious. Psychic elements, it is agreed, become religious only insofar as they become associated with one or another aspect of institutional religion. Nothing that has been said so far contradicts this position, with which I am in complete agreement.

Nonetheless, the view that there are no uniquely religious psychic elements does not preclude the possibility that there may be uniquely religious adaptations. Adaptations, by definition, are neither innate nor acquired but are instead the products of interaction between subject (individual or society) and environment. Every adaptation is thus a construction that bears the stamp of both nature and nurture, yet is reducible to neither one. The same holds true for religious adaptations. The concept of God, Spirit, or, more generally, the Transcendent, cannot be reduced to the search for conservation any more than it can be traced to the phenomenon of death. Contrariwise, neither the search for conservation nor the phenomenon of death is in itself religious, although it may well take part in the production of religious elements. Like a Gestalt, such as a painting or a melody, the Transcendent is greater than the sum or product of its parts.

As suggested above, once the concept of God or Spirit is accepted as the ultimate conservation, it necessarily entails genuinely religious problems for the other emerging need capacities. These problems can, in turn, be immediately resolved by the ready-made constructions afforded by institutional religion, such as scripture, worship, and theology. From the standpoint of the individual, therefore, the concept of God or of the Transcendent lies at the very core of personal religion. At the same time, however, whether the concept of God is a personal construction or one acquired from institutional religion, it is always superordinate, transcending the particular individual or social needs as well as the phenomenal facts out of which it arose.

10

Adolescent Religious Attitudes*

Lawrence R. Hepburn

Although religious attitudes recently have drawn considerable attention from sociologists, the teenager's religious disposition has not attracted much scholarly interest. One writer claims that "what he [the adolescent] thinks about his religion and the degree to which he observes its rules, and why, is possibly one of the least researched areas in contemporary American life" (Rosen, 1965). In their review of research into adolescent religion, Bealer and Willets (1967) note that the significance of this knowledge lack is increased in light of the fact that "today's young people are the target of many efforts in religious education. Nevertheless, very little organized information about adolescent religious interests is available."

Modest attempts to inquire into the religion of adolescents began in the early days of modern psychology. Coe presented a seminal scientific study of religious beliefs and attitudes in 1900 and compared his findings with those of contemporary investigators such as Starbuck (1899). Coe's study is remarkable for its perceptive relating

*The unedited version of this article appeared originally in *Religious Education*, 1971, *66* (May-June): 173-79. Reprinted by permission of the publisher, The Religious Education Association, 409 Prospect St., New Haven, CT 06510. Membership and subscription available for $20.00 a year.

of religious factors to the general nature of adolescence. Noting that "adolescence . . . is a period of general mental fermentation, but with definite tendencies toward sociability, intellectual independence, a sense of duty and destiny, [and] self-consciousness," he reveals that the turn-of-the-century teenager was not unlike today's. For Coe, "the soil of adolescent religiousness, as far as feelings are concerned, is an undefined sense of incompleteness."

By 1931 the study of adolescent religion employed a more scientifically sophisticated approach than that of Coe. Donelly found much attitudinal inconsistency as he went about *Measuring Certain Aspects of Faith in God as Found in Boys and Girls, Fifteen, Sixteen, and Seventeen Years of Age.* His study of 933 adolescents found an almost complete lack of relationship among three aspects of religious commitment: attitude of trust in God, content of beliefs about God, and effect of faith on certain conduct situations. Thirty years later, opinion polls revealed similar inconsistencies. Whereas over 95 percent of teenagers polled indicated belief in God, less than 40 percent were willing to entrust their lives to God (Bealer and Willets, 1967). Remmers and Radler (1957) report that older teenagers were less willing to accept religion unquestioningly, but that the older adolescents were more ready to condemn atheists as "bad people" than were younger adolescents. These findings agree with the earlier observation of Allport (1950) that, while adolescents commonly feel alienated from the church, they are often moral absolutists and believe that a God must exist to guarantee the moral values to which they hold. Bealer and Willets, in their research summary, assert that adolescent religion is characterized by ritualistic performance and overt subscription to Judeo-Christian dogma. They apply the label "hedging" to the religious orientation of teenage youth.

In Great Britain, where government-sponsored education includes religious education, considerable research has been conducted. Here Loukes (1961) contends that adolescent beliefs are not inconsistent. He offers that "if a child has a clear Christian outlook on one issue, we may expect him to show it in another; an agnostic is a thoroughgoing agnostic; and a degree of open-mindedness will reveal itself in all situations. . . . These children are thinking for themselves." This is supported in the American experience by Allport, who claims that "youth is compelled to transform his religious attitudes . . . from second-hand fittings to first-hand fittings of his personality. He can no longer let his parents do his thinking for him." If the contentions of Loukes and Allport be true, then the "incompleteness" offered by Coe in 1900 is, perhaps, a more appropriate label for adolescent religion than the "hedging" offered by Bealer and Willets in 1967.

That adolescents may be thinking for themselves about religion is alluded to by a number of investigators. Coe (1900) noted that adolescence is a period of "general mental fermentation." Argyle (1958), summarizing research concerning British adolescent religious development, notes that intellectual doubts about religion begin at age twelve. Allport (1950) reports that "various studies show that for approximately two-thirds of all children there is a reaction against parental and cultural teaching. . . . Usually it is not until the stress of puberty that serious reverses occur in the evolution of the religious sentiment." Another British investigator, Goldman (1968) notes that, although adolescents may be disillusioned about religion, they show an interest in learning more about religion. "For many of them the subject never came alive until the freedom of the sixth form (senior high school level) discussion was experienced." Religion was the second (only to sex) most discussed topic of a group of California students queried by Hunt and Metcalf (1968). Though this was a college student population, the investigators claim that "probably much can be inferred about the beliefs of high school students through studying those of college students. The age gap is not great." That such interest in religion is indeed held by high school age youth is reported by Remmers and Radler (1957). They found that 89 percent of those questioned would like to know more about religion. Loukes (1961) contends that this interest in religion is sincere whether adolescents are Christians or agnostics. He found no trace of the desire to say the "correct thing."

Adolescent interest in religion is apparently reflected by overt manifestations of religious decision making. Coe observed that conversion decisions were usually made at age fifteen or sixteen. Conversely, Moreton later (1944) found that most people who ceased to attend religious services did so between the ages of fifteen and nineteen. Allport (1950) confirms this, noting that "the average age for conversion, like that for the rejection of parental systems of belief, is sixteen." Finally, Loukes points out that Billy Graham's twelve thousand British converts in 1954 were mostly clustered around the age of fifteen.

One should note that the thoughtful interest and "general mental fermentation" characteristically found by the above research endeavors were found among student populations. Two studies of somewhat older young people reveal marked differences from the typical adolescent population. A 1950 YMCA survey, reported by Ross, found that, among a largely nonstudent population aged eighteen to twenty-nine, religion was seldom included among matters youth were most interested in or concerned about. Material well-being, personal advantage, and success were more important than religion, which was mentioned by less than 10 percent of the sample. Ross concluded that "youth's life goals and methods of reaching these goals bear little relation to traditional religious concerns and practices." Additionally, a longitudinal study conducted by Nelson (1956) revealed that attitudes toward religion did not change appreciably, even during a period of great social change (1936-1950), once students had left college. Since Ross's study looked at an essentially nonstudent population's religious orientation, and Nelson's study examined attitudes of an ex-student population, it could be inferred that the interest, fermentation, and change found by other investigators is a special characteristic of adolescent-student religiousness.

Clues from a number of research efforts indicate that the special religious configuration of teenage students is due, not only to the innate psychological characteristics of adolescence, but also to the nature of education received by youth. From research in Great Britain and the United States, it seems that conflict appears early in adolescence between literal religious teachings and scientific views of the world. According to Goldman, many early adolescents try to separate the two modes of thinking into compartments, religious thinking being about remote times and places and scientific thinking being about here and now. Eventually, when this conflict has to be resolved, many seem to achieve this by rejecting religion as childish, unscientific, and unbelievable. Additional support for the assumption that studying science affects religious beliefs comes from a study that found the "greatest changes toward liberalism [in religious attitudes] among science students, the least among history students, social scientists being intermediate" (Argyle, 1958). That high school students perceive the religion-science conflict as a problem was also reported by Remmers and Radler (1957). The available research findings indicate that scientific thinking and scientific learning, which saturate the school curriculum, affect the religious beliefs of adolescents. Science may even cause some to reject religion. That religious beliefs affect learning about science is not clearly indicated, although rejection of evolution theory may be related to religious posture (Schneider, 1966).

The relationship of religious orientation to other factors in academic performance has not been established by existing research findings. Concerning the relationship of religion and intelligence, Argyle (1958) mentions the following:

> Studies of children show that the more intelligent children have a more accurate knowledge of the meaning of religious concepts. On the other hand, the more intelligent children start questioning these beliefs at an earlier age. . . . A number of American studies of children and students found negative correlations between intelligence and religious beliefs, attitudes, and experiences.

MEASURING THE RELIGIOUS FACTOR

In an investigation in which effects on or from religiousness of students are of primary interest, accurate and reliable measurement of that religiousness is vital. The researcher, of needs, must employ an objective data-gathering instrument. Unfortunately, those involved with the religious education of youth have not provided suitable instruments to gather needed information. The absence of appropriate instruments to measure religiousness has not, however, deterred investigators from seeking to account for religious effects. The simplistic methods employed, perhaps resulting from narrow conceptualizations of religiousness, have rendered many research projects suspect regarding their findings.

No single aspect of religious behavior should be used as the sole criterion of religiousness. A valid and reliable assessment of religious effects demands both a multidimensional assessment and an indirect assessment technique. Indirect techniques for measuring religious attitudes were pioneered by Thurstone and other researchers in the 1920s, and his attitude scales have been used by other investigators. However, until recently a systematically developed and empirically tested multidimensional conceptualization of religious commitment was not employed as the frame of reference for the measurement of the religious orientation of individuals.

Although religious commitment is widely acknowledged as the core of religion, the great diversity of conventional meanings applied to an individual's "being religious" demands that one define this quality. Though expressions of being religious vary among religious traditions, and individual adherents to a single tradition may emphasize in their being religious different aspects of that tradition, certain core dimensions are distinguishable as common to the general Judeo-Christian tradition. As defined by Stark and Glock (1968) these dimensions are: belief, practice, experience, knowledge, and consequences. Research applications by the developers have supported the conceptual soundness of their five-dimensional scheme.

While the individual's religiousness, or religious commitment, should be of special concern to the educator because pedagogical interest in "affective domain" evaluation is coupled with legal pertinency, religiousness is not the sum total of religious attitudes. If religion study is to be included in the public schools, it should be so because religion is important—it holds a significant place in our society—not because it is good or good for one. As something important and significant, religion elicits attitudinal responses from people whether or not they are "religious" people. An individual of no great religiousness nevertheless has religious attitudes. Religious attitudes of this type, too, will be affected by religion study in the social studies, regardless of, or perhaps in conjunction with, religious commitments. Educators will need tools to measure effects on these religious attitudes if they are to have the capacity to comprehensively evaluate their programs for study about religion.

11

Change and Stability of Religious Orientations during College *

Kenneth A. Feldman

I. Freshman-Senior Comparisons

Researchers have studied change and stability of college students during their undergraduate years along a wide variety of dimensions. This article is a review and integration of the research literature in one of these areas: religious change and stability of undergraduate college students.

COMPARING SENIORS AND FRESHMEN

As an initial step toward discovering the effects of colleges on the religious outlook of students, the following question may be posed:

*The unedited versions of the two articles used here appeared originally in *The Review of Religious Research*, 1969, *11*: 40-60 and 103-28. Copyright 1969 by The Religious Research Association. Reprinted by permission.

Do American students, regardless of who they are or where they go to college, typically change in certain ways in their orientation to religion during their undergraduate years? One way of answering this question is to determine the consistency in results of studies that either (1) cross-sectionally compare the religious attributes of freshmen and seniors at a certain college (or colleges) at a given point in time, or, preferably, (2) longitudinally compare the religious characteristics of students as entering freshmen with the characteristics of the same students when they are departing seniors.

In reviewing these studies, I shall assume—for the moment—full reliability and validity of the measures (including single-item indicators of religiosity) used in the studies. I shall also assume complete meaningfulness of the various findings. Certain measurement problems and interpretive difficulties, as well as concomitant conceptual issues, will be raised in later pages.

Importance of Religious Values

One goal of research in this general area of freshman-senior comparisons has been that of finding out whether college students are likely to change in certain ways in the degree to which religious concerns serve as an important value to them relative to other values.

The Allport-Vernon-Lindzey Study of Values (1960) offers an instrument for measuring the relative importance of six types of values. Described in terms of "types of men," the six values are as follows: (1) Theoretical, (2) Economic, (3) Aesthetic, (4) Social, (5) Political, (6) Religious. This instrument measures the relative importance of these values to the individual, rather than the "absolute" importance of each value. For this reason, it is impossible to score highly on all six values; a preference for certain values must always be at the expense of the other values.

The strongest and most consistent changes across the studies using these six scales to compare freshmen and seniors—most of which are longitudinal in design—occur on the religious and aesthetic scales (Gordon, 1967; Heath, 1968; Huntley, 1965; Miller, 1959; Stewart, 1964; Thompson, 1960; Twomey, 1962; and Tyler, 1963). Nearly without exception, aesthetic values are of higher relative importance to seniors, whereas religious values are of lower importance. When students other than those who are in their senior year are compared to freshmen, results are the same: the average score on the religious scale decreases, and the average score on the aesthetic scale increases, with year in college (Hilton and Korn, 1964; Klingelhofer, 1965; Plant and Telford, 1966; Telford and Plant, 1963).

Another way of gauging the importance of religious values to students is to ask them to compare the importance of a number of possible life goals and life satisfactions. Research in this area—at least as conducted during the 1950s and the earlier years of the 1960s—reveals that the typical American student plans to search for the rich, full life within his future family and from his friendships and his job or career. Of somewhat less importance, though still a major source of expected life satisfaction, are recreational and leisure activities. The student is much less likely to feel that he will derive major life satisfactions from religious beliefs and activities, participation in community affairs, or participation in activities directed toward national or international betterment.

However, the amount and nature of change during the college years in the importance of religious activities and beliefs (in comparison with other sources of life satisfactions) cannot be determined. The few studies that do present freshman-senior comparisons in this area—all done, incidentally, during either the early or middle years of the 1960s—most generally reveal that religious beliefs and activities are of quite low importance to freshmen and are still unimportant in the senior year (Katz, 1967; Katz et al., 1968; Krulee, O'Keefe, and Goldberg, 1966).

The studies reviewed so far focus on change and stability in the general importance of religious values, beliefs, and activities—either relative to other values or in some nonrelativistic sense. These studies do not tell us about change (or stability) of religious orientations in more specific terms, to which the discussion now turns.

RELIGIOUS ORIENTATION

There have been a number of studies dealing with average change in students' religious orientations, as determined by average change in scores on multi-item scales. These scales are usually interpreted in terms of religious "liberalism" and nonorthodoxy, or conversely, in terms of religious "conservatism" and orthodoxy (Brown and Lowe, 1951; Bryant, 1958; Burchard, 1964, 1965; Ferman, 1960; Flacks, 1963; Hall, 1951; Hassenger, 1965, 1966; Havens, 1964; Hites, 1965; King, 1967; Trent, 1964, 1967; West, 1965; Young, Dustin, and Holtzman, 1966). These studies generally show mean changes indicating that seniors, compared with freshmen, are somewhat less orthodox, fundamentalistic, or conventional in religious orientation, somewhat more skeptical about the existence and influence of a Supreme Being, somewhat more likely to conceive of God in impersonal terms, and somewhat less favorable toward the church as an institution.

Other studies report cross-sectional differences or longitudinal changes on either a single questionnaire item or a series of such items not combined into a scale (Hassenger, 1965; Heath, 1968; MacNaughton, 1966; Spady, 1967; Trent, 1964; Webster, 1958; Webster, Freedman, and Heist, 1962). These studies, too, generally show that seniors, as a group, are somewhat less likely to believe in God and more likely to be indifferent or opposed to religion; somewhat more likely to conceive of God in impersonal terms; somewhat less orthodox or fundamentalistic in religious orientation; and somewhat more religiously "liberal." There are, however, a number of items showing no differences between seniors and freshmen, and a few reveal net religious changes in directions that are the reverse of those just given.

From the few studies in the above two sets that present information about attendance at religious services and participation in church-related activities, average change in behavior is consistent with average change in attitudes and beliefs. That is, church attendance and religious participation typically decrease between the freshman and senior years in college.

UNIFORMITY AND PATTERNING OF STUDENTS' RELIGIOUS CHARACTERISTICS

Average scale scores are not the only group characteristics of interest in the study of freshman-senior differences. For example, changes in the size of standard deviations (as indicators of the dispersion of scores around mean scores) give useful information from which to make inferences about the impact of college on students. Even if there are no mean differences between freshmen and seniors on some variable, it is still possible that there is a significant increase or decrease in the dispersion of scores. That is, even though a group of students has not shifted in average score, the college may still have had an impact of either "homogenization" or "heterogenization."

Change in the distribution of scores is another type of change in samples of students as a whole that merits future research. Scores may be distributed unimodally, with the highest frequencies of scores around the mean of the sample, as well as in other shapes, such as bimodal or even multimodal. Even if a group of seniors, compared to itself as a group of freshmen, has not changed in mean score or on dispersion of scores, it is still possible that the scores of these students now bunch in two (or more) peaks, rather than in one (as when they were freshmen). This might be called "factionalization." The change might be in the reverse direction—from factionalization in the freshman year to "integration" in the senior year. There are still other possibilities—say, from a curve approximating a "normal curve" to one approximating a rectangular distribution. Of course, any of these changes in distribution of scores may be accompanied by various combinations of directional trends in mean change and in changes in the dispersion of scores. Future investigations are needed to determine whether one of these kinds of changes typically predominates across different types of colleges, or whether certain kinds of changes occur at certain kinds of colleges.

TIMING OF CHANGE AND CHANGE PATTERNS

Many of the studies giving average scores for freshmen and seniors on the several religious-value and religious-orientation scales also present mean scores for sophomores and juniors. This information can be used to examine the timing of change and to explore patterns of change.

Comparison of the means of contiguous college-class levels can, then, be used to find out in what year change is typically the greatest. It might be expected that freshman-sophomore differences (in means) would be larger than either sophomore-junior or junior-senior differences (in means), thereby leading to the inference that the impact of college is greatest in the early months or the first year. This expectation is congruent with the view that the first year of college, more than any other year, is the major period of adjustment. More than one investigator has argued that the major changes in college occur early in the college experience due to the special sensitivity of freshmen (and perhaps sophomores) to the influences they encounter. Juniors and seniors, in particular, are considered to be in a different developmental phase, one when change is leveling off.

On the other hand, there are grounds for not expecting to find, as an invariable occurrence, that college effects are greatest during the freshman year. In the first place, there is no reason to anticipate that the curves of change will be the same in all change areas or in all colleges. For some dimensions, the early college years may indeed provide the greatest impetus for change, but other areas of potential change may not become salient or relevant to students until their later college years. Likewise, at some colleges the challenges of the early years may be greater than those of the later years, whereas the structural arrangements of other colleges may create greater pressures for change on upper division than on lower division students.

Second, the timing of change depends upon individual rhythms of adaptations. Even if most students find the challenges of their first year to be heavier than those of later years, they may still differ in the degree and timing in which such challenges are "registered" in terms of change. For some, change may be almost immediate; for others, there may be a longer period of "working through," with observable change evidenced only later. It is even possible that some students find the challenges of their freshman year so heavy that they become resistant to change, only to become less defensive and more likely to change in their junior or senior year.

Because of possibilities such as these, Feldman and Newcomb (1969) were not particularly surprised to find no indication that freshman-sophomore differences are larger than sophomore-junior or junior-senior differences in most of the change areas they surveyed—including religious orientation.

SOME PROBLEMS OF INTERPRETING FRESHMAN-SENIOR DIFFERENCES

Multidimensionality of Responses

Comparisons of average freshman and senior scores (or comparisons between any other college-class levels) on scales measuring religious outlook are not without interpretive problems. One such problem occurs when scales assumed (but not proven to be) unidimensional are in reality multidimensional. These differentials are hidden in the average change score for a group of students, so that interpretation of an overall difference is not fully meaningful and may be misleading. One way of discovering the basic dimensions that underlie a multi-item questionnaire or testing instrument is through the use of factor analysis or a similar methodological technique. In the same spirit of attempting to more fully and accurately interpret average-score change, it may be useful to determine on which individual items of a scale students change most and on which least. It is also possible that one category of students changes primarily on one set of items on a multi-item scale or questionnaire, while a second category changes primarily on a different set.

Multidimensionality of scales presumed to be unidimensional probably underlies the criticism that is sometimes made of the interpretation of change on scales measuring authoritarianism and politicoeconomic liberalism — and, by extension, religious liberalism and religious nonorthodoxy. The general criticism is that change scores on tests in these areas may be indicating changes in test-wiseness, sophistication, and the like, rather than changes in authoritarianism and various kinds of liberalism.

What seems likely is that these scales are scored as though they were unidimensional when they may be measuring two or more underlying characteristics. Two likely characteristics that are being measured are liberalism (or authoritarianism) and sophistication (including attitude-scale-wiseness). Unfortunately, we rarely know the proportions in which the two are combined. One awaits similar studies in the religious area.

MASKING INDIVIDUAL CHANGES

A further problem of using differences between freshman and senior mean scores is that such differences may conceal the amount and nature of individual changes. Any observed freshman-senior difference is affected by both extensity and intensity—that is, by the number of individuals who change and by the degree to which each of them changes. If, for purposes of simplicity, group scores of freshman-senior differences are categorized as either high or low, the four cells in Table 1 show the possible combinations. Assuming for the moment that all changes are in the same direction, then a large change score necessarily points to both high extensity and high intensity (Cell D), just as a small change score indicates small degrees of both (Cell A). Intermediate change scores, however, may result from high-low combinations of extensity and intensity, as in either Cell B or Cell C.

Table 1. Type of Group Change within a Population, According to Extensity and Intensity of Change

| | | Intensity of Change | |
		Low	High
Extensity	Low	Cell A	Cell B
of			
Change	High	Cell C	Cell D

The paradigm, though oversimple, illustrates the point that the processes by which change occurs are not the same when mean differences reflect large shifts by a comparatively few individuals and when they represent modest changes by many persons. Within most populations that are being studied, extensity will be somewhere between minimal and maximal, and there will be wide variations in individual intensity. One is not likely, therefore, to know what is responsible for observed differences in mean scores without information about both extensity and intensity.

The problem of interpreting overall freshman-senior differences is even more complex when—as seems to be especially the case in the religious area—change among students is in more than one direction. A difference either between average scale scores or between the percentage of students (at different college-class levels) endorsing a particular religious statement indicates net change in a particular direction. As such, these differences mask the amount and direction of individual change.

Additional evidence of the masking of individual change by net change is offered by studies in which college students are asked directly whether or not they have changed in religious orientation while they have been in college and, if so, in what way. A large number of students in these studies feel that they have changed their orientation toward religion during college; in almost all of the studies, at least half or more of the students in the samples specify a perceived change. Moreover, students clearly do not picture themselves as changing uniformly in one direction. In some studies the net perceived change is in the direction of strengthened religious beliefs and more interest in religion; in others the net perceived change is toward weakened religious faith and lessened religiosity (Burchard, 1965; Jacob, 1957; Lehmann and Dressel, 1962; Morgenstern et al., 1965; Newcomb et al., 1967; Trent and Medsker, 1968).

The obscuring of individual change by net change is further revealed in data on students' conceptions of God (Ferman, 1960). Students at Cornell were asked as freshmen and again as juniors to indicate which of the following statements of faith most clearly described their ideas about the Deity:

I believe in a divine God, Creator of the Universe, who knows my innermost thoughts and feelings and to whom one day I shall be accountable.

I believe in a power greater than myself, which some people call God and some people call nature.

I believe in the worth of humanity, but not in a God or a Supreme Being.

I believe in natural law, and that so-called universal mysteries are ultimately knowledge according to scientific method.

I'm not quite sure what I believe.

I'm an atheist.

Other.

If one simply referred to net percentage change based on the percentage of students endorsing each conception of the Deity as freshmen and as juniors, it would appear that very little happened during the students' years in college. As freshmen, 76 percent of the students endorsed one of the first three conceptions of God, while as juniors, 75 percent of these Cornell students selected one of these three categories. The largest net change was in the category of "Divine God," which received endorsement by 40 percent of the freshmen and 35 percent of the juniors—a net loss of 5 percent. But these net changes camouflage the amount and direction of change. For example, the net loss of 5 percentage points for the "Divine God" category—representing a net loss of 43 persons—came about because 113 persons who originally chose this conception no longer did as juniors, while 70 persons who did not choose this conception as freshmen did so as juniors. To give another example, the 2 percent or 14-person increase in the choice of the conception of God as a "Power greater than myself" is based on a defection of 113 students from this category and a recruitment of 127 students to this category. All told, of the 893 students of the sample, 397 (or 45 percent) changed their responses to the question about conceptions of the Deity.

If one had information solely about net percentage changes, one obvious inference would be that the "Divine God" category had the largest net loss because it had the highest defection rate of the seven categories. This is not true. Comparing defection rates of the seven conceptions of the Deity, "Divine God" actually had the lowest defection rate—that is, the proportion of the original students selecting a category who then changed to another category was the lowest for "Divine God." The conception of "God as humanity," in contrast, had the highest net change (in absolute numbers) but also a very high defection rate. What is at work here is that the rate of recruitment into these categories differed; thus all the defectors from the "Divine God" category were obviously not replaced, whereas the defectors from the "God as humanity" category were more than replaced. The "Divine God" category had the lowest and the "God as humanity" had the highest rate of recruitment by this index. Similarly, the latter category had the highest ratio of recruits to defectors while the former had the lowest ratio.

In sum, data from studies using a methodology that does not obscure the amount of religious change indicate that there is rather extensive change during the college years, but not in a uniform direction. This extensity of change is shown by freshman-senior changes on scale scores as well as by the fact that one-half or more of the students at most colleges are likely to say that they have changed their religious orientation during college. The fact that religious changes are in more than one direction most likely indicates that the influences of most colleges on religious orientations are neither direct nor uniform but, not surprisingly, are indirect and diffuse.

NEED FOR COMPARISON GROUPS

Noncollege students. From the studies reviewed to this point—at least as they have been summarized here—it cannot be determined whether the changes that occur during the college years are due to the college experience per se. The question therefore arises whether comparable changes are also occurring in young people of college age who do not attend college. If these persons change in ways similar to those of college attenders, it could be argued that the changes in both groups either reflect general maturational development within American society or are determined by general society-wide cultural forces at work during the years under study and thus reflect a societal trend. To determine whether, and to what degree, change during the college years can be attributed to the experiences in college requires the availability of research data collected in ways designed to answer such questions. One way is to observe changes in a control group of noncollege persons at the same time that students at college are being studied.

Only two studies—by Plant (1962, 1965) and Trent and Medsker (1968)—have systematically studied four-year changes of control groups in addition to changes by college students. From these studies, the best generalization that can be made is that, on such dimensions as intellectual dispositions and authoritarianism (and related variables), college experiences have a "facilitative effect," while similar changes occur in lesser degree in the noncollege group (although, in a few cases, the noncollege group is not changing at all).

Little is known about the comparison between college and noncollege groups with respect to change in religious attributes. Trent and

Medsker (1968) longitudinally studied 10,000 young adults from thirty-seven high schools in sixteen communities from California to Pennsylvania—comparing (among other things) the group of persons who were to be consistently in college for four years with the group who were to remain consistently employed during that time. Unlike their information on other dimensions of change, their data on religious attitudes was not longitudinal. However, they did ask persons in both groups (four years after high school) to give their opinions as to whether they valued religion the same, more, or less than they had in high school—with the following results:

> Proportionately more of those in college . . . than those in jobs reported a change in their religious values, and in both directions. Among the men, a greater proportion of the college students compared with the workers reported valuing religion less . . . and also valuing it more. . . . Twenty-four percent of the college women placed less value on religion, and 7 percent of the employed women valued religion less, but proportionately more employed than college women valued religion more (59 percent and 50 percent, respectively).

Comparing change over a two-year period by students who attended one of six public junior colleges (in California) with change during the same period by persons who applied to one of these same colleges but did not enter it or any other school, Plant and Telford (1966) found very little in the way of differential average change by the two groups on the Religious Scale of the Allport-Vernon-Lindzey Study of Values. Scores of college females decreased on this scale in about the same average amount as those of noncollege females. Both male groups also scored lower on the average, although in this case scores of the noncollege males, having started lower, decreased slightly more than those of the college groups—perhaps in this case indicating a slight facilitative effect of the noncollege environment.

Alumni. Apart from noncollege comparisons, freshman-senior differences will also take on additional meaning when we know more about change and stability of college alumni. Bender (1958) has shown that, between their senior year and fifteen years later, Dartmouth alumni typically increased their scores on the Religious Scale of the Study of Values. Since it is not known how these men scored as freshmen, it cannot be determined whether this average postcollege change on their part is an extension or a reversal of the average trend during their college days. (It probably is a reversal, since almost all studies—as presented earlier in this article—have shown average freshman-senior decreases on this scale.)

Nelson (1956) also found that in 1950 some nine hundred college alumni were on the average more proreligious than they had been fourteen years earlier, when they were either freshmen, sophomores, juniors, or seniors at eighteen different colleges and universities. Although there was much stability in religious attitudes during that fourteen-year period, what change there was tended on balance to be in the direction of increased favorability toward the church and increased belief in the reality and influence of God. Given the cross-sectional freshman-senior comparisons of these same persons (and their peers) when they were in college, this change probably represents a reversal of within-college change.

Longitudinal investigations of the same persons, comparing average freshman-senior change with average senior-alumni change, are needed to document these suggestions of a reversal in direction of religious change between that in college and that afterwards. Insofar as such reversals are genuine, they are probably to be accounted for primarily in terms of a shift from college environments, where students reinforce one another in questioning home and family values, to communities in which, as young adults, they are more subject to influences toward accepting than rejecting such values.

But what is really needed—more than comparisons between average freshman-senior differences and average senior-alumni differences—is exactly what Newcomb and his associates (1967) have given us in their study of the political and economic attitudes of female students when they were students at Bennington College and during their postcollege life. These investigations separated out women who changed in different ways during college, then traced the change and stability of attitudes for these different alumnae, and finally determined the conditions of differential postcollege change and stability. This has not yet been done for change in religious outlook. When it is, there will be answers to such questions as the following: Under what conditions do students who become less religiously orthodox during college persist in their new attitudes or make even further decreases (rather than reverting to prior orthodoxy) after college?

ONLY A BEGINNING

The above focused on the ways in which American students typically change in their orientations to religion during their undergraduate years. In a very real sense, however, this is not the most important question to be posed or answered in the analysis of the effects of colleges on the religious attributes of students. American colleges are diverse, and so are their students—even within a single institution. Thus no generalizations could be expected to apply to all colleges, nor, a fortiori, to all individual students. Moreover, the more interesting questions (and probably the more clearly answerable ones) are more specific—for example, What kinds of students change in what kinds of ways, following what kinds of experiences, mediated by what kinds of institutional arrangements? It is to such concerns that the second part of this article is devoted.

II. Social-Structural Correlates

COLLEGES

DIFFERENCES AMONG COLLEGES

Colleges clearly differ with respect to their social structures, types of control, faculty attributes, and environmental characteristics and pressures. Moreover, there are typical differences among students at different colleges on a variety of attitude, value, and personality dimensions. As part of this variation in student attributes, there are average differences in religious values, attitudes, and beliefs.

These differences, of course, do not suddenly spring up, full-blown, after students are in college. Students are already typically different in their religious commitments and outlooks as they enter different colleges. These entrance differences in some cases stem from direct causes: students of certain religious beliefs and orientations seek out particular colleges where they feel they will fit in, given the image of the college. For instance, Chickering (1965; Chickering et al., 1968) found relatively high congruence between certain of the institutional characteristics of thirteen small colleges and the typical attitudes and personality traits of students who entered each of them. Most relevant here is the finding that students with the most conservative religious beliefs attended those colleges with a strong emphasis of that kind. Moreover, within this group, the most altruistic students picked those church-related colleges where service was emphasized.

Although direct selection effects do occur—whereby students of similar religious views intentionally pick out similar colleges—variations among colleges with respect to the religious characteristics of their entering students are probably due more to indirect than to direct causes. A number of considerations are generally more important to most students than religious considerations in their choice of a college. These include the intellectual and social emphases of the college; general peer popularity of the school and its general prestige; and a number of practical considerations, including the location

131

of the school, its proximity to the student's home, and the cost of attendance.

It is altogether possible, however, that the nonreligious criteria students use in picking a college may be associated empirically with certain religious views. Therefore, even though religious matters do not come directly into play in college choice, variations in religious outlook of students entering different colleges would still appear as an indirect consequence. Furthermore, religious variables are correlated with many of the sociological and psychological variables (such as socioeconomic status, intellectual ability, and certain personality variables) that have been shown to be related, in turn, to the particular college or type of college attended (Feldman and Newcomb, 1969). Thus, as an indirect outcome, there is initial variation in students' religious attributes across colleges.

ACCENTUATION OF INITIAL DIFFERENCES

What happens to the initial religious diversity among schools as students progress through their four (or more) years of undergraduate college? One logical and theoretical possibility is that these initial differences among colleges decrease. Another is that they are maintained at about the same level. What little evidence we have suggests that the likelihood of either of these two is less than that of a third possibility, in which the initial religious differences among colleges are accentuated or amplified over the four years of college. At least this appears to be true when the comparison is between students entering sectarian colleges and those entering nonsectarian schools.

Data in Trent (1967) and Chickering (1965) show not only that students who enter sectarian colleges are, on the average, more favorable in attitude toward organized religion and more religiously orthodox to begin with than are students entering other kinds of colleges, but also that they decrease less in favorableness and orthodoxy than these other students during their years at college; in a few cases they even increase while the others are decreasing.

One next step in the study of this accentuation phenomenon is to trace out what happens to entrance differences among just those colleges that are nonsectarian and among just those colleges that are sectarian. What little evidence that now exists does not give consistent results. Data from a recent unpublished longitudinal study of students at eight colleges show a strong accentuation effect of initial differences for female students entering five different sectarian colleges. There is also accentuation of initial differences for women entering three nonsectarian colleges. However, the same study does not show this accentuation phenomenon for colleges within either of these two sets of schools when males rather than females are considered. If anything, initial average differences among sectarian schools and nonsectarian schools become smaller.

When accentuation occurs, the fact that groups of students entering different colleges differ (on the average) from each other not only initially but even more so (in the same direction) when they leave suggests that in such cases the processes of attraction and selection are interdependent with the processes of college effects. It seems reasonable to suppose that differences in the environments of different colleges play a major role in the heightening of initial diversity among student bodies. In this regard, the distinctive influences of the college stem from the mutually reinforcing impacts of similarly minded students as well as the intentional and unintentional influences of teachers, curricula, and administrative policies.

It can be argued that accentuation is also influenced by the operation of personality dynamics. For example, persons already high (or distinctive) on some characteristic may be the very ones who tend to make the greatest change. Also, persons differing on some characteristic, say religious orientation, are likely to differ on other personality and background characteristics. These other characteristics may be causing differential change on the religious variable. Since students differing on these personality and background variables, as well as on religious variable, are not uniformly distributed among colleges at entrance, these colleges would show differences in religious change. Quite probably, both sets of influences—environmental pressures and personality dynamics—contribute to the accentuation outcome. The relative contribution of each, along with the dynamics of the interplay between them, will have to be determined in future research.

DISTINCTIVE IMPACTS OF INDIVIDUAL COLLEGES

Determining the extent to which, and the conditions under which, entrance differences among schools are accentuated is, of course, only one aspect of interest in the study of the impacts of colleges. There are only a handful of investigations that compare the change and stability of students in different colleges in any systematic and methodologically rigorous way. Moreover, even those studies using the comparative approach in the study of college effects have not ordinarily included religious variables as part of the set of dependent variables under analysis.

One exception is the research of Ramshaw (1966), who studied changes in frequency of attendance at religious services of students at the University of Illinois and at Monteith College (an "experimental" college affiliated with Wayne State University, which, unlike the University of Illinois, is composed primarily of students who commute to school). Students at each school were divided into four categories: (1) those who were religiously active during high school and who continued to be as active in college; (2) those who increased in religious activity—from limited or no religious activity in high school to relatively high activity in college; (3) those who reduced their religious activities during college in comparison to their high school days; and (4) those who were religiously inactive during high school and remained so in college.

Compared with students at the University of Illinois (the residential school), students at Monteith (the nonresidential school) either were more likely to have reduced religious participation or were more likely to have maintained low levels of participation. Likewise, Monteith students either were less likely to have increased religious participation or were less likely to have maintained high participation. In searching for environmental differences between the two schools that may have caused these variations in change and stability of religious participation, one interesting set of conclusions that Ramshaw reached is as follows:

> The power of the campus at large, the classroom and the life outside the classroom as well, to affect beliefs was noted both at Illinois and Monteith. The total impact of the campus atmosphere at Monteith is attributed by Monteith students to the faculty and to the fact that a university leads students to be self-critical. Illinois students found a three-way influence composed of the faculty, the religious founda-

tions, and the diversity of students to account for the campus atmosphere which leads to the exploration or examination of religious beliefs. . . . While the nonresident [Monteith] student may be peripheral to the influences of student activities and organizations, informal contacts with others on the campus, the life of residence facilities, Greek-letter groups, and religious foundations, he may not be distant from or indifferent to the formal aspects of his educational life. It appears that it is toward these he responds more positively than to other aspects of student life which are partly beyond his reach. The resident [University of Illinois] student who shares fully in both the formal and informal life of the university finds his exposure to classroom and faculty only one aspect of the educational experiences which compete for his attention. Consequently, he looks to these formal aspects of his education for less than the nonresident student does, and is, these results suggest, less influenced by them when it comes to examining his religious beliefs in the light of his educational experiences.

A study by Skager, Holland, and Braskamp (1966) included changes in the importance of religious goals as part of the examination of college effects on selected student goals and self-ratings. Among other things, these investigators asked students at ten colleges—as freshmen and approximately one year later—to rate the importance to them of the goal of "following a formal religious code." The investigators were interested in determining in what ways which features of the environments were related to changes in goals and self-ratings. They concluded that—

for both sexes, change in the relative importance of the religious goal is negatively related to expenditure (per student) and selectivity (of admission policy), characteristics that are likely to imply institutional prestige as well as sophistication of the student body. Several other institutional measures have opposite effects for the two sexes. For male students, change on the religious goal shows relatively low positive relationships with (size of) enrollment, proportion of students majoring in practical and technical fields, and proportion of students with business or business-related majors. The same relationships are somewhat higher and in the opposite direction for females. Indeed, female students behave more as we might hypothesize, since the climate at a large institution with relatively strong emphasis on technical or business-related training would probably not be conducive to the increased importance of religious values.

It should also prove fruitful in the study of college effects to attempt to uncover the conditions under which the dispersion of a student body's religious positions does not increase during the four years at college. Generally speaking, standard deviations of scores on almost every kind of value, attitude, and personality trait (including religious attributes) are as likely to increase as to decrease over four years. In short, increasing homogeneity is a variable rather than a constant outcome.

Increases in homogeneity of scores on religious (or other) instruments may indicate an impact of the college. That is, students may influence each other so that they become more similar to one another. Such influences, as well as other normative and environmental pressures, may act on religious orientation directly or (perhaps more likely) on other kinds of attitudes that then have repercussions on religious views. These homogenizing influences are probably more likely at small, cohesive colleges with well-worked-out goals than at large, complex universities with a multiplicity of not fully consistent goals.

There are many possible conditions under which dispersion of scores—religious or otherwise—does not decrease. A given college may have a public image that attracts students who already fit the image and are quite similar to one another, leaving little room for change. Or perhaps a characteristic with respect to which students typically change in some colleges is simply irrelevant in other colleges; there are no college norms to induce change. Even when such norms do exist, students who do not find them congenial may tend to drop out, so that a longitudinal comparison between freshmen and seniors who do remain shows no difference in dispersion. Instead of dropping out, students who do not find these norms congenial may join groups of similar-minded individuals, and hence original dispersion is maintained or increased during the college years. Finally, most likely in large multiversities, there may be no overall dominant norms in the school, but rather, different clusters of norms inhering in different subgroups on the campus. Different types of students are attracted differentially to these subgroups, creating a situation where initial student differences within the school are maintained or even increased by the normative pressures within each group.

ACADEMIC MAJORS

DIFFERENCES AMONG MAJOR FIELDS

Within a college, students do not have the same kinds of experiences. An important locus of differential experiences is that of activities connected with students' major fields. The initial point of interest in this section is whether students enrolled in different major fields have distinctive characteristics. A number of studies have asked exactly this question, which of course has only an indirect bearing upon the matter of impacts because of the likely possibility that each field attracts students who are already different in distinctive ways (cf. Tisdale, 1967c). Nevertheless, it logically precedes the question of impacts, which could hardly be demonstrated in the absence of distinctively different characteristics of students in the several academic majors.

To summarize specifically the results of studies of major-field differences with respect to the relative importance given by students to the six values as measured by the Allport-Vernon-Lindzey Study of Values, there is some consistency across studies of the Religious Scale, although not of the same magnitude as on some of the other scales. Students in teacher preparation clearly rank high on the religious value, and students in the humanities are in the high and middle thirds. Although the general classification of natural science falls into the medium or low rankings, the specific classifications of physics, chemistry or mathematics rank high. Social science is medium or low, and business is clearly low.

One problem of interpretation here is that students with different backgrounds are more likely to enter some majors than others. The relative importance of religious values may be associated with such variables, and thus it is not known whether these differences exist *because of* or *in spite of* the students' backgrounds. If gender might be taken as an example of background, then we note that women generally score higher on the Religious Scale of the Study of Values than do men (Allport, Vernon, and Lindzey, 1960; Spoerl, 1952, Thompson,

1960; Tisdale, 1965; and Warren and Heist, 1960). They also are proportionately overrepresented in the humanities and in education (the very fields that rank high on the Religious Scale) and proportionately underrepresented in business and in natural science (the fields that tend to rank low). Thus, the differential distribution of the sexes may inflate the magnitude of religious differences among major fields, if not totally account for these differences. Most of the studies reviewed use a combined male-female sample (a few use either a male or female sample but not both) in which results are not presented separately for males and females. Therefore it is not currently known either to what degree the ranking of the fields would still be the same for each gender separately or to what degree the differential distribution of the sexes accounts for major-field differences on the Religious Scale.

It is difficult to summarize the results of studies comparing students in the several major fields with respect to their religious "liberalism" on the one hand and their "conservatism" on the other. The findings do not "add up" to much consistency across studies. No general curriculum has the majority of its cases in the high third (representing in relative terms a high degree of religious liberalism), although the natural science curriculum comes the closest. Students in the humanities range across the three rankings, as do students in the social sciences—although in the latter case, there is a slight tendency to be medium or low in religious liberalism. Students in business administration, engineering, and education clearly rank medium or low and thus are the most religiously orthodox and "fundamentalistic," compared to students in other fields.

DIFFERENTIAL CHANGE IN THE VARIOUS MAJOR FIELDS

In contrast to such "static" comparisons among major fields (at one point in time), very little is currently known about the differential change and stability of students' religious outlooks over time. Feldman and Newcomb (1969) have shown that, in general, accentuation of initial major-field differences is much more likely than is the minimization of such differences. In fact, for certain variables—particularly political and economic orientation and intellectual dispositions—such accentuation seems to occur almost invariably. The fact that, on religious variables, accentuation is not nearly so predictable an occurrence (Huntley, 1965; Webster, Freedman and Heist, 1962) most likely indicates at least two things: (1) religious considerations are not particularly important for most students in their choice of a major, and (2) whatever effects major fields do have on the religious outlooks of students are primarily the result of indirect, diffuse, and unintentional influences.

RESIDENTIAL SETTINGS

Campuses vary in the extent and directions of typical religious differences among students either entering or already living in the several kinds of residential settings. Bohrnstedt (1966) reports that, at the University of Wisconsin, men who seek membership in fraternities attend religious services less than those who do not seek entrance. Ramshaw (1966) has shown that fraternity and sorority members at the University of Illinois are less likely than other students to hold definite positions on religious topics or to express strong religious beliefs.

Contrary to the above, fraternity men at Stanford (at least those living on campus), as well as men living in dormitories, were somewhat more religiously active than men who had other living arrangements (Lozoff, 1967). Intriguingly, at the University of Wisconsin, Jewish male freshmen pledging a fraternity scored significantly higher on a scale measuring conventional religiosity than did Jewish freshmen not pledging a fraternity; non-Jewish fraternity pledges, however, were not significantly different from non-Jewish nonpledges on this scale (Bohrnstedt, 1969).

Scott (1965) did not find any differences between University of Colorado male (or female) freshmen pledging and those not pledging fraternities (or sororities) with respect to scores on a religiousness scale that measures the degree to which a subject reports that he is a religious person in belief and practice, attends church regularly, abides by the Bible's teachings, and so forth. Neither did random samples of Independent males and females (from all college-class levels) differ on this scale from samples of already active fraternity and sorority members. Similarly, Young, Dustin, and Holtzman (1966) found no statistically significant difference in degree of favorability toward organized religion between students at the University of Texas belonging and those not belonging to a fraternity or sorority.

Information on differential religious change of students in several kinds of residential settings is more sparse. In the study above of University of Colorado students (Scott, 1965), males pledging a fraternity and those already active typically decreased in religiousness during a one-year period, whereas nonaffiliates remained at about the same level. For women, only the pledge group tended to show average change (again, a decrease).

At Stanford (Lozoff, 1967), a somewhat smaller percent of male seniors in the Greek-letter system (living either on campus in fraternity houses or in off-campus apartments) than men in other residence groups reported that they changed "much" in their religious views.

Finally, in Ramshaw's study (1966), Greek-letter members (male and female) at the University of Illinois were more likely than Independents either to have decreased their attendance at religious services or to have maintained a low level of attendance (from their high school days); conversely, the Greek-letter members were less likely to have increased their attendance or to have maintained their relatively high level of attendance. The same trend appeared at Monteith, although the differences were not so pronounced. Interestingly, the nature of discussions about religion tended to be different in the Greek and non-Greek settings at the University of Illinois. The fraternity discussions on religion were not of a particularly serious nature; they were more likely to be in the form of humor or attack. In the residence halls and elsewhere, however, the discussions were more likely to be heated and argumentative confrontations and exchanges of information. Ramshaw concludes that the "fraternities (at Illinois) appear to create their effect by the atmosphere they establish in which religious individuality does not flourish."

FRIENDS, ACQUAINTANCES, AND
EXTRACURRICULAR ACTIVITIES

If we are to gain a deeper understanding of the way in which the college experience affects the student's religious outlook, we must move past a consideration of the impacts of major fields and residence (as formally defined, using conventional categorizations) to an analysis of the specific extracurricular activities (formal and informal) in which the student participates and the friendships and circles of acquaintances of which he is a part.

Students often pick certain extracurricular activities with an awareness of how such activities will mesh with their religious dispositions. No doubt this awareness of "fit" is generally higher than when they pick their major or when they select a residential setting. It seems obvious that students in different college activities will typically differ from each other in religious orientation—but documentation of the obvious is needed. More than this, it seems especially likely that initial differences among students entering different activities will be accentuated during the student's years at college—particularly when students engaging in religious or near-religious campus organizations and activities are compared with those joining other kinds of organizations and activities. Again, empirically gathered data on whether or not, and exactly how, this accentuation takes place are needed.

Students report that fellow students are important sources of influence on their religious thinking (*Educational Review*, 1963; Ramshaw, 1966). Religious matters do serve as one topic of conversation in student bull sessions (Bolton and Kammeyer, 1967; Ramshaw, 1966). Although religion tends to be discussed less than other matters—the proportion varying by campus and the particular students involved—it may be hypothesized that such conversations have effects disproportionate to their length and the frequency of their occurrence.

It is known that similarity of values and attitudes plays an important part in the formation and maintenance of friendships (see Feldman and Newcomb, 1969). Similarity along the religious dimension is involved in friendships—at least this may be inferred from the fact that friends tend to be alike in religious views and religious affiliation (Broderick, 1956; Glick and Jackson, 1967; Lindzey and Urdan, 1954; Mitchell, 1951; Reilly, Comins, and Stefic, 1960). The underlying processes resulting in such religious similarity need to be discovered.

DIFFERENCES IN BACKGROUND

The change and stability of religious outlook is determined by students' background characteristics in addition to the structural and substructural influences found in college. For instance, almost all studies show that Catholic students have lower apostasy rates than other students, typically make smaller decreases in religiosity, and are less likely to move toward religiously liberal, nonorthodox positions.

Burchard (1965) and Lehmann and Dressel (1962) present data showing that, when asked about religious changes, female students are less likely than male students to speak in terms of decreased religiosity and more likely to report increased religiosity. However, on scales measuring religious orientation (with respect to degree of liberality or nonorthodoxy) results vary for the sexes by college. At some schools, women are more likely than men to increase in religious liberality, at others they are more likely to decrease, and at still others they make about the same amount of average change (Burchard, 1965; Trent, 1964, 1967).

The socioeconomic background of the student can influence changes in college, although the degree and direction of this change seem to depend on such things as the college studied, the indicators of social class used in the study, the particular instrument employed to measure religious orientation, and the like. Hassenger (1965, 1966) found that working-class students—as indicated by the type of occupation of their fathers—showed the greatest freshman-senior differences in religious orientation. These students, more than any others, moved toward religious liberality and a less moralistic religious orientation. On the other hand, in a study of religious changes by Cornell students, Ferman (1960) found that, the higher the socioeconomic status (as indicated by educational level of their fathers), the more likely were the students to become less religious during college.

Particularly intriguing, and in need of further study, are the interaction effects between the student's background and the distinctive pressures of the type of college he attends. For example, Ramshaw (1966) has shown that the following background characteristics predicted the maintenance of religious interest and participation during college for Protestant students attending Monteith, but not for Protestant students attending the University of Illinois: (1) high degree of Sunday School training, (2) high religious interest of parents, and (3) much prior experience of daily religious practices in their families. Trent (1967) found that, in general, Catholic students attending Catholic colleges are much more religiously orthodox and conservative in their religious attitudes than are Catholics in secular colleges—even when entering college. Moreover, although the attitudes of the first group became somewhat more liberal (on the average) during college, these students did not change nearly as much as did the Catholics (or the non-Catholics) in secular colleges.

Entering college students vary in the degree to which their prior environment is continuous with that of the college and in the degree to which their orientations are congruent with the dominant orientation of the college. Although it has often been hypothesized that students whose backgrounds are most incongruent or discontinuous with that orientation found in college will experience the greatest change, Feldman and Newcomb (1969) found little evidence that this is true. Rather, the best guess at the moment is that the college is most likely to have the largest impact on students—both in general and in religious outlook (as a specific instance of the general case)—when a student experiences a continuing series of not-too-threatening discontinuities. Too little divergence between student and college might create no challenge for the student and thus might mean no impetus for change. Too great a divergence, especially initially, might result in the student's marshaling of resistances (searching out like-minded individuals to support initial attitudes, setting up psychological defenses against change, dropping out of college, transferring to another school, and so on). Moderate challenges, together with social support for change, will probably produce the largest amount of change.

In addition to general social background differences, variations in specific personality attributes also condition college impacts. An especially interesting personality variable is that of "openness to change"—that is, an openness to novelty and new experiences, a readiness and willingness to nondefensively explore and confront ideas, values, and attitudes dissimilar from one's own (see Feldman and Newcomb, 1969). It may be hypothesized that the college experience will have the greatest effects on the religious views of those students who are highly open to change in general when they enter college.

OVERVIEW

A large number of studies have shown that, between their freshman and senior year, college students on the average come to attach less importance to religious values, become more skeptical about God, the church, and religious activities, and become less religiously orthodox and fundamentalistic. These average trends are often small. They camouflage the fact that many students do not change in their religious views during college and that many others change in quite opposite directions from those specified. Indeed, at some colleges the number of students experiencing increased religiosity more than counterbalances the number manifesting a decrease.

There is no one general area of attitude and value change during college in which change is uniformly in one direction for all students. However, within this multidirectionality of change, religious changes are more likely to be multidirectional than changes in almost any other area. One obvious reason for this is that most colleges and curricula are not designed to have specified impacts on religious views. Whereas there may be relatively high agreement among a college staff about the way in which college should affect students in certain areas—say, increased academic achievement and intellectual disposition; increased commitment by the student to certain principles of tolerance, rationality, and high-mindedness; increased personal maturity and autonomy; and the like—there is little consensus about the way in which (or even if) college should influence a student's religious views.

Whether or not colleges intend to have impacts on the religious views of their students, they do have effects. Students themselves report such impacts and locate their sources in college experiences. They speak of direct challenges to, as well as direct reinforcements of, their religious positions. More than this, colleges may have religious impacts as an indirect consequence of their influence on students in other areas. Increasing independence from home and parents, increased knowledge and other academic achievements, changes in intellectual disposition and interpersonal and intrapersonal adjustments at college may all have repercussions on the student's thoughts and feelings about religion. The ways in which the impact of the college experience on nonreligious dimensions affects in turn the religious dimensions is clearly a particularly fruitful area for future research.

Religious change and stability have been shown to have social-structural and background correlates. The amount and direction of change are associated with (1) the type of total college environment, as well as the formal and informal subsettings within that environment; and (2) variations in the student's socioeconomic status, religious affiliation, gender, and the like. But additional study is needed to establish the sociopsychological linkages between the student's background and social structure, on the one hand, and the change (or stability) of his religious attitudes, on the other. We need to know exactly how students from given backgrounds perceive, experience, and react to the environmental influences of the college, some of which they themselves have helped to create. Included in this explanation should be a consideration of extracollege influences (parents, general societal pressures, and so forth) as well as college influences including the relative importance of each of the two sets of influences and the interplay between them.

One conclusion is inescapable. As much as we know about the general change and stability of students' religious views during college, and about some of the social-structural correlates of this change, we are only beginning to understand the processes by which colleges have impacts on students' religious orientations.

12

Sociology of Religion and the Aged: The Empirical Lacunae*

Edward F. Heenan

Theoretically, one would expect a great deal of intellectual cross-fertilization between sociologists of religion and gerontologists. However, there is in fact minimal cross-fertilization. Moberg is the only sociologist of religion who has consistently explored the relationship between religion and the aged. He is the only sociologist of religion who has drawn adequate samples of the aged, and he is the only such sociologist who has published his findings in the two major gerontological journals (Moberg, 1953a, 1953b, 1965b, 1965c). However, even Moberg has limited himself to empirically exploring one or two of the dimensions of religiosity among the aged.

In addition to general works and summaries of research findings and miscellaneous studies, the research in the area of religion and the aged may be conveniently divided into four categories: (1) organizational participation, (2) the meaning of religion to the aged, (3)

*The unedited version of this article appeared originally in *The Journal for the Scientific Study of Religion*, 1972, *11*: 171-76. Copyright 1972 by the Society for the Scientific Study of Religion. Reprinted by permission.

religion and personal adjustment for the aged, and (4) religion and death.

ORGANIZATIONAL PARTICIPATION

In the literature, organizational participation is generally restricted to the frequency with which the elderly attend church and belong to church groups. Of these areas, aging and church attendance is the better documented. It has been explored in eighteen articles or books since 1950 (Bahr, 1970; Beard, 1969; *Catholic Digest*, 1953, 1966; Glock, Ringer, and Babble, 1967; Hammond, 1969; Lazerwitz, 1961, 1962; McGreevey, 1966; Moberg, 1965c; Moberg and Taves, 1965; Orbach, 1961; O'Reilly, 1957; Riley and Foner, 1968; Stark, 1968; Stere, 1966; Wilensky, 1961; Wingrove and Alston, 1971). However, fourteen of the studies appeared after the White House Conference on the Aging in 1961. Therefore, more than half the studies of church participation among the aged conducted since 1961 have been concerned primarily with one subdimension of religiosity—church attendance. Moreover, during the same period of time, sociologists of religion were discovering the multidimensionality of the religious variable. For example, when Stark (1968) examines the relation between age and five dimensions of religious commitment, he concludes that the relationships between older age and piety are confined to private devotionalism, denominational differences, and belief in immortality. In contradistinction, most researchers who have focused on church attendance have considered neither the physical disabilities nor the private devotions of the aged.

THE MEANING OF RELIGION TO THE AGED

Although there are numerous scattered references to the relation of values and the meaning of religion to the aged, only four articles are directly focused on the subject (Albrecht, 1958; Barron, 1958; Covalt, 1960; Ludwig and Eichorn, 1967). Three of the articles appeared before 1961. This is clearly an oversight in research, and it indicates an implicit assumption among researchers that no important religious changes occur from the time an individual is defined as elderly until he dies. Of course, that assumption is subject to empirical test, especially since geriatricians have observed that many older persons become interested in essentially religious questions concerning the meaning of life (Butler, 1964).

RELIGION AND PERSONAL ADJUSTMENT

A total of seven studies on religion and the personal adjustment of the aged have been conducted (Barron, 1958; Moberg, 1953a; Moberg, 1953b; Moberg, 1956; Moberg and Taves, 1965; O'Reilly, 1957; Pan, 1950). Of these, only one appears after 1961, and four involved the same author. This body of literature is again open to the criticism of having limited the dimensionality of the religious variable. Unfortunately, the literature since 1961 on religious and personal adjustment in old age does not utilize the more recent refinements in the measurement of religiosity.

RELIGION AND DEATH

Most recently, the relation between religion and death has been explored (Martin and Wrightsman, 1964, 1965; Templar and Dotson, 1970; Williams and Cole, 1968). These studies can be criticized for the age of the subjects used in their samples. In general, they do not study the elderly directly but extrapolate from data collected from younger segments of the population. Since death is more salient to older persons, these studies would have been greatly improved if they had used the aged as their target population.

DISCUSSION

Sociologists of religion have, for the most part, neglected the final stages of the life cycle. There is no coherent body of literature on the interrelationships among religion, death, and aging. Beyond that, the work that has been done is open to several criticisms. First, it is not cumulative; in most of the literature one finds little reference to the works of others. For example, the work of sociologists of religion has not been disseminated in gerontological journals. Second, most studies impose on their aged subjects a research design and questions created for younger subjects. Third, the samples of the aged are small and regionally based, which makes generalizations risky. Fourth, sociologists of religion have overlooked the relation between denominationally affiliated institutions and care for the aged. Fifth, they have neglected the possibility that religiosity takes new forms among the elderly as they approach death. Finally, there is a total lack of cross-cultural research on religion and aging.

CONCLUSION

A question that cannot be answered from the survey of the literature is why sociologists of religion have not shown more interest in aging. Four reasons come readily to mind. First, gerontology as a subdiscipline of sociology is relatively young. Second, as a result of its short history and to some extent its subject matter, it is a low-status subdiscipline within the field. Perhaps the sociologist of religion, a member of another low-status subdiscipline, does not receive sufficient academic prestige for researching this area and reporting his findings in gerontology journals. Third, the aged are not the most attractive subjects to study, and they are not found in attractive settings. Nor do they offer the prospect of exciting or esoteric findings. Finally, we should not eliminate the possibility that sociologists of religion do not have the methodological techniques for researching this unique segment of the population.

The last point leads us to conclude that sociologists of religion and gerontologists alike would profit from academic reciprocity. The goal of the gerontologist is a scientific one—to comprehend the phenomena and process of aging. To do this he must have more sophistication in researching the religious variable. That sophistication can be provided by the sociologist of religion. The goal of the sociologist of religion, on the other hand, is to understand the nature and dynamics of religion in whatever setting it manifests itself. He cannot afford to neglect a segment of the population that is closest to the ultimate crisis that plays such a large part in his theories about why people need religion. However, in order to do research on the aged he must depend upon the gerontologist for workable techniques of interviewing the elderly. If this reciprocity is not developed, an important segment of the religious life cycle might well continue to be neglected.

13

Personality and Attitude Correlates of Religious Conversion*

Gordon Stanley

INTRODUCTION

It has been shown in a number of studies that about 30 percent of religious people report a more-or-less-sudden conversion experience, while the others become gradually more religious as a result of social influences (Argyle, 1958). Religious conversion has often been considered to be caused by a type of temporary neurotic condition, resolution of which results in the establishment of a "new life." Definitions of the term "conversion" generally emphasize this aspect, e.g.:

> A genuine religious conversion is the outcome of a crisis. Though it may occur to persons in a variety of circumstances and forms, and though we may find many preparatory steps and long-range consequences, the event of conversion comes to focus in a crisis of

*The unedited version of this article appeared originally in *The Journal for the Scientific Study of Religion*, 1964, 4: 60-63. Copyright 1964 by the Society for the Scientific Study of Religion. Reprinted by permission.

ultimate concern. There is in such conversion a sense of desperate conflict in which one is so involved that his whole meaning and destiny are at stake in a life-or-death, all-or-none significance (Johnson, 1959, p. 117).

> To be converted . . . [is] the process, gradual or sudden, by which a self hitherto divided, and consciously wrong, inferior and unhappy, becomes unified and consciously right, superior and happy, in consequence of its firmer hold upon religious realities (James, 1902, p. 189).

This suggests, then, *Hypothesis 1: There is a negative correlation between neuroticism and religious conversion; i.e., people who report conversion tend to have a lower neuroticism score than people who have not been converted.*

Sargant (1957), in a monograph dealing with the mechanics of indoctrination, brainwashing, and thought control, has likened religious conversion to an hysteric neurotic breakdown. Accepting a Pavlovian model to explain differences in breakdown, he considers that "among the readiest victims of brainwashing or religious conversion may be the simple healthy extravert." *Hypothesis 2: There is a positive correlation between extraversion and religious conversion.*

The religious beliefs of parents have been shown to relate positively to the subsequent beliefs of their children (Putney and Middleton, 1961). Since religious beliefs are inculcated as part of the general socialization process, it is likely that in those homes where religion is a strong influence such beliefs will tend to be emphasized, with a resulting greater likelihood of acceptance on the part of the children.

Those who have a strong religious background would have been inculcated with religious beliefs over a long period of time and hence would be less likely to have had a conversion experience, except perhaps where such an experience manifests itself in an institutionalized form (e.g., heightened religious experience at confirmation). Presumably people who are converted to religion are not likely to have had a strong religious background (Argyle, 1958). *Hypothesis 3: There is a negative correlation between the amount of parental religious belief and religious conversion.*

Festinger (1957) has produced a theory of personality and attitude functioning based upon the reduction of "cognitive dissonance":

after making a decision, people tend to engage in activities that confirm the wisdom of making that decision and to avoid suggestions or communications indicating that they were wrong. Hence, on the basis of this theory, one would expect people who have made a definite decision in favor of religion to develop a closed mind in relation to dissonant attitudes and beliefs. Rokeach (1960) has produced an operational measure of closed-mindedness (the Dogmatism Scale) that has been shown to differentiate among groups of religious believers. *Hypothesis 4: There is a positive correlation between dogmatism and religious conversion.*

Religious groups who hold beliefs that are somewhat incompatible with the general sociocultural milieu would be expected to manifest a greater incidence of conversion experience among their adherents than other groups (Festinger, Riecken, and Schachter, 1956). Fundamentalists accept a very literal view of the Bible, a view incompatible with most modern scholarship, both sacred and secular, and thus may be expected to report more conversions than other religious groups. Moreover, because they take the Bible literally, they may also be more concerned with its commands to convert than liberal believers. *Hypothesis 5: There is a positive correlation between fundamentalism and religious conversion.*

METHOD

SAMPLE

The results to be reported were obtained from questionnaires administered to 347 Australian theological students representing eight Christian denominations. Questionnaires were completed by the students of ten theological seminaries under supervision of the college authorities, who returned them to the author for processing.

THE MEASURES

Subjects were administered the extraversion and neuroticism scales of the Maudsley Personality Inventory, Rokeach's Dogmatism Scale, and measures of conversion, parental religious belief, and fundamentalism. The conversion item was:

Of the following please check the statement which most nearly describes your own experience:

(a) I consider that my present religious commitment is a gradual outgrowth of many years of religious instruction and training and that I cannot point to any single event in my life which wrought a definite change from unbelief to belief.

(b) Although there was a time in my life when I had no religious belief, the change from unbelief to belief has been a gradual one.

(c) Although I have always held some religious beliefs I can vividly recall the occasion when I became more vitally committed to these beliefs.

(d) There was a time in my life when religion had no interest for me and I can attribute my present religious commitment to a distinct point in my life at which I made a definite decision in favor of religion.

If the student checked (a) and/or (b) he was called "nonconverted"; if he checked (c) and/or (d) he was called "converted."

For purposes of assessing parental religious belief, the subject was asked to check two items:

On the whole would you say that your father was:
very religious
religious
indifferent to religion
antagonistic to religion
very antagonistic to religion
(Underline which one applies)

The second item was identical except that *mother* was substituted for *father*. Each item was scored from 0 to 4 (4 representing high religiosity) and a combined score for the two items obtained by addition.

The fundamentalist item was a direct question about the literal truth of the Bible:

Which one of these two statements most closely represents your own belief? (Please pick one statement only.)

(a) I believe in a God to whom one may pray for help, but I do not believe that every word of the Bible should be accepted as literal truth.

(b) I believe in a God to whom one may pray for help and I believe that all of the Bible is divinely inspired and literally true.

People checking item (b) were classified as fundamentalists.

RESULTS

Table 1 lists the various correlations that were calculated between conversion and the personality and attitude variables.

TABLE 1
Correlations Between Conversion and Personality and Attitude Variables.

	C	N	E	P	D	F
Conversion (C)	1.00	− 15**	.11 *	.34 **	.19 **	.33 **
Neuroticism (N)		1.00	− 02	− 01	.26 **	.04
Extraversion (E)			1.00	−.02	.05	.20
Parental Belief (P)				1.00	.03	.00
Dogmatism (D)					1.00	.58 **
Fundamentalism (F)						1.00

  * significant at .05 level
** significant at .01 level

The correlations are significant and support the five hypotheses under consideration. Thus there is a tendency for the converted theological student to be more extraverted, to have a lower neuroticism score (less emotionally unstable?), to be more dogmatic, to come from a less religious home than the nonconverted theological student, and to be conservative and literalistic in his religious beliefs.

DISCUSSION

A certain degree of caution must be exercised in the interpretation of the results. The correlations are small, although statistically significant because of the large sample used. The correlations between the measures used are similar to those obtained in validation studies and do not suggest the operation of any obvious response bias.

The present findings may be interpreted as supportive of the theories from which the hypotheses were derived. Further research is needed with groups of laity in order to determine the extent to which the results may have been attenuated by sampling factors.

SUMMARY

From a review of the psychological literature on conversion five hypotheses were proposed: (1) There is a negative correlation between neuroticism and religious conversion. (2) There is a positive correlation between extraversion and religious conversion. (3) There is a negative correlation between amount of parental religious belief and conversion. (4) There is a positive correlation between dogmatism and religious conversion. (5) There is a positive correlation between fundamentalism and religious conversion.

These hypotheses were tested on 347 theological students on the basis of their replies to a questionnaire comprising the N and E scales of the Maudsley Personality Inventory, Rokeach's D Scale, and conversion, parental religious belief, and fundamentalism measures. All were confirmed at the 5 percent level or better. However, it was pointed out that the study should be viewed as suggestive rather than definitive: replications with groups of laity are necessary to determine the generality of the results.

14

Religious Conversion: Regression and Progression in an Adolescent Experience*

Joel Allison

Peaks of insight and inspiration and dramatic alterations of states of consciousness leading to major shifts in outlook and behavior are characteristic of adolescence. At times such experiences take a primarily positive, ecstatic form and, like creative inspiration, are felt to be joyful, transitory, unexpected, rare, valued, and extraordinary to the point of seeming as if derived from a source outside the normal course of events. At other times there are unexpected, abrupt alterations that reflect more violent and disruptive shifts in thought, affect, and action. Although the regressive and pathological aspects of these latter experiences are usually highlighted, they too have important, even though misguided, progressive components. Intense religious conversion experiences—most often a phenomenon of ado-

*The unedited version of this article appeared originally in *The Journal for the Scientific Study of Religion*, 1969, *8*: 23-38. Copyright 1969 by the Society for the Scientific Study of Religion. Reprinted by permission.

lescence—possess important characteristics in common with both the ecstatic and violent states in which consciousness is altered and sudden transformations occur in thought, feeling, and action. For the religious conversion experience, especially the more sudden and dramatic variety, is felt to be a unifying and joyful spiritual awakening; it has a special intensity that often includes strong emotional arousal and hallucinationlike phenomena, and it often leads to significant, even drastic, disruptive modifications in subsequent behavior.

Furthermore, it is the thesis of this paper that the [male] conversion experience—like other sudden, abrupt, disruptive alterations in adolescence—reflects efforts both to curtail sharply and also to realize and gratify an intense longing to fuse with the maternal figure in an undifferentiated matrix. In this regard an internal representation of a strong and principled father serves a crucial role in helping to counteract the yearning to retain the fusion with the mother, in aiding differentiation and separation, and in providing the basis for a coherent masculine identification. For in large part the degree to which the fusion is curtailed appears to depend on the possibility of supplying, via religious belief, a substitute paternal figure to replace a deficient, weak, or absent father who in various ways was seen as unable to promote separation from the mother and to enable the establishment of a clear and secure masculine identity.

The focus here is on the positive role of the sudden and dramatic conversion experience in bringing the adolescent into adulthood and in transforming a sense of diffusion, division, and fragmentation into a sense of order, integration, wholeness, and inner harmony—the adaptive, integrative, maturing aspects of conversion.

PROCEDURE

In order to investigate these aspects of conversion, a study was conducted employing students in a Northern, university-affiliated divinity school with a largely Methodist student body.

Subjects (Ss) included:

seven students who had reported an intense conversion experience in an autobiographical statement in their applications to divinity school (in all cases the conversion experience was an important factor in facilitating religious growth but did not in itself lead to a decision to enter the ministry);

seven other students with relatively mild, weak conversions (like being heartwarmed at a church service);

six students who reported no religious conversions either in their autobiographies or during later interviewing and who had indicated no "unusual" or "mystical" experiences on a routinely administered questionnaire of their religious motivations.

Ss were matched in age, religious denomination, geographical background, and marital status and were found not to differ in IQ.

All Ss were preselected, contacted by phone, and asked to participate in a study of the psychological characteristics of divinity students. In this way no specific interest in conversion was indicated, and the different groups of Ss, therefore, had similar expectations about the study.

Each S was seen for a total of seven hours in three separate sessions during which a battery of psychological tests was administered, followed by an interview oriented around S's life history.

Some preliminary findings of this study indicated that conversion can occur in a setting of adaptive realization (Allison, 1968). In terms of the characteristics of the thought processes of the Ss, it was found that those with more intense conversion experiences showed a significantly greater capacity for adaptive regressive thinking (regression in the service of ego). Furthermore, the adaptive, progressive role of a conversion experience was also indicated by the cultural support and relevance of the conversions and by the short duration of the experience, the rapid return of an earlier or improved mental organization, and an increase in self-esteem.

The present paper also approaches the conversion experience in terms of its adaptive aspects. For this purpose, relevant details of the conversion experience and the life and family relationships of one of the seven divinity students with an intense conversion experience will be presented in order to demonstrate in fuller depth the adaptive, integrative, and progressive potentiality of the conversion experience.

P: A RELIGIOUS CONVERT

P's religious conversion experience occurred several months prior to his graduation from college and shortly after his marriage to another student. His plans at the time were to go on to graduate school with the aim of preparing to teach history in college.

PRECIPITATING CRISIS

Unexpectedly, however, an event occurred that played a major role in precipitating his conversion experience. P and his wife were confronted with the possibility that they might have to be separated for some time so that she could return to a foreign university and complete preparation for her degree. Although P wished to accompany her, it became apparent that he might be drafted if he tried to leave the country. In addition, P discovered that it was virtually impossible for her to complete her academic work except by the unlikely possibility of having a faculty member at P's university sponsor her research project.

Much of this information that P acquired he somewhat angrily conveyed to his wife, blaming her for her failure to get the facts about her situation. He felt he only increased her upset, which he then was unable to calm. He left the house and began walking, criticizing himself for his anger toward his wife, which he believed reflected his selfish desire to assert himself and to establish himself as the man of the family, "the head, the big power." Even though he had been an atheist since junior high school, as he walked down the street he thought he would go into the church he had occasionally attended with his more devout wife, "just to sit and think." But he was surprised to find the church doors locked. Ordinarily, the thought that it was necessary to lock church doors to "keep God safe from vandals" would have angered him, but he found himself amused instead at the little degree of faith the locked doors reflected.

EXPERIENCE

As I was walking, I started praying. I started talking as I walked. I must have looked fairly stupid walking along the streets talking to myself. And I had—I was just looking at the ground—at the sidewalk—and I suddenly felt that I was being heard, and that there was

God. God is—and this was all I could think of—the whole—this just captured my entire being—that God is. . . . I didn't know anything about God—I didn't know who the hell he was, what he was, what it meant, but there was something relevant. No matter how irrelevant and absurd everything seemed, there was something that was the exact opposite of this absurdity—that was centered in the middle of the universe. Everything revolved around it. Even though it didn't appear to have meaning it did with God. Then I sat down on the bench in the woods near school and prayed for about a half hour or forty-five minutes. Simply a prayer of thanksgiving, just thanking God for being. I just thought it was the greatest thing that ever happened. There I was, and this was a tremendous, it was a fantastic feeling which I never felt before or since.

This came to him as "sure knowledge" that transcended logic or proof.

Following this experience, P returned to his wife and apologized for upsetting her. He thought that he must look as changed as he felt, as if he now had "a long, flowing white beard—great white hair, like Charlton Heston in the *Ten Commandments*, because I'd been up to the Mount." But this change was not immediately perceptible to his wife. At first the newness of his beliefs made them feel very fragile to P, who feared they might "disintegrate" at any moment; in fact, he initially felt embarrassed in directly referring to "God" and instead he and his wife called God "our sponsor"—a term they also used in reference to the potential sponsor at P's university who could enable his wife to stay in this country. Several months after the experience, as he gradually integrated his new knowledge, P decided to study for the ministry. "I always said, if I could believe all that crap I'd be a preacher."

Childhood

Early Years. P was born in a Midwestern city, the first son of a middle-aged white Southern Baptist couple who had recently migrated from the South. The only other child, a much older sister, married shortly after his birth. His early years he recalls as very lonely ones, due to the fact that his parents both worked long hours, leaving him in the care of an elderly housekeeper in a relatively unpopulated part of town somewhat secluded from children his own age. P recalls spending considerable amounts of time counting cars in anticipation of his parents' return home; then he would feel increasingly separated from them when they returned with lavish gifts to "buy" his love.

His sense of separation from his parents is more fully elaborated in his belief that he was not a wanted child, particularly because of the lengthy interval between his birth and his sister's. P, however, does not appear to connect his birth with its likely relationship to a preceding major family scandal that concerned his father's affair with a secretary. This resulted in a split between P's father and his close-knit family, in a temporary separation of his parents, and in their reconciliation and move north shortly afterwards, following which P was born.

Parents' Background.   Both parents were from poor Southern working-class families; as they prospered financially, they tried increasingly to dissociate themselves from their background, although their ultimate religious attitudes differed. P's father's separation from his parents and siblings was sudden. In his religious attitudes, P's father had gradually moved from a fundamentalist religious background toward an agnostic position and a cynicism concerning the cultural tendency to separate religious teachings and religious practice.

His mother (P's grandmother), in fact, had wanted him to be a minister, and, even when he turned to agnosticism, he remained "superstitious enough"—according to P—to believe that his mother's wish for a minister in the family would be realized. P's decision for the ministry, then, fulfilled the "superstition" of his father.

P's mother's origins were equally poor and fundamentalist; her father was an ordained minister who worked as a salesman to support his family. However, P's mother, unlike her husband, remained a "rip-roaring Christian" who played hymns in the mornings to rouse her family to go to church. "I would be late getting dressed, and she'd be in there playing hymns. She would get mad, and she would play hymns loud and fast."

When P was ten, increased financial success enabled his parents to move to a more fashionable residential area. They continued to be determined to reject their lower-class origins, and one expression of this determination was their efforts (as earlier) to restrict P from associating with children from the "wrong side of the tracks," where P was in fact increasingly finding his friends.

ADOLESCENCE

At this point in his life, P reports, there was "a metamorphosis from being a lovely, well-mannered good student to something else." He began to rebel against his mother's strong but naive fundamentalism, her daily morning Bible readings to him, and the terror of sexuality she instilled in him (for example, the belief that masturbation causes mental illness).

At the same time that he began to try to evade her religiosity, he also began to flee her obvious seductiveness. "I can remember being somewhat repulsed kissing my mother 'cause she'd want to kiss me on the lips. And after I got in high school I didn't want this at all. I found this—I wanted to and I was repulsed, frightened. I had feelings of repulsion because I thought this wasn't the right thing."

In high school, P had his first sexual experiences with the daughter of a woman who worked as a secretary for his father—a woman, interestingly enough, who P's mother believed her husband to be sexually involved with at that very time.

Increasingly P became associated with alienated fellow high school students and began actively to emulate James Dean, to espouse a kind of philosophical existentialism, to drink, to acknowledge himself fully as an atheist, and to attend school classes only on occasion. Yet he never completely committed himself to these alienated activities and attitudes. His closest friend, for example, remained a sober, "security-minded," diligent person. Rather, his life took on an increasingly dichotomous quality in which contrasting identities competed for ascendence.

RELATION TO FATHER

It is also about this time—toward the end of high school—that P dates his most vivid, single proud and pleasant memory of his father.

Despite his father's effectiveness and success in his business, P portrays his father in the home as weak, infantilized, dominated by and subservient to P's mother. Moreover, not only is his father presented as impotent psychologically, but for years, claims P, it was common knowledge in the family that he was sexually impotent with his wife. We do not know the character and successfulness of P's father's extramarital affairs, however—only that P related that his mother openly confessed to him her concern that his father was an adulterer. P is puzzled by and unable to account for the discrepancy between his perception of his father's impotence at home and his alleged sexual prowess elsewhere.

P felt that, in a variety of ways, he superseded his father in his closeness with his mother. Not only did he feel that his mother loved him (P) more; he also recalls incidents in which his father vented his helpless, tearful, frustrated rage at a wife and son who were pitted against him. With a mixture of pride, embarrassment, and sadness, P recounts his victory over his father, the essential hollowness of it, the resentment about feeling that he came between his parents, and the terrible sense of loss he experienced in having had a father who did not want him to be born, made him feel he was never able to do anything, and who further rejected him by lacking strong, assertive, commanding qualities. In fact, P reports that his father's impotence disappeared only with P's final departure from the home to get married and his resulting absence as a threat to his father.

On one occasion, however, and somewhat unexpectedly, P's father came through in the commanding way P had often wished he would. It was in the final week of P's senior year in high school. P and some friends had gotten drunk and because of this missed an important school activity the following day. On his return to school, the principal, assistant principal, and counselor in turn chastised P for the generally bad reports about his behavior of the entire year and for his turning to drink. As P was shifted from one to another of these school authorities, he became increasingly frightened about not being allowed to remain in school.

> I was really terrified by this time. And I looked out the window. This school is located on a high hill. And I saw the most beautiful sight I've ever seen. There was my 6-foot-3-1/2-inch dad, straight white hair, getting out of the Cadillac. He had just come. He had decided that maybe I might be having a little trouble. It was the *first* time—the first time I ever felt that he was wholly on my side and

doing what I wanted him to do—that is, take command. And this has been a big problem in my family. I've always wanted my Dad to take command—to be, you know, *my* dad. And he was this time. He came in, and I said, "Boy am I glad to see you!" and I told him what was happening. This irritated him! It really made him angry. Which pleased me no end. I mean, he was teed off with me—very, very angry with me for having done this, but now he, you know, turned his anger, and he went in and talked to the principal. And he used very blunt language for my dad. And the principal assured him everything would be okay.

COLLEGE

P managed to pull himself together sufficiently to graduate and then go off to college, where the split in his life became more pronounced. During his freshman year, he reverted to being "a good studious little boy" who studied hard even during vacations and got high grades. Then in his sophomore year, when he began to live on his own away from the dorm, his life veered in the direction of "booze and parties," "drinking and debauching."

In his junior year, he swung back in part by moving back into a dorm, working harder at his studies, and simultaneously keeping up his contacts with his boozing, partying friends out in town. "I then lived in sort of a dichotomy between out in town and the dorm. And I had friends—pretty close friends, as much as you can have, out in town and in the dorm. Just so different! And the morals—the mores—and the morals too were different. And I had to reconcile the two. It was impossible. I was constantly bouncing back and forth."

P also embarrassedly admits that at about this time he was a staunch supporter of Barry Goldwater, who he feels reflected his father's values.

Towards his last year in college, he met his future wife. This was during a time when he considered himself to be a "devil-may-care, king-of-the-mountain kind," involved with a girl from whom he broke away with difficulty in order to become more openly involved with his future wife. With her, for the first time, he did not feel dirty or guilty at the point of sexual climax, but felt "some sort of achievement or fulfillment." Shortly afterward they were married.

Since she was a churchgoer, although of a different Protestant denomination than P, and because he loved and respected her, P began to feel that all Christians could not be as rotten as he had thought. Whereas he "really didn't dislike J.C." who "was okay, a nice nut running around two thousand years ago who had some pretty decent ideas," to him Christians were "just such hypocrites—it's pathetic." His wife went to church regularly, and P accompanied her, at first with the aim of "mentally criticizing the performance of the ministers as they danced around in front of the altar." P never felt moved but got to like the church, which was quiet and cool inside; he "enjoyed going and sitting and thinking occasionally."

But he also felt a keen sense of embarrassment about going into a church. "One time when I was drunk, I and the guy I went around with—one of the things we did that night, for some unknown reason, we stole things from automobiles. . . . We didn't sell them or anything. It was just vandalism. And one of the things—one of the acts that we did that night was to—I urinated on the chapel door. This was my great statement." Nevertheless, while he overtly depreciated religion, P also secretly felt attracted to it; he repeatedly denounced himself for his persuasibility at revivals and sermons during the time he was an alleged atheist; at the age of eighteen, for example, he had felt a keen sense of embarrassment because of an urge to go down the aisle and dedicate himself to Christ at a Billy Graham revival. "This is a bunch of crap. Why do I feel so involved?" Several months after his religious experience, these conflicting attitudes were reconciled, and he was in fact sufficiently involved to be a believer and enrolled in divinity school.

DISCUSSION

Aggressive Themes

In the events immediately preceding P's conversion experience, typical aspects of the preconversion struggle as seen in the six other Ss are illustrated. The appearance of guilt, self-blame and "a sense of sin" has been noted in many earlier writings about conversion.

Also prominent is the association of this guilt with specifically aggressive thoughts and/or deeds, which more recently has been emphasized. This hatred figures prominently either in the immediately antecedent conditions of the intense conversions or in the content of the actual experience, although it is clear that the hatred is often felt to be unacceptable and is accompanied by considerable guilt.

The conversion experiences of two Ss, for example, directly related to their implication in the death of other people. In one instance, a woman was killed in an automobile accident for which S was responsible; in the other, S felt that his acceding to a girl friend's undergoing an abortion was equivalent to murder. A third S portrayed the aggression more in the content of his actual conversion experience, in which he saw an image of the agonized, suffering face of Jesus on the cross being cruelly jeered at.

In a final S the aggression was also strong and was highlighted by an event that occurred shortly before his conversion experience. In his conversion he had experienced a sudden and intense sense of omnipotent magical power in being able to control the specific events of a crucial baseball game. He associated this experience with the replacement in his church of an older minister by a younger, more dynamic minister, who seemed in S's account to be actively taking power away from and replacing the older man.

In an additional way, the preconversion experience of most Ss also touches on issues around aggression. In comparison to Ss who do not report conversions, Ss with intense conversions reveal a history of marked rebelliousness toward religious values and observances during adolescence following a long period of steady belief during childhood. Sometimes openly blasphemous behavior was recounted, such as P's urinating on a chapel door, but usually the rebelliousness took the form of atheism and a move away from stricter earlier religious beliefs through drinking or premarital heterosexual activity.

OEDIPAL THEMES

As analytic writers have sometimes suggested, the aggression that is intimately related to the conversion experience also has direct links with content reminiscent of the Oedipus complex, in particular with the need to reconcile hatred toward paternal authority. We can trace this in P's account of his religious experience and his earlier life. He directly relates his guilt with his wife prior to his conversion experience to a wish to assert himself aggressively and to be "the head, the big power.'' Subsequently, however, by means of his conversion he shifted conspicuously in the direction of submitting himself to God without, however, abandoning his need for a strong masculine identity. For he returned feeling like Moses—too often rebellious, quick-tempered, but a strong and commanding liberator and leader of people, the giver of laws.

We know too from P's account that he probably links this single, sudden conversion experience with the equally unique and sudden appearance of his tall, commanding, white-haired father on the hill of his school to rescue, protect, chide, and lead his son.

Thus, the conversion experience in the light of these events could be viewed as a compromise solution to P's hatred toward his father. By submitting himself to a higher, stronger, more awesome authority, he vicariously shares in the father's strength and is able thereby to forestall the terrors of fearsome retribution for his supposed victory over his father and greater favor in his mother's eyes.

In this regard, his postconversion attitudes and behavior are especially relevant. After his conversion, P experienced a greater sense of responsibility ("I'm not the center of the universe"), a greater sense of freedom at the same time ("I belong to God, not to man"), a feeling of being released to a certain extent from the burden of guilt, and a feeling of being less bound by the world:

> It can't hurt me, and it can't kill me; it can't capture me or enslave me because I belong ultimately to God. I am responsible to the world and must love it as God does. But I'm not bound within it. That is why I don't have to become so panicked about Barry Goldwater. He can win the election and establish a Gestapo. But he can never enslave me because I don't belong to myself or him but to God.

The degree to which his submission to God makes him unthreatened by and invulnerable to an angry, sadistic paternal figure is noteworthy, especially since that figure takes the form of Barry Goldwater, who is closely identified with his father's values and was at the time striving to be president (father) of the country.

Including P, four of the seven Ss who had intense conversions, but none of the Ss without conversions, had fathers who were either adulterers or alcoholics or committed suicide. In each of these four, there is the suggestion that the father's actual absence or unavailability or the perception of him as weak or immoral by an intensely religious wife is associated with a special closeness between the Ss and their mothers.

Even in the cases of the conversion Ss whose fathers were less obviously absent or inadequate, there is a suggestion that the Ss felt particularly close to their mothers and relatively remote from their fathers during much of their lives. While some nonconversion Ss also allude to a greater degree of closeness with their mothers, they tend to be more outspokenly negative toward and critical of their mothers than the conversion Ss, who may, like P, be disturbed by the closeness but do not openly devalue their mothers for it.

If we consider the especially intense relationships the conversion Ss report with their mothers, we could conjecture that the resolution of the Oedipus complex was particularly complicated because of the degree to which these Ss—like P—felt themselves actually to have been victorious over their fathers and because of the murderous, castrating retribution they may have anticipated for their victory. This hypothesis then could indicate one source of the necessity for these Ss to submit themselves to God.

Although few studies of conversion have shown an interest in the relationship between conversion Ss and their mothers, we could in the above way bring our findings into accord with the general emphasis in the psychoanalytic literature on the role in the conversion experience of hatred toward paternal authority stemming from the Oedipus complex.

On the other hand, there are themes in the interviews with P and with the other conversion Ss that suggest a need to revise the hypothesis that conversion primarily reflects an attempt to settle problems of hatred toward the Oedipal father restimulated during adolescence. The nature of the revision is suggested in P's account of his subjective experience, particularly in his persistent emphasis on his wish for a strong, protective, commanding, and aggressive father—the kind of father he and most conversion Ss felt they lacked, the lawmaker and lawgiver symbolized in the person of Moses, with whom P identified in his conversion experience.

THEMES OF STRENGTH AND WEAKNESS

In addition to the Oedipal themes, the Ss who experienced intense conversions betray ambivalent feelings of both strength and weakness. These Ss, unlike the others, responded to their psychological tests—the Rorschach in particular—with a special focus on things in a vulnerable or helpless condition: falling apart, sinking, crumbling, chopped up, exposed, cut open, limp, dominated, and menaced. Often, however, major efforts were made to shift from such images of vulnerability to images of strength, dominance, loftiness, and ascendence. At other times, there were equally conspicuous shifts away from images of sadistic strength and brutality to those of helplessness and weakness.

To a much greater degree than Ss without conversions, the conversion Ss show a striking tension between strength and weakness, being on top and being on the bottom, rising and sinking, fearfulness and fearlessness, intactness and fragmentation. This tension is likely to reflect the predominance in their psychological make-up of major issues around passivity, helplessness, and weakness vs. strength, power, and fearlessness.

LONGING FOR PROTECTIVE FATHER

The wish on the part of P and other subjects with intense religious conversions for a strong protective father and for a consistent, organized set of values and ideals can be viewed in terms of recent efforts to broaden the conceptualization of the role played by the actual father in superego development, in aiding differentiation of the ego from reality, and in facilitating the child's progressive urge to counter regressive longings for the maintenance of symbiotic ties to the mother.

The remainder of this paper will be concerned with these issues. As regards superego development, Schafer (1964) has demonstrated how the concept of the superego as living and protective and not solely criticizing and feared began to appear throughout Freud's later writings. A monograph by Lederer (1964), in addition, has focused on how an "actually strong, decisive, assertive and principled father contributed to the benevolent and beneficial aspect of super-ego development and through that development to the strengthening of positive ego identity and its expression in adaptive orientation and action'' (Schafer, 1964).

Lederer, moreover, has argued that the concept of a protective father does not derive solely from the transformation of an image of a feared, dreaded father, but stems as well from identification with an actual father who combines within himself the capability for good and evil, creation and destruction, but who has learned to ''tame his savagery.'' Fathers who lack these qualities, who are good but have no strong principles, willing but ineffective, who are immoral or ludicrous, weak or absent—such fathers fail to supply modes for aggressive, assertive, effective maleness, for a sense of ''direction of mission and purpose,'' for a sense of responsibility to oneself and to others, for self-sacrifice, and for a capacity to take care of and care for others.

One point in Lederer's monograph of special relevance is that people without a stable identity show their strongest parental relationship with their mothers. This is a necessity, Lederer claims, because in lieu of a strong father, the mother is the only remaining source of acceptance and security to fall back on. However, in this respect, she also serves as a threat, because the concentrated relationship with her entails a ''powerful seduction into regression.'' In another context, in discussing the relationship of ego to external reality, Loewald (1951) has also pointed to the role of the powerful but positive paternal figure in counteracting ''the threatening possibility of remaining in or sinking back into the structureless unity from which the ego emerged,'' that is, the undifferentiated matrix of the mother-child symbiosis. This threat, moreover, is seen as predating the castration fear of the Oedipus complex and is particularly noteworthy ''in cases where there is no father or where the father has remained an insignificant and weak figure.'' Inasmuch as a strong paternal figure can serve as a major safeguard against a fear of being engulfed and overpowered by the mother, ''the positive identification with the father cannot be reduced to the fearful submission to his castrating threat,'' but ''lies before and beyond submission as well as rebellion.''

Thus, a strong ''active, nonpassive'' father aids in the establishment of boundaries between ego and external reality and serves in the development of "differentiation and objectivity."

The centrality for P of pre-Oedipal issues involving longings for unity and fusion with a maternal figure is particularly well illustrated by a story he told about a card of the Thematic Apperception Test.

> TAT No. 5 [A woman standing by a half-opened door looking into the room]: This picture depicts a woman who is leaving it for the last time. The room is very repugnant to her. She has lived in this house for many, many years and is the spinster daughter of an old widow. The widow's own personality has permeated that of the house; it is a very dominating, clutching personality, like a vast wind that bends everything in its path. And everything bends and conforms to this wind as everything in this home has conformed to the will of the girl's mother. The girl is about thirty or thirty-five, though she looks older because of her severe life, and at last she has made a decision to leave this house, to leave her mother, who has supposedly been an invalid for many, many years. And for the last time the girl has cleaned the house and has set everything in order, just as her mother would want and with a repugnant look on her face, and this by the way I sense is a defiant act. And she is looking at the room; it is the last glance one takes when one is leaving something forever, except that one usually has a nostalgic, fond feeling, and she has none of this. She is filled with a great deal of determination. It is not a snap decision but something that has been building up and building up. And she closes the door with a great purpose and leaves the house, and when she gets into the world she discovers that all vitality—the life that she had—was coming from the house just as trees that grow in high places where there is a great wind bend with the wind but gain strength from it. And so she returns to the house. Only to discover in the meantime that her mother has died, for she too depended upon the girl for her own force as if she had to have something to blow against. The end.

Routinely, this card elicits themes concerning relationships with a maternal figure, and P is no exception to this expectation. What is striking about his story, however, is the particular focus on the intense interconnectedness between mother and daughter. The old widow's personality is said to "permeate" the house; the daughter's vitality and the mother's force are said to be mutually dependent and interfused. This story sets forth in bold detail the difficulties attendant upon separating from a strong interdependent relationship—a relationship that in P's language seems at times to blend into symbiosis, since each person in the absence of the other essentially perishes. The foreshortened time perspective regarding the girl's future, the hint that the mother's death is also the girl's "end," additionally reflect the powerful regressive longings for the symbiotic union with the mother.

There is then, a strong suggestion from P that the religious conversion experience may serve to supply a benevolent, protective, strong, and firm paternal figure to replace a father who was seen as deficient in these respects. Moreover, in line with Loewald's hypothesis, it is also suggested that this positive and powerful paternal figure is a crucial protector against the regressive nostalgia for the undifferentiated union with the mother and serves thereby in aiding the process of individuation and differentiation.

The conversion experience largely puts an end to a variety of insecure and shifting commitments by enabling frequently strong religious roots to prevail (evident in P's mother and in both sets of grandparents). We have also seen how subjects prior to this intense conversion fluctuate with regard to professional choice, sexual expressiveness, their degree of narcissistic relatedness to others, and the openness of expression of their hostile or antisocial impulses. In P's case, for instance, we know that he was continually disturbed by his dichotomous life and by his frequent alternations of value and belief. He has suggested the sources of these contradictory attitudes and behaviors in his perceptions of his parents: in his mother's conflicting naive morality and her seductiveness; his father's weakness at home in contrast to his business and presumed sexual strength elsewhere; the general discrepancy in values and beliefs between his "rip-roaring religious" mother and his agnostic, cynical father; and the discrepancy between his parents' lower-class origins and the middle-class respectability to which they aspired. In P's conversion experience, however, the sense of dichotomy was finally resolved, the bouncing back and forth ended. P, like Moses, returned from the Mount with a clear, consistent set of values and precepts (the Ten Commandments). God as lawmaker and lawgiver is further emphasized in P's use of the term *sponsor* to refer both to God and to the professor who might sponsor his wife's research and enable them to stay together.

Thus we find that the conversion experience moves subjects toward a more organized, differentiated, yet consistent set of values that supplies the foundation for the beginnings of a stable identity, the capacity for enduring relatedness to others, and even impetus toward the choice of a profession—one concerned with caring for others and supplying them a model of active, effective, and paternal behavior.

Moreover, like Augustine before them, these subjects were able by means of a dramatic conversion experience to crystallize out order, meaning, and strength in a society beset by turbulence, disorder, and the breakdown of traditional values.

Yet it would be incorrect to imply that the experience of these Ss supplied a totalistic, final, and closed solution to their search for order, value, and meaning. As P pointed out, there is at the time of the experience a feeling of having moved from sin and darkness into light, but afterward P realized, "The light is not a 200-watt bulb—it's only about a 50-watt bulb—and I grope around here on the outer edges; so it's not all light anymore."

Nor is it correct that the conversion experience moved the Ss away from their mothers in any absolute way. In the case of P, for example, his conversion experience clearly shifted him in the direction of an identification with his mother's religious orientation. Moreover, the crucial event that directly preceded his conversion experience was the possibility of a protracted separation from a woman (his wife)—an event that probably restimulated his anxieties about separating from his mother. The effect of his conversion, furthermore, was in supplying a sponsor (God and the professor) who could keep him and his woman together. Another conversion subject, whose father had committed suicide "just at the point a boy is coming out of being a mother's child and turns to one's father" and who clearly was moving via his conversion toward independence from his mother, nevertheless also placed considerable stress on his necessity for a good woman who could help him "hold the center" and without whom he would be fated to self-destruction. If we recall Loewald's (1951) thesis that the mother aids the ego's striving toward unification and synthesis, we can see that another facet of the mother's role in the conversion is in aiding the convergence of divergent beliefs and feelings and in supplying the central sense of unity and wholeness to replace a sense of division and contradiction.

Our earlier, but only partial, conclusion held that the conversion experience adaptively facilitates the emergence of an adolescent into adulthood by replacing a weak, ineffective or absent father with a representation of a strong, principled, protective paternal figure who offsets a powerful urge toward reestablishing or maintaining a sense of symbiotic union with the mother. Now we add that the conversion experience simultaneously permits a partial expression of the early unity, a partial return to "the paradise of wholeness which once gave liberal provision but which, alas, was lost leaving forever an undefinable sense of evil division, potential male violence and deep nostalgia" (Erikson, 1954). The return to religion itself suggests a return to the sources of faith, hope, and trust—vital aspects both of the earliest aspects of the relationship with the mother and of religion in a most basic sense. Thus, the conversion experience forges a new psychological organization in which the early ties with the maternal wellsprings of faith, hope, wholeness, and union are maintained and a strong, guiding paternal figure with clear, organized values and firm judgments is also acquired.

For Further Reading

Without much doubt, you should examine *Research on Religious Development* (ed. Merton Strommen [New York: Hawthorne, 1971]) if you wish to consult a wide variety of chapters bearing on this general topic. If you are interested specifically in knowing more about Jean Piaget and are looking for a place to begin, perhaps John L. Phillips's *The Origins of Intellect: Piaget's Theory* (San Francisco: Freeman, 1964) will serve you well. However, the best single source probably still is John H. Flavell's *The Developmental Psychology of Jean Piaget* (Princeton, N.J.: Van Nostrand, 1963). Some comparisons of developmental theories can be found in either Jonas Langer's *Theories of Development* (New York: Holt, Rinehart, and Winston, 1969) or Henry W. Maier's *Three Theories of Child Development* (rev. ed. [New York: Harper and Row, 1965]).

If you are a bit more interested in religious development and want to look at something other than the Strommen book, perhaps a volume reporting on some British research, *Religious Thinking from Childhood to Adolescence* by Ronald Goldman (London: Routledge and Kegan Paul, 1964), or Charles William Stewart's *Adolescent Religion* (Nashville: Abingdon, 1967) will be helpful. *Growing Up to God* (Abingdon, 1975) by John J. Gleason attempts to relate Erikson's developmental stages with stages of religious development. Roy Zuck and Gene Getz report some survey data specifically on evangelical Protestants in their *Christian Youth* (Chicago: Moody, 1968). Orlo Strunk's *Mature Religion* (Nashville: Abingdon, 1965) pulls together insights on religious maturity from half a dozen different theorists and is the only book I know of its kind on that topic.

Conversion has had no full-length treatment for quite some time, with the exception of Albert I. Gordon's *The Nature of Conversion* (Boston: Beacon, 1967), an interview study of forty-five individuals who changed their formal religious affiliations.

Part Three

Mysticism and Altered States of Consciousness

INTRODUCTION

The study of mysticism was one of the earliest topics to catch the attention of psychologists of religion. The mystical experience, an intensely personal one in which one apprehends himself to be in touch with Ultimate Reality, may be the essential ingredient of all religions. James (1902) thought so, and his interest in it led to a formulation of the characteristics of the mystical experience that has been widely influential ever since. Although there are others, the two most important aspects of this experience, he believed, are its ineffability—the fact that the nature of the experience cannot be communicated to others—and its noetic quality—its function as a knowledge-imparting state. He noted as well that it is usually fairly transient in character and an event during which the participant feels passive.

Evelyn Underhill (1911), writing less than a decade later, attempted to correct James's formulation with four characteristics of her own. She noted, first, that mysticism is active, insofar as entrance into the mystical state requires considerable preparatory activity and effort. It is also entirely spiritual, in the sense that the mystic is not concerned with the immediate world of our normal sense data. The heart of mysticism is love, perhaps the most important characteristic of all. Finally, the mystical experience eventually involves a distinct reorganization of the personality as a result.

There have been regular and consistent attempts recently to specify the heart of the religious experience. Stace's (1960) work is reflected in that portion of Pahnke's article (see chapter 15) in which he describes the essence of both the extravertive and introvertive mystical experiences. Maslow's (1964) description of the peak experience is touched upon in my article that closes this section.

Both Stace and Maslow are in reality describing altered states of consciousness, as were James and Underhill before them. This is a relatively new interface between psychology and religion, and it is showing considerable vitality. It is not clear, really, just what kind of research to expect in this area, since traditional techniques may prove inadequate to the task. Tart (1975), for instance, argues very persuasively for the recognition of research methods and communication modes that are "state specific." He may be right. In any case, the dialogue has been encouraged by the experiences of many using psychedelic drugs, by some fantasy and regressive techniques used by the human potential movement, by a renewed general interest in meditation and Eastern religions, and by the increasing respectability of investigating altered and normal states themselves. Indeed, the *Journal of Transpersonal Psychology* is devoted to areas in psychology that would look familiar (with perhaps some vocabulary changes) to religionists.

Describing a study that has become nearly a classic, Pahnke opens the section with a report on an experiment using psilocybin at a Boston University Good Friday service. First he traces out a detailed typology of the mystical experience, and then he describes the data gathering itself. A number of his recommendations in the concluding section are excellent, but few have been carried out—largely because of the negative climate currently surrounding psychedelic research.

Exactly what happens in the mystical experience is not yet settled. In an attempt to examine this question, Deikman suggests that many of the phenomena that are reported can be regarded as bringing to awareness many of the perceptual processes of which we are usually unaware, and thus opening us for alternative ways of experiencing our world.

While Pahnke and Deikman look at the mystical experience itself, Hood examines one aspect of the place this kind of experience may have in the emotional economy of the individual. He finds that such intense personal experiences are found much more often in individuals who see themselves as personally religiously committed than in persons who are institutionally religiously committed. There is a clear implication here that mysticism is not often found in most of our churches—an observation with which I agree. Hood's work is not inconsistent with Allison's beliefs about conversion in the final article of the preceding group.

Ornstein expands the context of discussion to an examination of states of consciousness in general, rather than specific psychological processes. Noting that historical and experimental evidence are both strong for the existence of two basic modes of consciousness, he finds it easy to place mystical experiences within one of them. He makes a clear case for the biological grounding of this mode in the brain's right cerebral lobe.

Finally, I try to bring together explicitly the relations among some of these apparently diverse strands—and in so doing, give myself less to say in these introductory paragraphs. The article points out this new area of potential collaboration between religion and psychology and underlines the importance of the mystical experience to fully human functioning.

15

Drugs and Mysticism*

Walter N. Pahnke

The claim has been made that the experience facilitated by psychedelic (or mind-opening) drugs such as LSD, psilocybin, and mescaline can be similar or identical to the experience described by the mystics of all ages, cultures, and religions. This paper will attempt to examine and explain this possibility.

There is a long and continuing history of the religious use of plants that contain psychedelic substances. In some instances, such natural products were ingested by a priest, shaman, or witch doctor to induce a trance for revelatory purposes; sometimes, they were taken by groups of people who participated in sacred ceremonies. For example, the dried heads of the peyote cactus, whose chief active ingredient is mescaline, were used by the Aztecs at least as early as 300 B.C. and are currently being employed by over fifty thousand Indians of the North American Native Church as a vital part of their religious ceremonies. Both *ololiuqui*, a variety of morning glory seed, and certain kinds of Mexican mushrooms were also used for divinatory and religious purposes by the Aztecs. These practices have continued to the present among remote Indian tribes in the mountains of Oaxaca

*The unedited version of this article appeared originally in the *International Journal of Parapsychology*, 1966, *8*: 295-315. Copyright 1966 by the Parapsychology Foundation, Inc. Reprinted by permission.

Province in Mexico. Modern psychopharmacological research has shown the active chemicals to be psilocybin in the case of the mushrooms, and several compounds closely related to LSD in the case of *ololiuqui*.

AN EXPERIMENTAL EXAMINATION OF THE CLAIM THAT PSYCHEDELIC DRUG EXPERIENCE MAY RESEMBLE MYSTICAL EXPERIENCE

Some of the researchers who have experimented with synthesized mescaline, LSD, or psilocybin have remarked upon the similarity between drug-induced and spontaneous mystical experiences because of the frequency with which some of their subjects have used mystical and religious language to describe their experiences. These data interested the author in a careful examination and evaluation of such claims. He undertook an empirical study (Pahnke, 1963) designed to investigate in a systematic and scientific way the similarities and differences between experiences described by mystics and those facilitated by psychedelic drugs. First, a phenomenological typology of the mystical state of consciousness was carefully defined, after a study of the writings of the mystics themselves and of scholars who have tried to characterize mystical experience. Then, some drug experiences were empirically studied, not by collecting such experiences wherever an interesting or striking one might have been found and analyzed after the fact, but by conducting a double-blind, controlled experiment with subjects whose religious background and experience, as well as personality, had been measured *before* their drug experiences. The preparation of the subjects, the setting under which the drug was administered, and the collection of data about the experience were made as uniform as possible. The experimenter himself devised the experiment, collected the data, and evaluated the results without ever having had a personal experience with any of these drugs.

A nine-category typology of the mystical state of consciousness was defined as a basis for measurement of the phenomena of the psychedelic drug experiences. Among the numerous studies of mysticism, the work of W. T. Stace (1960) was found to be the most

helpful guide for the construction of this typology. His conclusion—
that in the mystical experience there are certain fundamental characteristics that are universal and not restricted to any particular religion
or culture (although particular cultural, historical, or religious conditions may influence both the interpretation and the description of
these basic phenomena)—was taken as a presupposition. Whether or
not the mystical experience is "religious" depends upon one's definition of religion and was not the problem investigated. Our typology
defined the universal phenomena of the mystical experience, whether
considered "religious" or not.

The nine categories of our phenomenological typology may be
summarized as follows:

CATEGORY I: *UNITY*

Unity, the most important characteristic of the mystical experience, is divided into internal and external types, which are different
ways of experiencing an undifferentiated unity. The major difference
is that the internal type finds unity through an "inner world" *within*
the experiencer, while the external type finds unity through the
external world *outside* the experiencer.

The essential elements of *internal unity* are loss of usual sense
impressions and loss of self without becoming unconscious. The
multiplicity of usual external and internal sense impressions (including time and space), and the empirical ego or usual sense of individuality, fade or melt away while consciousness remains. In the most
complete experience, this consciousness is a pure awareness beyond
empirical content, with no external or internal distinctions. In spite
of the loss of sense impressions and dissolution of the usual personal
identity or self, the awareness of oneness or unity is still experienced
and remembered. One is not unconscious but is rather very much
aware of an undifferentiated unity.

External unity is perceived outwardly with the physical senses
through the external world. A sense of underlying oneness is felt
behind the empirical multiplicity. The subject or observer feels that
the usual separation between himself and an external object (inani-
mate or animate) is no longer present in a basic sense; yet the subject
still knows that on another level, at the same time, he and the objects

are separate. Another way of expressing this same phenomenon is that the essences of objects are experienced intuitively and felt to be the same at the deepest level. The subject feels a sense of oneness with these objects because he "sees" that at the most basic level all are a part of the same undifferentiated unity. The capsule statement "all is One" is a good summary of external unity. In the most complete experience, a cosmic dimension is felt, so that the experiencer feels in a deep sense that he is a part of everything that is.

Category 2: Transcendence of Time and Space

This category refers to loss of the usual sense of time and space. This means clock time but may also be one's personal sense of his past, present, and future. Transcendence of space means that a person loses his usual orientation as to where he is during the experience in terms of the usual three-dimensional perception of his environment. Experiences of timelessness and spacelessness may also be described as experiences of "eternity" or "infinity."

Category 3: Deeply Felt Positive Mood

The most universal elements (and, therefore, the ones that are most essential to the definition of this category) are joy, blessedness, and peace. The unique character of these feelings in relation to the mystical experience is the intensity that elevates them to the highest levels of human experience, and they are highly valued by the experiencers. Tears may be associated with any of these elements because of the overpowering nature of the experience. Such feelings may occur either at the peak of the experience or during the "ecstatic afterglow," when the peak has passed but while its effects and memory are still quite vivid and intense. Love may also be an element of deeply felt positive mood, but it does not have the same universality as joy, blessedness, and peace.

Category 4: Sense of Sacredness

This category refers to the sense of sacredness that is evoked by the mystical experience. The sacred is here broadly defined as that which a person feels to be of special value and capable of being profaned. The basic characteristic of sacredness is a nonrational, intuitive, hushed, palpitant response of awe and wonder in the presence of inspiring realities. No religious "beliefs" or traditional theological terminology need necessarily be involved, even though there may be a sense of reverence or a feeling that what is experienced is holy or divine.

CATEGORY 5: OBJECTIVITY AND REALITY

This category has two interrelated elements: (1) insightful knowledge or illumination felt at an intuitive, nonrational level and gained by direct experience; and (2) the authoritative nature of the experience, or the certainty that such knowledge is truly real, in contrast to the feeling that the experience is a subjective delusion. These two elements are connected because the knowledge through experience of ultimate reality (in the sense of being able to "know" and "see" what is really *real*) carries its own sense of certainty. The experience of "ultimate" reality is an awareness of another dimension unlike the "ordinary" reality (the reality of usual, everyday consciousness); yet the knowledge of "ultimate" reality is quite real to the experiencer. Such insightful knowledge does not necessarily mean an increase in facts, but rather in intuitive illumination. What becomes "known" (rather than merely intellectually assented to) is intuitively felt to be authoritative, requires no proof at a rational level, and produces an inward feeling of objective truth. The content of this knowledge may be divided into two main types: (a) insights into being and existence in general and (b) insights into one's personal, finite self.

CATEGORY 6: PARADOXICALITY

Accurate descriptions and even rational interpretations of the mystical experience tend to be logically contradictory when strictly analyzed. For example, in the experience of internal unity there is a loss of all empirical content in an *empty* unity that is at the same time *full* and complete. This loss includes the loss of the sense of self and the dissolution of individuality; yet something of the individual entity remains to experience the unity. The "I" both exists and does not exist. Another example is the separateness from, and at the same time unity with, objects in the experience of external unity (essentially a paradoxical transcendence of space).

CATEGORY 7: ALLEGED INEFFABILITY

In spite of attempts to relate or write about the mystical experience, mystics insist either that words fail to describe it adequately or that the experience is beyond words. Perhaps the reason is an embarrassment with language because of the paradoxical nature of the essential phenomena.

CATEGORY 8: TRANSIENCY

Transiency refers to duration and means the temporary nature of the mystical experience in contrast to the relative permanence of the level of usual experience. There is a transient appearance of the special and unusual levels or dimensions of consciousness as defined by our typology, their eventual disappearance, and a return to the more usual. The characteristic of transiency indicates that the mystical state of consciousness is not sustained indefinitely.

CATEGORY 9: PERSISTING POSITIVE CHANGES IN ATTITUDE AND BEHAVIOR

Because our typology is of a healthful, life-enhancing mysticism, this category describes the positive, lasting effects of the experience and the resulting changes in attitude. These changes are divided into four groups: (1) toward self, (2) toward others, (3) toward life, and (4) toward the mystical experience itself.

1. Increased integration of personality is the basic inward change in the personal self. Undesirable traits may be faced in such a way that they may be dealt with and finally reduced or eliminated. As a result of personal integration, one's sense of inner authority may be strengthened, and the vigor and dynamic quality of a person's life may be increased. Creativity and greater efficiency of achievement may be released. An inner optimistic tone may result, with a consequent increase in feelings of happiness, joy, and peace.

2. Changes in attitude and behavior toward others include more

sensitivity, more tolerance, more real love, and more authenticity as
a person by virtue of being more open and more one's true self with
others.

3. Changes toward life in a positive direction may involve philosophy of life, sense of values, sense of meaning and purpose, voca-
tional commitment, need for service to others, and new appreciation
of life and the whole of creation. Life may seem richer. The sense of
reverence may be increased, and more time may be spent in devotional life and meditation.

4. Positive change in attitude toward the mystical experience
itself means that it is regarded as valuable and that what has been
learned is thought to be useful. The experience is remembered as a
high point and an attempt is made to recapture it or, if possible, to
gain new experiences as a source of growth and strength. The mystical experiences of others are more readily appreciated and
understood.

The purpose of the experiment in which psilocybin was administered in a religious context was to gather empirical data about the
state of consciousness experienced. In a private chapel on Good
Friday, twenty Christian theological students, ten of whom had been
given psilocybin one-and-a-half hours earlier, listened over loud-
speakers to a two-and-a-half-hour religious service that was in actual
progress in another part of the building and that consisted of organ
music, four solos, readings, prayers, and personal meditation. The
assumption was made that the condition most conducive to a mystical experience should be an atmosphere broadly comparable to that
achieved by tribes who actually use natural psychedelic substances in
religious ceremonies. The particular content and procedure of the
ceremony had to be applicable (i.e., familiar and meaningful) to the
participants. Attitude toward the experience, both before and during,
was taken into serious consideration in the experimental design.
Preparation was meant to maximize positive expectation, trust, confidence, and reduction of fear. The setting was planned to utilize this
preparation through group support and rapport; through friendship
and an open, trusting atmosphere; and through prior knowledge of
the procedure of the experiment in order to eliminate, if possible,
feelings of manipulation that might arise.

In the weeks before the experiment, each subject participated in five hours of various preparation and screening procedures that included psychological tests, medical history, physical examination, questionnaire evaluation of previous religious experience, intensive interview, and group interaction. The twenty subjects were graduate student volunteers, all of whom were from middle-class Protestant backgrounds and from one denominational seminary in the free-church tradition. None of the subjects had taken psilocybin or related substances before this experiment. The volunteers were divided into five groups of four students each on the basis of compatibility and friendship. Each group had two leaders who knew from past experience the positive and negative possibilities of the psilocybin reaction. The leaders met with their groups to encourage trust, confidence, group support, and fear reduction. The method of reaction to the experience was emphasized (i.e., to relax and cooperate with, rather than to fight against, the effects of the drug). Throughout the preparation, an effort was made to avoid suggesting the characteristics of the typology of mysticism. The leaders were not familiar with the typology that had been devised.

A double-blind technique was employed in the experiment, so that neither the experimenter nor any of the participants (leaders or subjects) knew the specific contents of the capsules, which were identical in appearance. Half of the subjects and one of the leaders in each group received psilocybin (30 milligrams each for ten of the twenty experimental subjects and 15 milligrams apiece for five of the ten leaders). Without prior knowledge of the drug used, or of its effects, the remaining ten subjects and the other five leaders each received 200 milligrams of nicotinic acid, a vitamin that causes transient feelings of warmth and tingling of the skin, in order to maximize suggestion for the control group.

Data were collected during the experiment and at various times up to six months afterwards. On the experimental day, tape recordings were made both of individual reactions immediately after the religious service and of the group discussions that followed. Each subject wrote an account of his experience as soon after the experiment as was convenient. Within a week all subjects had completed a 147-item questionnaire that had been designed to measure the various phenomena of the typology of mysticism on a qualitative, numerical scale. The results of this questionnaire were used as a basis for a one-and-one-half-hour, tape-recorded interview that immediately followed. Six months later each subject was interviewed again after completion of a follow-up questionnaire in three parts with a similar scale. Part 1 was open ended; the participant was asked to list any changes that he felt were a result of his Good Friday experience and to rate the degree of benefit or harm of each change. Part 2 (fifty-two items) was a condensed and somewhat more explicit repetition of items from the postdrug questionnaire. Part 3 (ninety-three) was designed to measure both positive and negative attitudinal and behavioral changes that had lasted for six months and were due to the experience. The individual descriptive accounts and Part 2 of the follow-up questionnaire were content-analyzed with a qualitative, numerical scale by judges who were independent of the experiment and who knew only that they were to analyze twenty accounts written by persons who had attended a religious service.

Prior to the experiment, the twenty subjects had been matched in ten pairs on the basis of data from the predrug questionnaires, interviews, and psychological tests. Past religious experience, religious background, and general psychological makeup were used for the pairings, in that order of importance. The experiment was designed so that by random distribution one subject from each pair received psilocybin and one received the control substance, nicotinic acid. This division into an experimental and control group was for the purpose of statistical evaluation of the scores from each of the three methods of measurement that used a numerical scale: the postdrug questionnaire, the follow-up questionnaire, and the content analysis of the written accounts.

A summary of percentage scores and significance levels reached by the ten experimentals and ten controls, for each category or subcategory of the typology of mysticism, is presented in Table 1. The score from each of the three methods of measurement was calculated as the percentage of the maximum possible score if the top of the rating scale for each item had been scored. The percentages from each method of measurement were then averaged together. A comparison of the scores of the experimental and control subject in each pair was used to calculate the significance level of the differences observed by means of the nonparametric Sign Test. As can be seen from Table 1, for the combined scores from the three methods of measurement, p was less than .020 in all categories except deeply felt positive mood (love) and persisting positive changes in attitude and behavior toward the experience, where p was still less than .055.

Although this evidence indicates that the experimentals as a group achieved to a statistically significant degree a higher score in each of the nine categories than did the controls, the degree of completeness or intensity must be examined.

In terms of our typology of mysticism, ideally the most "complete" mystical experience should have demonstrated the phenomena of all the categories in a maximal way. The evidence (particularly from the content analysis and also supported by impressions from the interviews) showed that such perfect completeness in all categories was not experienced by all the subjects in the experimental group. The closest approximation to a complete and intense degree of experience was found for the categories of internal unity, transcendence of time and space, transiency, paradoxically, and persisting positive changes in attitude and behavior toward self and life. The evidence indicated that the second group of categories showed almost but not quite the same degree of completeness or intensity as the first group. The second group consisted of external unity, objectivity and reality, joy, and alleged ineffability. There was a relatively greater lack of completeness for sense of sacredness, love, and persisting positive changes in attitude and behavior toward others and toward the experience. Each of these last eight categories or subcategories was termed incomplete to a greater or lesser degree for the experimentals but was definitely present to some extent when compared with the controls. When analyzed most rigorously and measured against all possible categories of the typology of mysticism, the experience of the experimental subjects was considered incomplete in this strictest sense. Usually such incompleteness was demonstrated by results of the content analyses.

The control subjects experienced few phenomena of the mystical typology and even these reached only a low degree of completeness. The phenomena for which the scores of the controls were closest to (although still always less than) the scores of the experimentals were:

Table 1

Summary of Percentage Scores and Significance Levels
Reached by the Experimental and Control Groups
for Categories Measuring the Typology of
Mystical Experience

	Percent of Maximum Possible Score for Ten Ss		
	Exp.	Cont.	p*
Category			
1. Unity	62	7	.001
a. Internal	70	8	.001
b. External	38	2	.008
2. Transcendence of Time and Space	84	6	.001
3. Deeply Felt Positive Mood	57	23	.020
a. Joy, Blessedness and Peace	51	13	.020
b. Love	57	33	.055
4. Sacredness	53	28	.020
5. Objectivity and Reality	63	18	.011
6. Paradoxicality	61	13	.001
7. Alleged Ineffability	66	18	.001
8. Transiency	79	8	.001
9. Persisting Positive Changes in Attitude and Behavior	51	8	.001
a. Toward Self	57	3	.001
b. Toward Others	40	20	.002
c. Toward Life	54	6	.011
d. Toward the Experience	57	31	.055

blessedness and peace, sense of sacredness, love, and persisting
positive changes in attitude and behavior toward others and toward
the experience.

---

*Probability that the difference between experimental and control scores was due to chance.

The design of the experiment suggested an explanation for the fact that the control subjects should have experienced any phenomena at all. The meaningful religious setting of the experiment would have been expected to encourage a response of blessedness, peace, and sacredness. In the case of love and persisting changes toward others and toward the experience, observation by the controls of the profound experience of the experimentals and interaction between the two groups on an interpersonal level appeared, from both post-experimental interviews, to have been the main basis for the controls' experience of these phenomena.

The experience of the experimental subjects was certainly more like mystical experience than that of the controls, who had the same expectation and suggestion from the preparation and setting. The most striking difference between the experimentals and controls was the ingestion of thirty milligrams of psilocybin, which it was concluded was the facilitating agent responsible for the difference in phenomena experienced.

After an admittedly short follow-up period of only six months, life-enhancing and -enriching effects similar to some of those claimed by mystics were shown by the higher scores of the experimental subjects compared to the controls. In addition, after four hours of follow-up interviews with each subject, the experimenter was left with the impression that the experience had made a profound impact (especially in terms of religious feeling and thinking) on the lives of eight out of ten of the subjects who had been given psilocybin. Although the psilocybin experience was unique and quite different from the "ordinary" reality of their everyday lives, these subjects felt that this experience had motivated them to appreciate more deeply the meaning of their lives, to gain more depth and authenticity in ordinary living, and to rethink their philosophies of life and values. The data did not suggest that any "ultimate" reality encountered had made "ordinary" reality no longer important or meaningful. The fact that the experience took place in the context of a religious service, with the use of symbols that were familiar and meaningful to the participants, appeared to provide a useful framework within which to derive meaning and integration from the experience, both at the time and later.

The relationship and relative importance of psychological preparation, setting, and drug were important questions raised by our results. A meaningful religious preparation, expectation, and environment appeared to be conducive to positive drug experiences, although the precise qualitative and quantitative role of each factor was not determined. For example, everything possible was done to maximize suggestion, but suggestion alone cannot account for the results because of the different experience of the control group. The hypothesis that suggestibility was heightened by psilocybin could not be ruled out on the basis of our experiment. An effort was made to avoid suggesting the phenomena of the typology of mysticism, and the service itself made no such direct suggestion.

IMPLICATIONS FOR THE
PSYCHOLOGY OF RELIGION

The results of our experiment would indicate that psilocybin (and LSD and mescaline by analogy) are important tools for the study of the mystical state of consciousness. Experiences that previously have been possible only for a small minority of people, and that have been difficult to study because of their unpredictability and rarity, are now reproducible under suitable conditions. The mystical experience has been called by many names that are suggestive of areas that are paranormal and not usually considered easily available for investigation (e.g., an experience of transcendence, ecstasy, conversion, or cosmic consciousness); but this is a realm of human experience that should not be rejected as outside the realm of serious scientific study, especially if it can be shown that a practical benefit can result. Our data would suggest that such an overwhelming experience, in which a person existentially encounters basic values such as the meaning of his life (past, present, and future), deep and meaningful interpersonal relationships, and insight into the possibility of personal behavior change, can possibly be therapeutic if approached and worked with in a sensitive and adequate way.

Possibilities for further research with these drugs in the psychology of religion can be divided into two different kinds in relation to the aim: (1) theoretical understanding of the phenomena and psychology of mysticism, and (2) experimental investigation of possible social application in a religious context.

The first or theoretical kind of research would be to approach the mystical state of consciousness as closely as possible under controlled experimental conditions and to measure the effects of variables such as the dose of the drug, the preparation and personality of the subject, the setting of the experiment, and the expectation of the experimenter. The work described above was a first step in the measurement of these variables, but more research is needed. The results should be proved to be reproducible by the same and by different experimenters under similar conditions. Such work could lead to a better understanding of mysticism from a physiological, biochemical, psychological, and therapeutic perspective.

Several experimental approaches can be envisioned for the second kind of research, to determine the best method for useful application in a religious context. One suggestion would be the establishment of a research center where carefully controlled drug experiments could be done by a trained research staff which would consist of psychiatrists, clinical psychologists, and professional religious personnel. Subjects, ideally, would spend at least a week at the center to facilitate thorough screening, preparation, and observation of their reactions, both during and after drug experiments. Another suggestion would be the study of the effect of mystical experience on small natural groups of from four to six people who would meet periodically, both prior to and after a drug experience, for serious personal and religious discussion, study, and worship. The reactions of a varied range of subjects with different interests could be studied, but perhaps a good place to start would be with persons professionally interested in religion, such as ministers, priests, rabbis, theologians, and psychologists of religion.

Such research may have important implications for religion. The universal and basic human experience that we have called mystical is recorded from all cultures and ages of human history, but mysticism has never been adequately studied and understood from a physiological, biochemical, sociological, psychological, and theological perspective.

Perhaps there is more of a biochemical basis to such "natural" experiences than has been previously supposed. Certainly many ascetics who have had mystical experiences have engaged in such practices as breathing and postural exercises, sleep deprivation, fast-ing, flagellation with subsequent infection, sustained meditation, and sensory deprivation in caves or monastic cells. All of these techniques have an effect on body chemistry. There is a definite interplay between physiological and psychological processes in the human being. Some of the indolic substances in the body do not differ greatly from the psychedelic drugs.

Many persons concerned with religion are disturbed by drug-facilitated mystical experiences because of their apparent ease of production, with the implication that they are "unearned" and therefore "undeserved." Perhaps the Puritan and Calvinistic element of our Western culture—especially in the United States, where most of the controversy about psychedelic drugs has centered—may be a factor in this uneasiness. Although a drug experience might seem unearned when compared with the rigorous discipline that many mystics describe as necessary, our evidence has suggested that careful preparation and expectation play an important part, not only in the type of experience attained, but in later fruits for life. Positive mystical experience with psychedelic drugs is by no means automatic. It would seem that the "drug effect" is a delicate combination of psychological set and setting in which the drug itself is the trigger or facilitating agent—i.e., in which the drug is a *necessary* but not *sufficient* condition. Perhaps the hardest "work" comes after the experience, which in itself may only provide the motivation for future efforts to integrate and appreciate what has been learned. Unless such an experience is integrated into the ongoing life of the individual, only a memory remains rather than the growth of an unfolding renewal process that may be awakened by the mystical experience. If the person has a religious framework and discipline within which to work, the integrative process is encouraged and stimulated. Many persons may not need the drug-facilitated mystical experience, but there are others who would never be aware of the undeveloped potentials within themselves, or be inspired to work in this direction, without such an experience. "Gratuitous grace" is an appropriate theological term, because the psychedelic mystical experience can lead to a profound sense of inspiration, reverential awe, and humility, perhaps partially as a result of the realization that the experience *is* a gift and not particularly earned or deserved.

Mysticism and *inner* experience have been stressed much more by

Eastern religions than by Western. Perhaps Western culture is as far off balance in the opposite direction—with its manipulation of the external world, as exemplified by the emphasis on material wealth, control of nature, and admiration of science. Mysticism has been accused of fostering escapism from the problems of society, indifference to social conditions, and disinterest in social change. While the possibility of such excesses must always be remembered, our study has suggested the beneficial potential of mystical experience in stimulating the ability to feel and experience deeply and genuinely with the full harmony of both emotion and intellect. Such wholeness may have been neglected in modern Western society.

The subjects in our experiment who were given psilocybin found the religious service more meaningful, both at the time and later, than did the control subjects. This finding raises the possibility that psychedelic drug experiences in a religious setting may be able to illuminate the dynamics and significance of worship. Increased understanding of the psychological mechanism involved might lead to more meaningful worship experiences for those who have not had the drug experience. The analogy with the efficacy of the Sacraments is one example of what would have to be considered for a better psychological understanding of what goes on during worship. Such considerations raise the question of the place of the emotional factor, compared to the cognitive, in religious worship. An even more basic question is the validity of religious experience of the mystical type, in terms of religious truth. Reactions to such religious implications will vary with theological position and presuppositions, but one value of our study can be to stimulate thoughtful examination of the problems.

Although our experimental results indicated predominantly positive and beneficial subjective effects, possible dangers must not be underestimated and should be thoroughly evaluated by specific research designed to discover the causes and methods of prevention of physical or psychological harm, both short-term and long-term. While physiological addiction has not been reported with psychedelic substances, psychological dependence might be expected if the experience were continually repeated. The intense subjective pleasure and enjoyment of the experience for its own sake could lead to escapism and withdrawal from the world. An experience that is capable of changing motivation and values might cut the nerve of achievement. Widespread apathy toward productive work and accomplishment could cripple a society. Another possible danger might be suicide or prolonged psychosis in very unstable or depressed individuals who are not ready for the intense emotional discharge. If it can be determined that any of these forms of harm occurs in certain types of individuals, research could be directed toward the development of pretest methods to screen out such persons. Our evidence would suggest that research on conditions and methods of administration of the drugs might minimize the chance of harmful reactions. Spectacular immediate advance must be sacrificed for ultimate progress by careful, yet daring and imaginative, research under adequate medical supervision.

The ethical implications also cannot be ignored. Any research that uses human volunteers must examine its motives and methods to make certain that human beings are not being manipulated like objects for purposes they do not understand or share. But in research with powerful psychoactive chemicals that may influence the most cherished human functions and values, the ethical problem is even more acute. The mystical experience, historically, has filled man with wondrous awe and has been able to change his style of life and values; but it must not be assumed that greater control of such powerful phenomena will automatically result in wise and constructive use. Potential abuse is just as likely. Those who undertake such research carry a heavy responsibility.

This is not to say that research should be stopped because of the fear of these various risks in an extremely complex and challenging area that has great promise for the psychology of religion. But while research is progressing on the theoretical or primary level, and before projects for testing useful social applications in a religious context become widespread, serious and thoughtful examination of the sociological, ethical, and theological implications is needed without delay.

Not the least of these implications is the fear that research that probes the psyche of man and involves his spiritual values may be a sacrilegious transgression by science. If the exploration of certain phenomena should be prohibited, should the mystical experiences made possible by psychedelic drugs be one of the taboo areas? Such restrictions raise several relevant questions. Who is wise enough to decide in advance that such research will cause more harm than good? If such restrictions are applied, where will they end, and will they not impede knowledge of unforeseen possibilities? This attitude on the part of religion is not new. Galileo and Servetus encountered it hundreds of years ago. The issue should not be whether or not to undertake such research, but rather how to do so in a way that sensitively takes into consideration the contribution, significance, and values of religion. A better scientific understanding of the mechanisms and application of mysticism has the potential for a greater appreciation and respect for heretofore rarely explored areas of human consciousness. If these areas have relevance for man's spiritual life, this should be a cause for rejoicing, not alarm. If the values nurtured by religion are fundamental for an understanding of the nature of man, then careful and sensitive scientific research into the experiential side of man's existence has the potential for illumination of these values. The importance of such research should be emphasized, especially because of its possible significance for religion and theology.

Many unknown conscious and unconscious factors operate in the mystical experience. Much investigation is needed in this area, and drugs like psilocybin can be a powerful tool. Experimental facilitation of mystical experiences under controlled conditions can be an important method of approach to a better understanding of mysticism. Better understanding can lead to appreciation of the role and place of such experiences in the history and practice of religion.

16

De-Automatization and the Mystic Experience*

Arthur J. Deikman

To study the mystic experience, one must turn initially to material that appears unscientific, is couched in religious terms, and seems completely subjective. Yet these religious writings are data and not to be dismissed as something divorced from the reality with which psychological science is concerned. The following passage, from "The Cloud of Unknowing," a fourteenth-century religious treatise, describes a procedure to be followed in order to attain an intuitive knowledge of God. Such an intuitive experience is called mystical because it is considered beyond the scope of language to convey. However, a careful reading will show that these instructions contain within their religious idiom psychological ideas pertinent to the study and understanding of a wide range of phenomena not necessarily connected with theological issues.

Forget all the creatures that ever God made and the works of them, so that thy thought or thy desire be not directed or stretched to

*The unedited version of this article appeared originally in *Psychiatry*, 1966, 29: 324-38. Copyright 1966 by the William Alanson White Psychiatric Foundation, Inc. Reprinted by special permission of The William Alanson White Psychiatric Foundation, Inc.

any of them, neither in general nor in special. . . . At the first time when thou does it, thou findst but a darkness and as it were a kind of unknowing, thou knowest not what, saving that thou feelest in thy will a naked intent unto God. . . . Thou mayest neither see him clearly by light of understanding in thy reason, nor feel him in sweetness of love in thy affection.

. . . If ever thou shalt see him or feel him as it may be here, it must always be in this cloud and in this darkness. . . . Smite upon that thick cloud of unknowing with a sharp dart of longing love. (Quoted in Knowles, 1961)

Specific questions are raised by this subjective account: What constitutes a state of consciousness whose content is not rational thought ("understanding in thy reason"), affective ("sweetness of love"), or sensate ("darkness," "cloud of unknowing")? By what means do both an active "forgetting" and an objectless "longing" bring about such a state? A comparison of this passage with others in the classical mystic literature indicates that the author is referring to the activities of renunciation and contemplative meditation. This paper will present a psychological model of the mystic experience based on the assumptions that meditation and renunciation are primary techniques for producing it, and that the process can be conceptualized as one of de-automatization.

PHENOMENA OF THE MYSTIC EXPERIENCE

Accounts of mystic experiences can be categorized as (1) untrained-sensate, (2) trained-sensate, and (3) trained-transcendent. "Untrained-sensate" refers to phenomena occurring in persons not regularly engaged in meditation, prayer, or other exercises aimed at achieving a religious experience. These persons come from all occupations and classes. The mystic state they report is one of intense affective, perceptual, and cognitive phenomena that appear to be extensions of familiar psychological processes. Nature and drugs are the most frequent precipitating factors.

The "trained-sensate" category refers to essentially the same phenomena occurring in religious persons in the West and in the East who have deliberately sought "grace," "enlightenment," or "union" by means of long practice in concentration and renunciation (contemplative meditation, Yoga, and so forth). Visions, feelings of "fire," "sweetness," "song," and joy are various accompaniments of this type of experience.

The untrained-sensate and the trained-sensate states are phenomenologically indistinguishable, with the qualification that the trained mystics report experiences conforming more closely to the specific religious cosmology to which they are accustomed. As one might expect, an experience occurring as the result of training, with the support of a formal social structure, and capable of being repeated, tends to have a more significant and persisting psychological effect. However, spontaneous conversion experiences are also noteworthy for their influence on a person's life. Typical of all mystic experience is a more or less gradual fading away of the state, leaving only a memory and a longing for that which was experienced.

Mystics such as St. John of the Cross and St. Teresa of Avila, commentators such as Poulain, and Eastern mystic literature in general, divide the effects and stages through which mystics progress into a lesser experience of strong emotion and ideation (sensate) and a higher, ultimate experience that goes beyond affect or ideation. It is the latter experience, occurring almost always in association with long training, that characterizes the "trained-transcendent" group.

A similar distinction between lower (sensate) and higher (transcendent) contemplative states may be found in Yoga texts. "Conscious concentration" is a preliminary step to "concentration which is not conscious [of objects]." In the transcendent state, multiplicity disappears and a sense of union with the One or with All occurs, "when all lesser things and ideas are transcended and forgotten, and there remains only a perfect state of imagelessness where Tathagata ["spirituality"—ed.] and Thahata ["being"—ed.] are merged into perfect Oneness" (Goddard, 1938.) This state is described in all the literature as one in which the mystic is passive in that he has abandoned striving. He sees "grace" to be the action of God on himself and feels himself to be receptive. In addition, some descriptions indicate that the senses and faculties of thought feel suspended, a state Roman Catholic literature calls the *ligature*.

BASIC MYSTIC TECHNIQUES

How is the mystic experience produced? To answer this question, I will examine the two basic techniques involved in mystical exercises: contemplation and renunciation.

Contemplation is, ideally, a nonanalytic apprehension of an object or idea—nonanalytic because discursive thought is banished and the attempt is made to empty the mind of everything except the percept of the object in question. Thought is conceived of as an interference with the direct contact that yields essential knowledge through perception alone. The renunciation of worldly goals and pleasures, both physical and psychological, is an extension of the same principle of freeing oneself from distractions that interfere with the perception of higher realms or more beautiful aspects of existence. The renunciation prescribed is most thorough and quite explicit in all texts. The passage that begins this paper instructs, "forget all the creatures that ever God made . . . so that thy thought . . . be not directed . . . to any of them." In the Lankavatra Scripture one reads, "he must seek to annihilate all vagrant thoughts and notions belonging to the externality of things, and all ideas of individuality and generality, of suffering and impermanence, and cultivate the noblest ideas of egolessness and emptiness and imagelessness" (Goddard, 1938). In most Western and Eastern mystic practice, renunciation also extends to the actual life situation of the mystic. Poverty, chastity, and the solitary way are regarded as essential to the attainment of mystic union. Zen Buddhism, however, sees the ordinary life as a proper vehicle for *satori* (a state of mystic illumination) as long as the "worldly" passions and desires are given up, and with them the intellectual approach to experience. "When I am in my isness, thoroughly purged of all intellectual sediments, I have my freedom in its primary sense . . . free from intellectual complexities and moralistic attachments" (Suzuki, 1959).

Instructions for performing contemplative meditation indicate that a very active effort is made to exclude outer and inner stimuli, to devalue and banish them, and at the same time to focus attention on the meditative object. In this active phase of contemplation, the concentration of attention upon particular objects, ideas, physical movements, or breathing exercises is advised as an aid to diverting attention from its usual channels and restricting it to a monotonous focus. Breathing exercises can also affect the carbon dioxide content of the blood and thus alter the state of consciousness chemically.

Elaborate instructions are found in Yoga for the selection of objects for contemplation and for the proper utilization of posture and breathing to create optimal conditions for concentration. Such techniques are not usually found in the Western religious literature except in the form of the injunction to keep the self oriented toward God and to fight the distractions that are seen as coming from the devil.

The active phase of contemplative meditation is a preliminary to the stage of full contemplation, in which the subject is caught up and absorbed in a process he initiated but that now seems autonomous, requiring no effort. Instead, passivity—self-surrender—is called for, an open receptivity amidst the "darkness" resulting from the banishment of thoughts and sensations and the renunciation of goals and desires directed toward the world.

It should not be forgotten that the techniques of contemplation and renunciation are exercised within the structure of some sort of theological schema. This schema is used to interpret and organize the experiences that occur. However, mere doctrine is usually not enough. The Eastern texts insist on the necessity for being guided by a guru (an experienced teacher), for safety's sake as well as in order to attain the spiritual goal. In Western religion, a "spiritual advisor" serves as guide and teacher. The presence of a motivating and organizing conceptual structure and the support and encouragement of a teacher are undoubtedly important in helping a person to persist in the meditation exercises and to achieve the marked personality changes that can occur through success in this endeavor. Enduring personality change is made more likely by the emphasis on adapting behavior to the values and insights associated both with the doctrinal structure and with the stages of mystical experience.

How can one explain the phenomena and their relation to these techniques? Most explanations in the psychological and psychoanalytic literature have been general statements emphasizing a regression to the early infant-mother symbiotic relationship. These statements range from an extreme position such as Alexander's (1931)—in which Buddhist training is described as a withdrawal of libido from the world to be reinvested in the ego until an intrauterine narcissism is achieved—to the basic statement of Freud (1929) that "oceanic feeling" is a memory of a relatively undifferentiated infantile ego state.

In recent years hypotheses have been advanced uniting the concepts of regression and of active adaption. This paper will attempt an explanation of mystic phenomena from a different point of view, that of attentional mechanisms in perception and cognition.

DE-AUTOMATIZATION

In earlier studies of experimental meditation, I (1963, 1966) hypothesized that mystic phenomena were a consequence of a *de-automatization* of the psychological structures that organize, limit, select, and interpret perceptual stimuli. I suggested the hypotheses of sensory translation, reality transfer, and perceptual expansion to explain certain unusual perceptions of the meditation subjects. At this point I will try to present an integrated formulation that relates these concepts to the classical mystic techniques of renunciation and contemplation.

De-automatization is a concept stemming from Hartmann's (1958) discussion of the automatization of motor behavior:

> In well-established achievements they [motor apparatuses] function automatically: the integration of the somatic systems involved in the action is automatized, and so is the integration of the individual mental acts involved in it. With increasing exercise of the action its intermediate steps disappear from consciousness. . . . Not only motor behavior but perception and thinking, too, show automatization.

Gill and Brenman (1959) developed the concept of de-automatization:

> De-automatization is an undoing of the automatizations of apparatuses—both means and goal structures—directed toward the environment. De-automatization is, as it were, a shake-up which can be followed by an advance or a retreat in the level of organization. . . . Some manipulation of the attention directed toward the functioning of an apparatus is necessary if it is to be de-automatized.

Thus, de-automatization may be conceptualized as the undoing of automatization, presumably by *reinvesting actions and percepts* with attention. The de-automatization of a structure may result in a shift to a structure lower in the hierarchy, rather than a complete cessation of the particular function involved.

CONTEMPLATIVE MEDITATION

In reflecting on the technique of contemplative meditation, one can see that it seems to constitute just such a manipulation of attention as is required to produce de-automatization. The percept receives intense attention while the use of attention for abstract categorization and thought is explicitly prohibited. Since automatization normally accomplishes the transfer of attention *from* a percept or action to abstract thought activity, the meditation procedure exerts a force in the reverse direction. Cognition is inhibited in favor of perception; the active intellectual style is replaced by a receptive perceptual mode.

Automatization is a hierarchically organized developmental process, so one would expect de-automatization to result in a shift toward a perceptual and cognitive organization characterized as "primitive," that is, an organization preceding the analytic, abstract, intellectual mode typical of present-day adult thought. This kind of organization has been described by Werner (1957) as: (1) relatively more vivid and sensuous, (2) syncretic, (3) physiognomic and animated, (4) dedifferentiated with respect to the distinctions between self and object and between objects, and (5) characterized by a de-differentiation and fusion of sense modalities. Theoretically, de-automatization should reverse the developmental process in this direction.

It is striking, then, to note that classical accounts of mystic experience emphasize the phenomenon of unity. Unity can be viewed as a de-differentiation that merges all boundaries until the self is no longer experienced as a separate object and customary perceptual and cognitive distinctions are no longer applicable. In this respect, the mystic literature is consistent with the de-automatization hypothesis.

If one searches for evidence of changes in the mystic's experience of the external world, the classical literature is of less help, because the mystic's orientation is inward rather than outward and he tends to write about God rather than nature. However, in certain accounts of untrained-sensate experience, there is evidence of a gain in sensory richness and vividness. James (1902), in describing the conversion experience, states, "A third peculiarity of the assurance state is the object change which the world often appears to undergo, 'An appearance of newness beautifies every object.'" He quotes Billy Bray: "I shouted for joy. I praised God with my whole heart. . . . I remember this, that everything looked new to me, the people, the fields, the cattle, the trees. I was like a new man in a new world.''

It is hard to document this perceptual alteration because the autobiographical accounts that many cite are a blend of the mystic's spiritual feeling and his actual perception, with the result that the spiritual content dominates the description the mystic gives of the physical world. However, these accounts do suggest that a ''new vision'' takes place, colored by an inner exaltation. Their authors report perceiving a new brilliance to the world, of seeing everything as if for the first time, of noticing beauty that for the most part they may have previously passed by without seeing. Although such descriptions do not prove a change in sensory perception, they strongly imply it. These particular phenomena appear quite variable and are not mentioned in many mystic accounts.

However, direct evidence was obtained on this point in the meditation experiments of mine (1963) already cited. There it was possible to ask questions and to analyze the subjects' reports to obtain information on their perceptual experiences. The phenomena the subjects reported fulfilled Werner's criterial completely, although the extent of change varied from one subject to the next. They described their reactions to the percept, a blue vase, as follows: (1) an increased vividness and richness of the percept—''more vivid,'' ''luminous''; (2) animation of the vase, which seemed to move with a life of its own; (3) a marked decrease in self-object distinction, occurring in those subjects who continued longest in the experiments: ''I really began to feel, you know, almost as though the blue and I were perhaps merging, or that the vase and I were. . . . It was as though everything was sort of merging''; (4) syncretic thought and a fusing and alteration of normal perceptual modes: ''I began to feel this light going back and forth,'' ''When the vase changes shape I feel this in my body,'' ''I'm still not sure, though, whether it's the motion in the rings or if it's the rings [concentric rings of light between the subject and the vase]. But in a certain way it is real. . . . It's not real in the sense that you can see it, touch it, taste it, smell it, or anything, but it certainly is real in the sense that you can experience it happening.'' The perceptual and cognitive changes that did occur in the subjects were consistently in the direction of a more "primitive" organization.

Thus, the available evidence supports the hypothesis that a de-automatization is produced by contemplative meditation. One might be tempted to call this de-automatization a regression to the perceptual and cognitive state of the child or infant. However, such a concept rests on assumptions as to the child's experience of the world that cannot yet be verified. One might call the direction regressive in a developmental sense, but the actual experience is probably not within the psychological scope of any child. It is a de-automatization occurring in an adult mind, and the experience gains its richness from adult memories and functions now subject to a different mode of consciousness.

REUNICATION

The de-automatization produced by contemplative meditation is enhanced and aided by the adoption of renunciation as a goal and a life style, a renunciation not confined to the brief meditative period alone. Poverty, chastity, isolation, and silence are techniques traditionally prescribed for pursuing the mystic path: to experience God, keep your thoughts turned to God and away from the world and the body that binds one to the segments of the subject's life. The mystic strives to banish from awareness the objects of the world and the desires directed toward them.

To the extent that perceptual and cognitive structures require the "nutriment" of their accustomed stimuli for adequate functioning, renunciation would be expected to weaken and even disrupt these structures, thus tending to produce an unusual experience (Rapaport, 1951). Such an isolation from nutritive stimuli probably occurs internally as well. The subjects of the meditation experiment quoted earlier reported that a decrease in responsiveness to distracting stimuli took place as they became more practiced. They became more effective, with less effort, in barring unwanted stimuli from awareness. These reports suggest that psychological barrier structures were established as the subjects became more adept. EEG studies of Zen monks yield similar results (Kasamatsu and Hirai, 1963). The effect of a distracting stimulus, as measured by the disappearance of alpha rhythm, was most prominent in the novices, less prominent in those of intermediate training, and almost absent in the master. It may be that the intensive, long-term practice of meditation creates temporary stimulus barriers producing a functional state of sensory isolation.

On the basis of sensory isolation experiments, it would be expected that long-term deprivation (or decreased variability) of a particular class of stimulus "nutriment" would cause an alteration in those functions previously established to deal with that class of stimuli. These alterations seem to be a type of de-automatization, as defined earlier—for example, the reported increased brightness of colors and the impairment of perceptual skills such as color discrimination. Thus, renunciation alone can be viewed as producing de-automatization. When combined with contemplative meditation, it produces a very powerful effect.

Finally, the more renunciation is achieved, the more the mystic is committed to his goal of Union or Enlightenment. His motivation necessarily increases, for having abandoned the world, he has no other hope of sustenance.

PRINCIPAL FEATURES OF
THE MYSTIC EXPERIENCE

Granted that de-automatization takes place, it is necessary to explain five principal features of the mystic experience: (1) intense realness, (2) unusual sensation, (3) unity, (4) ineffability, and (5) trans-sensate phenomena.

REALNESS

It is assumed by those who have had a mystic experience, whether induced by years of meditation or by a single dose of LSD, that the truthfulness of the experience is attested to by its sense of realness. The criticism of skeptics is often met with the statement, "You have to experience it yourself and then you will understand." This means that if one has the actual experience he will be convinced by its intense *feeling of reality*. "I know it was real because it was more real than my talking to you now."

But "realness" is not evidence. Indeed, there are many clinical examples of variability in the intensity of the feeling of realness that is not correlated with corresponding variability in the reality. Psychosis, for instance, is often preceded or accompanied by a sense that the world is less real than normally, sometimes that it is more real or has a different reality. The phenomenon of depersonalization demonstrates the potential for an alteration in the sense of the realness of one's own person, although one's evidential self undergoes no change whatsoever. Thus it appears that (1) the *feeling* of realness represents a function distinct from that of reality *judgment*, although they usually operate in synchrony; (2) the feeling of realness is not inherent in sensations, per se; and (3) realness can be considered a quantity function capable of displacement and, therefore, of intensification, reduction, and transfer affecting all varieties of ideational and sensorial contents.

From a developmental point of view, it is clear that biological survival depends on a clear sense of what is palpable and what is not. The sense of reality necessarily becomes fused with the object world. When one considers that meditation combined with renunciation brings about a profound disruption of the subject's normal psychological relationship to the world, it becomes plausible that the practice of such mystic techniques would be associated with a significant alteration of the feeling of reality. The quality of reality formerly attached to objects becomes attached to the particular sensations and ideas that enter awareness during periods of perceptual and cognitive de-automatization. Stimuli of the inner world become invested with the feeling of reality ordinarily bestowed on objects. Through what might be termed "reality transfer," *thoughts and images become real.*

Unusual Percepts

The sensations and ideation occurring during mystic de-automatization are often very unusual; they do not seem part of the continuum of everyday consciousness. Perceptions of encompassing light, infinite energy, ineffable visions, and incommunicable knowledge are remarkable in their seeming distinction from perceptions of the phenomena of the "natural world." According to mystics, these experiences are different because they pertain to a higher transcendent reality. What is perceived is said to come from another world, or at least another dimension. Although such a possibility cannot be ruled out, many of the phenomena can be understood as representing *an unusual mode of perception*, rather than an unusual external stimulus.

In my studies of experimental meditation, two long-term subjects reported vivid experiences of light and force. For example:

> Shortly I began to sense motion and shifting of light and dark as this became stronger and stronger. Now when this happens it's happening not only in my vision but it's happening or it feels like a physical kind of thing. It's connected with feelings of attraction, expansion, absorption, and suddenly my vision pinpointed on a particular place and . . . I was in the grip of a very powerful sensation and this became the center. (Deikman, 1966)

This report suggests that the perception of motion and shifting light and darkness may have been the perception of the movement of attention among various psychic contents (whatever such "movement" might actually be). "Attraction," "expansion," "absorption," would thus reflect the dynamics of the effort to focus attention—successful focusing is experienced as being "in the grip of" a powerful force. Another example: "When the vase changes shape . . . I feel this in my body and particularly in my eyes. . . . There is an actual kind of physical sensation as though something is moving there which recreates the shape of the vase." In this instance, the subject might have experienced the perception of a resynthesis taking place following de-automatization of the normal percept. That is, the percept of the vase was being reconstructed outside of normal awareness and the *process* of reconstruction was perceived as a physical sensation. I have termed this hypothetical perceptual mode *sensory translation*, defining it as the perception of psychic action (conflict, repression, problem solving, attentiveness, and so forth) via the relatively unstructured sensation of light, color, movement, force, sound, smell, or taste.

The concept of sensory translation offers an intriguing explanation for the ubiquitous use of *light* as a metaphor for mystic experience. It may not be just a metaphor. "Illumination" may be derived from an actual sensory experience occurring when, in the cognitive act of unification, a liberation of energy takes place or when a resolution of unconscious conflict occurs, permitting the experience of "peace," "presence," and the like. Liberated energy experienced as light may be the core sensory experience of mysticism.

If the hypothesis of sensory translation is correct, it does present the problem of why sensory translation comes into operation in any particular instance. In general, this seems to occur when (1) heightened attention is directed to the sensory pathways, (2) controlled analytic thought is absent, and (3) the subject's attitude is one of receptivity to stimuli. Training in contemplative meditation is specifically directed toward attaining a state with those characteristics. Laski (1961) reports that spontaneous mystic experiences may occur during such diverse activities as childbirth, viewing landscapes, listening to music, or having sexual intercourse. Although her subjects gave little description of their thought processes preceding the ecstasies, they were all involved at the time in intense sensory activities in which the three conditions listed above would tend to prevail. Those conditions seem also to apply to the mystical experiences associated with LSD. The state of mind induced by hallucinogenic drugs is reported to be one of increased sensory attention accompanied by an impairment or loss of some intellectual functions. With regard to the criterion of receptivity, if paranoid reactions occur during the drug state they are inimical to an ecstatic experience. On the other hand, when drug subjects lose their defensiveness and suspiciousness so that they "accept" rather than fight their situation, the "transcendent" experience often ensues (Sherwood, Stolaroff, and Harman, 1962). Thus, the general psychological context may be described as *perceptual concentration*. In this special state of consciousness, the subject becomes aware of certain intrapsychic processes ordinarily excluded from or beyond the scope of awareness. The vehicle for this perception appears to be amorphous sensation, made real by a displacement of reality feeling ("reality transfer") and thus misinterpreted as being of external origin.

UNITY

Experiencing one's self as one with the universe or with God is the hallmark of the mystic experience, regardless of its cultural context. I have already referred to explanations of this phenomenon in terms of regression. Two additional hypotheses should be considered: on the one hand, the perception of unity may be the perception of one's own psychic structure; on the other hand, the experience may be a perception of the real structure of the world.

It is a commonplace that we do not experience the world directly. Instead, we have an experience of sensation and associated memories from which we infer the nature of the stimulating object. As far as anyone can tell, the actual *substance* of the perception is the electrochemical activity that constitutes perception and thinking. From this point of view, the contents of awareness are homogeneous. They are variations of the same substance. If awareness were turned back upon itself, as postulated for sensory translation, this fundamental homogeneity (unity) of perceived reality—the electrochemical activity— might itself be experienced as a truth about the outer world, rather than the inner one. Unity—the idea and the experience that we are one with the world and with God—would thus constitute a valid perception insofar as it pertained to the nature of the thought process, but need not in itself be a correct perception of the external world.

Logically, there is also the possibility that the perception of unity does correctly evaluate the external world. As described earlier, de-automatization is an undoing of a psychic structure permitting the experience of increased detail and sensation at the price of requiring more attention. With such attention, it is possible that de-automatization may permit the awareness of new dimensions of the total stimulus array—a process of "perceptual expansion." The studies of von Senden (1960) and Shapiro (1960) suggest that development from infancy to adulthood is accompanied by an organization of the perceptual and cognitive world that has as its price the selection of some stimuli and stimulus qualities to the exclusion of others. If the automatization underlying that organization is reversed, or temporarily suspended, aspects of reality that were formerly unavailable might then enter awareness. Unity may in fact be a property of the real world that becomes perceptible via the techniques of meditation and renunciation, or under the special conditions, as yet unknown, that create the spontaneous, brief mystic experiences of untrained persons.

INEFFABILITY

Mystic experiences are ineffable, incapable of being expressed to another person. Although mystics sometimes write long accounts, they maintain that the experience cannot be communicated by words or be a reference to similar experiences from ordinary life. They feel at a loss for appropriate words to communicate the intense realness, the unusual sensations, and the unity cognition already mentioned. However, a careful examination of mystic phenomena indicated that there are at least several types of experiences, all of which are "indescribable" but each of which differs substantially in content and formal characteristics. Error and confusion result when these several states of consciousness are lumped together as "the mystic experience" on the basis of their common characteristic of ineffability.

To begin with, one type of mystic experience cannot be communicated in words because it is probably based on primitive memories and related to fantasies of a preverbal (infantile) or nonverbal sensory experience. Certain mystical reports that speak of being blissfully enfolded, comforted, and bathed in the love of God are very suggestive of the prototypical "undifferentiated state," the union of infant and breast, emphasized by psychoanalytic explanations of mystical phenomena.

A second type of mystical experience is equally ineffable but strikingly different—namely, a revelation too complex to be verbalized. Such experiences are reported frequently by those who have drug-induced mystical experiences. In such states, the subject has a revelation of the significance and interrelationships of many dimensions of life; he becomes aware of the many levels of meaning simultaneously and "understands" the totality of existence. The question of whether such knowledge is actual or an illusion remains unanswered; however, if such a multileveled comprehension were to occur, it would be difficult—perhaps impossible—to express verbally. Ordinary language is structured to follow the logical development of one idea at a time, and it might be quite inadequate to express an experience encompassing a large number of concepts simultaneously.

TRANS-SENSATE PHENOMENA

A third type of ineffable experience is that which I have described earlier as the "trained-transcendent" mystical experience. The author of "The Cloud of Unknowing," St. John of the Cross, and others are very specific in describing a new perceptual experience that does not include feelings of warmth, sweetness, visions, or any other elements of familiar sensory or intellectual experience. They emphasize that the experience *goes beyond* the customary sensory pathways, ideas, and memories. As I have shown, they describe the state as definitely not blank or empty but as filled with intense, profound, vivid perception, which they regard as the ultimate goal of the mystic path.

If one accepts their descriptions as phenomenologically accurate, one is presented with the problem of explaining the nature of such a state and the process by which it occurs. Following the hypotheses presented earlier in this paper, I would like to suggest that such experiences are the result of dimensions of the stimulus array previously ignored or blocked from awareness. For such mystics, renunciation has weakened and temporarily removed the ordinary objects of consciousness as a focus of awareness. Contemplative meditation has undone the logical organization of consciousness. At the same time, the mystic is intensely motivated to perceive something. If undeveloped or unutilized perceptual capacities do exist, it seems likely that they would be mobilized and come into operation under such conditions. The perceptual experience that would then take place would be one outside of customary verbal or sensory reference. It would be unidentifiable, hence indescribable. The high value, the meaningfulness, and the intensity reported of such experiences suggest that the perception has a different scope from that of normal consciousness. The loss of "self" characteristic of the trans-sensate experience indicates that the new perceptual mode is not associated with reflective awareness: the "I" of normal consciousness is in abeyance.

CONCLUSION

A mystic experience is the production of an unusual state of consciousness. This state is brought about by a de-automatization of hierarchically ordered structures of perception and cognition, structures that ordinarily conserve attentional energy for maximum efficiency in achieving the basic goals of the individual: biological survival as an organism and psychological survival as a personality. Perceptual selection and cognitive patterning are in the service of these goals. Under special conditions of dysfunction, such as in acute psychosis or in LSD states, or under special goal conditions, such as exist in religious mystics, the pragmatic systems of automatic selection are set aside or break down, in favor of alternate modes of consciousness whose stimulus processing may be less efficient from a biological point of view but whose very inefficiency may permit the experience of aspects of the real world formerly excluded or ignored. The extent to which such a shift takes place is a function of the motivation of the individual, his particular neurophysiological state, and the environmental conditions encouraging or discouraging such a change.

A final comment should be made. The content of the mystic experience reflects not only its unusual mode of consciousness but also the particular stimuli being processed through that mode. The mystic experience can be beatific, satanic, revelatory, or psychotic, depending on the stimuli predominant in each case. Such an explanation says nothing conclusive about the source of "transcendent" stimuli. God and the unconscious share equal possibilities here, and one's interpretation will reflect one's presuppositions and beliefs.

The mystic vision is one of unity, and modern physics lends some support to this perception when it asserts that the world and its living forms are variations of the same elements. However, there is no evidence that separateness and differences are illusions (as affirmed by Vedanta) or that God or a transcendent reality exists (as affirmed by Western religions).

The available scientific evidence tends to support the view that the mystic experience is one of internal perception, an experience that can be ecstatic, profound, or therapeutic for purely internal reasons. Yet for psychological science, the problem of understanding such internal processes is hardly less complex than the theological problem of understanding God. Indeed, regardless of one's direction in the search to know what reality is, a feeling of awe, beauty, reverence, and humility seems to be the product of one's efforts. Since these emotions are characteristic of the mystic experience itself, the question of the epistemological validity of that experience may have less importance than was initially supposed.

17

Forms of Religious Commitment and Intense Religious Experience*

Ralph W. Hood, Jr.

A persistent problem within the area of religious research has been the conceptual and empirical identification of forms of religious commitment. While most authorities would argue for the multidimensionality of religious commitment, the problem remains in adequately delineating these dimensions. However, if there is a consistent theme among diverse investigators, it is in essentially separating religious commitment into a personal, private, experiential orientation versus a public, associational, institutional orientation. This division, however named, refers to a persistent distinction of some importance within the area of religious research. Unfortunately, one real problem with this tendency to dichotomize religious commitment as either personal or institutional is that it obscures a significant group of persons—those who are both institutionally and personally committed. The empirical problems of measurement with respect to these categories are substantial.

*The unedited version of this article appeared originally in *The Review of Religious Research*, 1973, *15*: 29-35. Copyright 1973 by the Religious Research Association. Reprinted by permission.

One simple solution to this measurement problem is the assumption that, among persons religiously committed, primary forms of religious commitment can be identified readily by self-report. It seems reasonable rather than naive to believe that religiously committed persons can identify themselves as to the form of their religious commitment, whether primarily personal, primarily institutional, or equally personal and institutional. In the absence of more adequate scales and conceptualizations of religious commitment, the author decided to utilize this radically simple method to categorize the religiously committed as to their primary form of religious commitment. No additional assumptions were made with respect to the relationship among these nominally identified forms of commitment.

Interest in the measurement of religious commitment has had as one minor focal point the presumption of an intense experiential awareness that is uniquely or profoundly religious, even though it has been difficult to conceptualize. In a series of studies, I (1970, 1971, 1972a) demonstrated a positive relationship between such reported religious experience and intrinsic religious orientation. However, I measured religious experience by my "Religious Experience Episodes Measure" (REEM), which is essentially a paper-and-pencil instrument. This makes the relationship between presumed intense experiential states and intrinsic religious orientation less impressive, since both variables are inferred from paper-and-pencil measures. In an effort to minimize this limitation, I (1972b) interviewed intrinsic and extrinsic subjects regarding their most intense personal experience. It was found that intrinsically oriented subjects had more experiences that could be coded as transcendent or mystical than extrinsically oriented subjects. These data are consistent with the claim that the primarily personally religiously committed person is more likely to have intense religious experiences than the primarily institutionally religiously committed person. However, it is difficult to relate intrinsic religious orientation as measured by Allport's scale with a simple notion of personal religious commitment independent of institutional commitment (Dittes, 1971; Hood, 1971; Hunt and King, 1971, and above, chapter 14).

In the present study, the major concern was to relate intense religious experience to forms of religious commitment, with two factors of most interest. First, a classification of religiously committed persons according to their form of religious commitment that would permit more than a simple two-part separation into either personally or institutionally committed was desired. This was achieved by allowing religiously committed subjects to self-classify themselves into primarily personally, primarily institutionally, or equally personally and institutionally religiously committed. Second, it was desired to explore the nature of intense personal experiences for each form of religious commitment, utilizing operational categories of mystical experience derived from Stace (1960) and previously proven to be empirically fruitful (Hood, 1972b; Pahnke, 1966, and above, chapter 15; Pahnke and Richards, 1966). Specifically, it was hypothesized that the primarily institutionally religiously committed would have less intense personal religious experiences codifiable as mystical than would either the primarily personally religiously committed or the equally personally and institutionally religiously committed.

METHOD

SUBJECTS

Subjects (Ss) were selected from a self-acknowledged group of religiously committed persons by a combination of two procedures. First, notices were made in several psychology and religion classes as well as in several campus religious groups that Ss were wanted to participate in a psychological interview for which they would be paid two dollars. However, it was emphasized that only persons who considered religion—however defined—personally important should apply. Second, persons who arrived to volunteer for the interview responded to three simple items indicating importance of religion. The first item required Ss to "estimate how important religion is to you" along a five-point continuum where 1 was "not at all important" and 5 was "extremely important." Only Ss who marked "3" or above were assigned an interview time. By this method, all Ss who participated in the experiment could be operationally defined as equally religiously committed. Two additional items were also completed at this time. One item requested Ss to "estimate how important the church is to you" along a five-point continuum where 1 was anchored as "not at all important" and 5 as "extremely important." The remaining item required Ss to "estimate how important personal religious experience is to you" along the same five-point continuum. Satisfactory retest reliability of these three single-item "scales" was determined in pilot work.

The importance-of-church and importance-of-personal-religious-experience items were used to divide Ss into three groups. The first, personally religiously committed, group (N-25) consisted of all Ss who responded to the importance-of-personal-religious-experience item with a greater score than that for the importance-of-church item. The second, primarily institutionally committed, group (N-14) consisted of all Ss who responded to the importance-of-church item with a greater score than that for the importance-of-personal-religious-experience item. The third, equally personally and institutionally committed, group (N-15) consisted of all Ss who responded to both the importance-of-personal-religious-experience and importance-of-church items with the same value. The classification of Ss into these three groups was thus based upon the relative relationship between responses to these two items and not upon the absolute magnitude of responses to these two items. Finally, it is worthy of note that the denominational preferences of Ss in this study were primarily Baptist and Methodist.

INTERVIEWS

Interviews were conducted over a five-week interval by a senior psychology student who was paid for his efforts. The interviewer was unaware of the specific nature of the experiment and had no knowledge of the Ss' religious classification based upon the procedures discussed above.

All fifty-four interviews were conducted in similar fashion and were tape-recorded with explicit S approval. Interviews varied in length from twenty-six to ninety-five minutes, with a median length of approximately thirty-eight minutes. Ss were instructed that the interview was confidential and would be heard only by the author and his research associates. When signing up for an interview time, all Ss had been forewarned that the interview would concern a description of the S's single most significant personal experience. During the actual interview, Ss were told that the purpose of the study was to obtain a phenomenological classification system for personally significant experiences. The interviewer then asked each S to describe his most significant experience. The interviewer allowed the S freedom to explore his experience and was essentially nondirective until the S exhausted his ability to describe his experience. At this point, the interviewer would prod the S further in terms of the eight code categories used in this study, if they had not already been spontaneously utilized by the S. The interviewer had a check sheet to assure coverage of each of the code categories. In all cases, the interviewer instructed and guided the S to focus upon the phenomenological nature of the experience itself and not upon detailed, extensive personal interpretations. If the S talked about more than one experience, the interviewer guided the S to focus eventually upon only that experience which was most significant, and in such cases only this experience was utilized for coding purposes.

CLASSIFICATION OF MYSTICAL EXPERIENCE

The following eight operational categories of mystical experience were utilized: ego quality, noetic quality, communicable quality, religious quality, unifying quality, temporal quality, affective quality, and affective intensity. These characteristics were basically derived from Stace's (1960) criteria for mystical experience, with certain modifications, most notably the exclusion of paradoxicality as a criterion due to the problem of coding it independent of the other categories. These criteria were made operational for use by the author and an additional rater, taking into account Stace's detailed discussions and previous efforts at making the criteria operational.

The tape-recorded responses for each S were scored by rating, for each of these criteria, the degree to which the experience fulfilled the operational specifications. For this purpose, a six-point scale was used, ranging from 1 ("this criterion is definitely not applicable to this experience") to 6 ("this criterion is definitely and fully applicable to this experience"). These judgments were made as the relevant criteria were discussed by the S, either spontaneously or after prodding by the interviewer. The score values for these eight criteria were then summed to form a single mysticism score, with a possible range of 8 (not mystical) to 48 (most mystical). The actual range of scores obtained in this study was 12 to 48. The rating of all taped interviews was done without prior knowledge of the S's religious commitment classification.

RELIABILITY

A senior psychology student and the author worked to determine the reliability of the eight criteria. After familiarity with these criteria was established, twenty tapes were randomly selected from the fifty-four completed, and these were independently coded by the author and the additional rater. The resulting interjudge reliabilities of .79 and up indicate that raters can be trained to make similar relative assessments with these criteria, even though their absolute assessments with respect to these criteria may, of course, vary. It is important to note that, for purposes of actual data analysis, only the scores obtained by the single rater who rated all fifty-four tapes were utilized. High internal consistency reliabilities were also discovered.

RESULTS

The design of this study resulted in the classification of the Ss according to form of religious commitment, with S's total mysticism score utilized as the dependent variable. The mean and standard deviation mysticism scores for each form of religious commitment are as follows: primarily personally religiously committed, M. = 31.4, S.D. = 9.7; primarily institutionally religiously committed, M. = 17.3, S.D. = 3.8; equally personally and institutionally religiously committed, M. = 27.2, S.D. = 9.7. These data were initially analyzed by means of a one-way analysis of variance. Analysis indicated that all possible differences among these three means were significant (.01 level).

In order to further clarify the relationship between intense religious experience and form of religious commitment, correlations were calculated between total mysticism score obtained from the interviews and responses to the items used to measure the importance of personal religious experience and importance of the church. The item to measure importance of the church negatively correlated with

total mysticism score (r= −.27) while the item to measure importance of personal religious experience positively correlated with total
mysticism score (r= +.46). These items did not significantly correlate with each other.

DISCUSSION

These data clearly support the hypothesis tested. The primarily
institutionally religiously committed person is less likely to have the
intense religious experience characterized as mystical than either the
primarily personally religiously committed or the equally institutionally and personally religiously committed. These data are consistent
with the large body of research literature suggesting that the person
who is perhaps merely institutionally oriented has adopted a religion
for reasons that are more utilitarian and functional than devoutly
experientially based (Allport and Ross, 1967; Dittes, 1969; Hunt and
King, 1971). These data are also consistent with previous research
indicating that extrinsically oriented persons are less likely to report
intense personal religious experiences than are intrinsically oriented
persons (Hood, 1970, 1971, 1972a, b).

However, it is important to note that the mysticism scores were
significantly different for each category of form of religious commitment, with the primarily personally religiously committed category
significantly more mystical than the equally personally and institutionally religiously committed category, which in turn was significantly more mystical than the primarily institutionally religiously
committed category. These data suggest that institutional religious
commitment may make the intense personal experience of mysticism
less likely, as long ago emphasized by James (1902).

We suggest, then, that the intense religious experience of mysticism is unlikely to maintain itself within church boundaries simply
because such experiences are unlikely to be normative in such institutions, as Dittes (1969) has also suggested. Perhaps, as persons
become more institutionally committed, their commitment to culti-
vating intense personal religious experiences declines. It may be that
our three groups scored as they did precisely because of an antithetical interaction between church commitment and this form of intense
personal religious commitment. This conjecture is especially reason-

able in light of the negative correlation between institutional commitment and mysticism and the positive correlation between personal religious commitment and mysticism. It is also worthy to note that these correlations hold within a sample of reasonably equally religiously committed persons. Although this conjecture is consistent with our data, a word of caution is in order. This conjecture suggests a developmental hypothesis that is not directly tested by the design of this study, which only documents differences in mystical experiences for forms of religious commitment measured at one point in time. A direct test of this developmental hypothesis would clearly be worthwhile.

Finally, we must note that our discussion is not meant to imply that all forms of religious experience are antithetical to institutional religious commitment. We have previously documented the normative effect of institutional religious commitment on the report of religious experience (Hood, 1972a). Likewise, Yinger (1970) has emphasized that certain forms of religious experience occur within institutional contexts and are likely to be overlooked simply because they affirm a person's contemporary religious views. What our data indicate is that a particular form of intense religious experience, mysticism, is perhaps unlikely to occur within institutional contexts. Precisely why this is the case is a matter for further empirical investigation.

18

Right and Left Thinking*

Robert E. Ornstein

The belief that there are two forms of consciousness has been with us for centuries. Reason versus passion is one of its guises; mind versus intuition is another. The feminine, the sacred, the mysterious historically have lined up against the masculine, the profane, and the logical. Medicine argues with art, yin complements yang. In fable and folklore, religion and science, this dualism has recurred with stunning regularity.

What is new is the discovery that the two modes of consciousness have a physiological basis. They are not simply a reflection of culture or philosophy. The evidence accumulates that the human brain has specialized, and that each half of that organ is responsible for a distinct mode of thought.

The difference between the right and left sides of the body gave researchers their main clue to the biological mechanisms of thought. In this regard, other cultures have been ahead of us. The Australian aborigines hold the "male" stick in the right hand and the "female" stick in the left hand. To the Mojave Indians, the left hand is the

*The unedited version of this article appeared originally in *Psychology Today*, May 1973, pp. 86-92. Copyright © 1973 by Ziff-Davis Publishing Company. Reprinted by permission of *Psychology Today* magazine.

passive, maternal side of the person, while the right hand represents the active father.

SPECIALTIES IN THE HALF-BRAIN

It turns out that such distinctions are not arbitrary. The cerebral cortex of the brain is divided into two hemispheres, joined by a large bundle of interconnecting fibers called the corpus callosum. The right side of the cortex primarily controls the left side of the body, and the left side of the cortex largely controls the right side of the body. The structure and the function of these two "half-brains" influence the two modes of consciousness. The left hemisphere is predominantly involved with analytic thinking, especially language and logic. This hemisphere seems to process information sequentially, which is necessary for logical thought since logic depends on sequence and order.

The right hemisphere, by contrast, appears to be primarily responsible for our orientation in space, artistic talents, body awareness, and recognition of faces. It processes information more diffusely than the left hemisphere does, and integrates material in a simultaneous, rather than linear, fashion.

But it is important to note that the activities of the right and left hemispheres are not exclusive of each other. Rather, we should think of each "half-brain" as a specialist in its functions. In children, each side possesses the potential for both modes of thought. Brain damage to the left hemisphere in young children often means that the right side will develop language, contrary to the normal course of events.

Scientists have determined the right-left specialization of the hemispheres from studies of right-handed people. Left-handers, who make up about 5 percent of the population, are less consistent. Some of them are no different from right-handers; others show a complete reversal of brain function; and yet others have a mixed pattern, e.g., both hemispheres have verbal ability.

Clinical and neurological investigators tend to label the left and right hemispheres the "major" and the "minor" respectively. This is more a societal than a neurological distinction. Our culture emphasizes verbal and intellectual abilities, and this bias intrudes into the most "objective" haunts of science. if an injury to the right hemisphere does not affect speech or reason, then many neurologists consider the damage minor. Since injury to the left hemisphere affects verbal ability, the left hemisphere must be "major."

I disagree with this cultural slant. I believe that each hemisphere is the major one, depending on the mode of consciousness under consideration. If one is a wordsmith, a scientist, or a mathematician, damage to the *left* hemisphere may prove disastrous. If one is a musician, a craftsman, or an artist, damage to the *right* hemisphere may obliterate a career.

SPLITTING THE BRAIN

Roger Sperry (1964) and his associates have done extensive work on the functions of the two hemispheres. They began by severing the corpus callosum, the bundle of fibers that joins the two hemispheres, in laboratory animals. Their work led them to adopt a radical treatment for human patients suffering from severe epilepsy. This treatment was to sever the corpus callosum. By isolating one hemisphere from the other, they hoped to reduce the amount of neural mass that could be involved in a seizure. In many cases, the procedure worked. Many severely disordered patients improved enough to leave the hospital.

Despite the radical surgery, these "split-brain" people showed almost no abnormalities in their everyday lives. However, Sperry and his associates discovered, through many subtle tests, that the operation clearly separated the specialized functions of the two hemispheres.

If, for instance, the patient held a pencil (hidden from his sight) in his right hand, he could describe it verbally as usual. But if he held the pencil in his left hand, he could not describe it at all. Recall that the left side of the body is connected with the right hemisphere, which does not possess much capability for speech. With the corpus callosum severed, the hemispheres cannot communicate. So the verbal mechanism of the patient *literally does not know* what is in his left hand. If, however, the experimenters offered the patient a selection of small objects—a key, a book, a pencil, etc.—and asked him to choose the one he had previously held in his left hand, he could select the correct item. The patient could recognize a pencil, he just couldn't talk about one.

Most right-handed people can to some extent write and draw with their left hands. Bogen tested the ability of right-handed patients to write and draw with either hand after their split-brain surgery. They were able to write English with the right hand as well as they could before the operation, but this hand could no longer draw very well. It seemed unable to carry out relational, spatial tasks. Given a square to copy, for instance, the patient might draw four corners stacked together. He could draw *only* the corners; his right hand could not link the segments. The left hemisphere, which controls the right hand, primarily operates in an analytic manner, yet has difficulty relating individual parts. But when patients used their left hands, their performance was reversed. The left could draw and copy spatial figures (the province of the right hemisphere) but had great difficulty copying a written word.

HEAD AND HEART DUALITY

Recent research with split-brain monkeys indicates that the two hemispheres can function simultaneously as well as independently. We can train a split-brain monkey to solve one learning problem with its right eye and left brain while it solves a second problem with its left eye and right brain. And one preliminary experiment with split-brain people shows that their two hemispheres can process more information at once than can those of a normal person. Sperry notes that apparently "surgery has left each of these people with two separate minds, that is, with two separate spheres of consciousness."

We all have decisions in which intellect suggests one course of action and "heart" or intuition suggests another. Split-brain patients provide a good example of this dual response. In one experiment, Sperry wanted to see whether the right (nonverbal) hemisphere could learn to respond verbally to different colors. He asked the patient to look at a dot directly in front of him. While the patient's eyes were fixated, Sperry flashed a light, either red or green, to the patient's left visual field, which the right half of each retina receives and sends to the right hemisphere. Sperry then asked the split-brain patients to guess out loud which color was flashed to them. He expected that each patient's number of correct guesses would be no better than chance, since the left hemisphere controls words and the color information had gone to the right hemisphere. The side that was doing the guessing, in short, was disconnected from the side that knew the answer.

After a few tests, however, the patients' scores improved whenever Sperry allowed a second guess. If the patient had guessed incorrectly, he would typically frown, shake his head, and then change his answer. It was as if the right hemisphere heard the left side give the wrong answer. Since it lacked the ability to speak, the right hemisphere then used the physical means at its disposal—a frown and a headshake—to tell the left hemisphere that it had made a mistake.

A VERY PECULIAR MACHINE

This experiment provides a loose analogy to the conflict between Freud's conscious and unconscious processes. Freud's famous dichotomy holds that the conscious mind largely controls language and rational discourse, while the unconscious is much less accessible to reason or to verbal analysis. The unconscious may communicate through gestures, face and body movements, or tone of voice. In split-brain patients, the verbal, rational system, disconnected from the source of information, may be countermanded by body language. A person may insist "I am *not* angry," yet his tone of voice and facial expression indicate that he is furious.

Sperry demonstrated the "Freudian conflict" that occurs when the right hemisphere gets emotional input that the verbal hemisphere does not. He showed a photograph of a nude woman, among a series of otherwise dull pictures, to the right hemisphere of a patient. At first the woman said that she saw nothing; but she immediately flushed, squirmed, and looked uncomfortable. Her "conscious" or verbal half was unaware of what had caused her emotional turmoil. All she knew was that something unusual was occurring in her body. Her words showed that the emotional reaction had been "unconscious," unavailable to her language apparatus. Finally she told Sperry that he had a very peculiar machine.

RIGHT AND LEFT LOOKING

Other experiments (Bakan, 1971) use eye movements to confirm the specialization of the two hemispheres. If you ask a friend a question such as How do you spell Mississippi? the chances are that he will shift his gaze off to one side while reflecting. My colleagues and I have found that the kind of question affects the direction of gazing. If the question is verbal-analytical (such as "Give the definition of the following word: *prejudice*"), more eye movements veer to the right than if the question is spatial (such as "Which way does an Indian face on the nickel?"). Similarly, David Galin and I (1972), along with other colleagues, are investigating the electroencephalograms (EEG) of normal people while they are thinking verbally and spatially. The corresponding changes in the EEG indicate that the normal human brain does indeed have specialized thought processes.

DESCRIBING A SPIRAL STAIRCASE

It is not at all clear how these two modes of thought interact in daily life. Galin and I (1972) believe that in most ordinary activities we simply alternate between the two modes, selecting the appropriate one and inhibiting the other. We do not know how this process occurs. The two systems may work continuously in parallel and merely alternate control of the body. Or they may divide the control according to some undiscovered time-sharing plan. Obviously most of us can work in both modes—we speak, we move about, we usually can do both at once. Yet if I attempt to describe with words each body movement I make while I am skiing, for example, I will meet disaster. The two modes of thought complement each other, but one does not readily replace the other. Try to describe a spiral staircase without using your hands. Or try to ride a bicycle based on verbal instruction only.

The specialization of the two hemispheres seems to be unique to human beings and to be related to the evolution of language; there is as yet no evidence that any other primates have specialized hemispheres. Jerre Levy-Agresti and Sperry (1968) argue that human beings have evolved in this manner because language and logic require sequential thought, which is not compatible with the simultaneous thought that spatial orientation demands. There is some evidence that the two hemispheres may differ in their physiological organization. Josephine Semmes (1968) and her colleagues of the National Institute of Mental Health studied 124 brain-injured war veterans. They tested the effects of brain injury on simple motor reactions, sensory thresholds, and ability to distinguish objects. Semmes found that injuries in quite specific areas of the left hemisphere interfered with performance of specific tasks, but they found no such specific disruption following right-hemisphere lesions. They concluded that the left hemisphere is organized in a more diffuse manner.

The complementary workings of our two thought processes permit our highest achievements, but most occupations value one mode over the other. Science and law, for example, emphasize linear thought and verbal logic. The arts, including music, and the religions are more present-oriented, aconceptual, and intuitive. The unfortunate result is that many intellectuals often disparage the nonverbal mind, while many mystics and poets often disparage the rational mind.

But a complete human consciousness should include both modes of thought, just as a complete day includes both light and darkness. Perhaps the knowledge that the two modes have a physiological basis will help science and psychology to regain their balance. We must not ignore the right-hemisphere talents of imagination, perspective, and intuition, which in the long run may prove essential to our personal and cultural survival.

19

Mystical Experience: Normal and Normative*

John R. Tisdale

To speak of religion without speaking of the intensely personal experience is not to speak of religion at all. Knowledge, belief, and institutional loyalties may be important, but beyond them lies another dimension. This is the deeply moving individual experience, of which William James was so fond, and which has appeared regularly in attempts to distinguish mystical from rational religion and to describe various dimensions of religion, as in the first section of this book. In a day when many religious institutions here in the West are losing their ability and desire to encourage this kind of experience, it is important to point out some fresh converging evidence from rather disparate sources that mysticism not only may be deeply rooted in the biological nature of man, but may also be a necessary part of his emotional health.

1.

There is the fact, first of all, that such mystical experiences are not unique to any particular religion, although creedal attempts to

*The unedited version of this article appeared originally in *Religion in Life*, 1975, 44 : 370-74. Copyright 1975 by Abingdon Press. Reprinted by permission.

describe them may obscure this. They are found in a wide variety of religious contexts. In itself, this is not a new observation. Further, underlying particular interpretations of such experiences are several definable characteristics upon which there is some general agreement.

In all religious cultures, for instance, the person experiences some kind of identity or unity with Creation or Reality (or God). This goes beyond a sense of continuity with all that exists to the point at which the individual reports that somehow he is one with or even the same as that which he believes to be Ultimate.

Moreover, he experiences insights into the nature of reality that he is absolutely convinced are true. It is not that he has gained new factual information necessarily, but that he now comprehends the true meaning of what information he has. The experience has opened up cognitive vistas that are felt to be self-authenticating. Incidentally, the nature of this reality is almost always felt to be unitary; dualities and apparent contradictions are resolved in a larger whole that encompasses without denying them.

He is also likely to experience a wide variety of unusual perceptual phenomena. These may take the form of "abnormal" bodily sensations and feelings, visual alterations, or even periods of what may appear to be hallucinations. The experience of time itself is often altered.

He has great difficulty as well in communicating or expressing the precise nature of this experience. Words somehow do not carry the necessary meanings with which to tell others of it. Metaphor and simile are often used in an attempt to make up for this inadequacy, but they do not entirely do so.

Finally, such experiences are usually felt to be extremely significant by those who have had them. Whether continual or occasional, they seem to provide touchstones by which individuals often reorder their thinking and their behavior. They are important experiences.

2.

Several years ago it became apparent not only that these states were common to a number of religions, but that they could also be produced by the administration of psychedelic or psychotropic drugs.

Clark's (1969) treatment of this phenomenon is probably the most comprehensive. He makes the point both that drugs and religious experience have been connected historically for a long time (e.g., the Delphic Oracle) and that drugs today can be a factor in many types of religious experience, whether found within church settings or not.

Others have noted this also. Pahnke (1966 and above, chapter 15; Pahnke and Richards, 1966) used psilocybin in a Good Friday service at Boston University, noticeably enhancing the service as a mystical experience for those who used the drug. Masters and Houston (1966) reported analogous experiences, some of which were not within conventional religious contexts at all. The evidence seems incontrovertible: drugs do produce intensely personal religious experiences with the same characteristics as nondrug mystical experiences.

3.

The recent work that promises to tie this together and that may in part help to explain why such experiences are found in such different contexts is that of Robert E. Ornstein (1972, 1973 and above, chapter 18). His direct concern is with consciousness, not religion. Drawing upon empirical research of his own and that of others, as well as a wide variety of other sources, he points out that there very clearly seem to be two modes of consciousness normally existing in every one. One of these is rational; this has to do with logic and sequential thinking. It is the sort of thinking upon which this article depends. The other is nonrational; it is intuitive and nonanalytic. It is the stuff of which artistic and mystical experiences are made.

Ornstein goes on to state persuasively that these functions are also neurologically specific, one to each hemisphere of the brain. As is generally known, the right side of the body is controlled by the left hemisphere, the left side by the right half of the cerebral cortex.

The left hemisphere (connected to the right side of the body) is predominantly involved with analytic, logical thinking, especially in verbal and mathematical functions. Its mode of operation is primarily linear. This hemisphere seems to process information sequentially. This mode of operation of necessity must underlie logical thought, since logic depends on sequence and order. Language and mathematics, both left-hemisphere activities, also depend predominantly on linear time. If the left hemisphere is specialized for analysis, the right hemisphere (again, remember, connected to the left side of the body) seems specialized for holistic mentation. Its language ability is quite limited. This hemisphere is primarily responsible for our orientation in space, artistic endeavor, crafts, body image, recognition of faces. It processes information more diffusely than does the left hemisphere, and its responsibilities demand a ready integration of many inputs at once. If the left hemisphere can be termed predominantly analytic and sequential in its operation, then the right hemisphere is more holistic and relational, and more simultaneous in its mode of operation. (Ornstein, 1972, pp. 52-53)

Clearly the experiential-mystical religious experience belongs to functions of the right lobe—whether triggered by drugs or not—and everyone comes genetically equipped with a right lobe.

4.

The work of Abraham Maslow provides the final extension of my argument; he suggests that such experience is necessary for the full realization of human potential. A humanistic psychologist, Maslow was long concerned to articulate the nature of healthy, self-actualizing human beings. One of the characteristics of those who are engaged in the self-actualizing process is that they regularly report "peak experiences." These are precisely the kinds of experiences under consideration here, which differ from religion to religion only in their cognitive interpretation. Those who are not actively self-actualizing do not seem to have them. Thus he finds a sort of "core-religious experience" that is an integral part of maximum personal development. "The two religions of mankind tend to be the peakers and the non-peakers, that is to say, those who have private, personal, transcendent, core-religious experiences easily and often and who accept them and make use of them, and, on the other hand, those who have never had them or who repress them and who, therefore, cannot make use of them for their personal therapy, personal growth, or personal fulfillment" (Maslow, 1964).

Some independent suggestive support for this same position has been appearing in studies by Hood (1970, 1973a, and above, chapter

17, 1974), in which he has found that persons with intrinsically oriented religion, personal religious commitments, or with high ego strength are more likely to report such intense personal religious experience than those with extrinsic religion, institutional religious commitments, or low ego strength.

Although these observations are not conclusive, they clearly point to an aspect of human experiencing that must not be overlooked. The human capacity for the nonrational mystical experience is universal to the species, seems to have clear physiological roots, and is necessary to man's fullest human development.

For Further Reading

Although Underhill's *Mysticism* is a classic, it is also lengthy and probably not the best place to begin. If you are looking for a general work, consider Stace's *Mysticism and Philosophy* (Philadelphia: Lippincott, 1960), a sound, extensive, and readable discussion cited by several authors in this section.

Abraham Maslow talks of the common elements in peak experiences in *Religions, Values, and Peak Experiences* (New York: Viking, 1964) and presents some further material on this in *The Further Reaches of Human Nature* (New York: Viking, 1971). Although neither is like Maslow's essays, I think you might also find it worth your while to read John Lilly's autobiography, *The Center of the Cyclone* (New York: Julian, 1972), and the guide by Baba Ram Das, *Be Here Now* (San Cristobal, N. M.: Lama Foundation, 1971).

Walter Houston Clark's *Chemical Ecstasy: Psychedelic Drugs and Religion* (New York: Sheed and Ward, 1969) is a balanced presentation of the relations between drugs and mystical experience, although it needs some updating. William Braden's *The Private Sea* (Chicago: Quadrangle, 1967) is a good companion to it, even though Braden does not deal with exactly the same thing. R. E. L. Masters and Jean Houston's *The Varieties of Psychedelic Experience* (New York: Holt, Rinehart, and Winston, 1966) presents interesting case material. No new volumes in this particular area have appeared so far in the 1970s.

Charles T. Tart has assembled two collections of readings that are relevant to this section. The first is *Altered States of Consciousness* (New York: Wiley, 1969). The second, *Transpersonal Psychologies* (New York: Harper and Row, 1975), is clearly at this growing edge of the psychology of religion. Although not all of the chapters in it have been equally valuable to me, the ones by Tart himself are very provocative. Robert Ornstein's *The Psychology of Consciousness* (San Francisco: Freeman, 1972) has also influenced my own thinking a good deal.

If you are interested in a discussion of meditation free of most of the jargon that often surrounds it, you will certainly want to look at Lawrence LeShan's *How to Meditate* (Boston: Little, Brown, 1974).

Part Four

Religion, Deviant Behavior, and Therapy

INTRODUCTION

The relationship between religion and deviant behavior of various types has intrigued many people over a long period of time. It is still one of the growing edges in the psychology of religion. It has, I think, been fed in part by the observations that religious delusions are sometimes found in psychotics, that historically some important religious leaders have shown signs of personality disorder, and that reports of mystical experiences may sound quite strange—and by the fact that ministers, priests, and rabbis are often contacted first by people in periods of emotional distress or crisis.

An even more influential reason for the continuation of this interest is the belief in a causal relationship between religiosity or "faith" and mental health or happiness. In a negative form, this belief may show itself as the assertion that religion and sound emotional health are incompatible. Freud (1928) is often cited as a proponent of this point of view because of his conviction that religious beliefs belong in the realm of untestable hypotheses (*illusions*, in his special terminology) that man would do better to give up in the face of a universe that is indifferent to his existence. I have found no empirically oriented articles that support this assumption, although a volume described at the end of this section tends to be slanted in this direction. Most support for the viewpoint seems to be found in writings that define religion in such a way that a person who is religious is for that reason alone unhealthy.

The opposite form of the same belief is the insistence that a person who is essentially "right" with God will not (therefore) fall heir to fears and anxieties. His faith has made him whole. Conversely, people who are anxious or upset may need above all to set right their relationship with their Divinity. Their difficulties stem from being out of tune with the Ultimate. I suspect that religionists—recognizing that the functions of religion and healing were at one time united in the same role (shaman, medicine man, priest, etc.)—may hold this position more frequently than therapists. However, I really have no data to support this impression.

I think you can see from what you have read already in this book that one's religious experiences are indeed a part of one's total experience. Even so, this position is not easy to maintain, for in doing so one is likely to face considerable evidence suggesting that many very religious people do suffer both emotionally and physically—which in turn is a direct lead-in to the whole theological problem of the existence of evil. Discussion is made even more difficult by the definitional problem: neither mental health nor religion (as we know) is a unitary entity. "We face the problem of two separate global realities: psychological health as well as religion in the person. Neither one can be presumed to be fairly appraised by simple measures" (Becker, 1971).

In the first article in this section, we can see that Stark is not so easily discouraged, however. He examines some of the theoretical background for the first alternative I referred to—that religiosity and poor emotional adjustment are directly related—and rejects it. He then presents data concerning some indicators of conventional religiosity and emotional disturbance that support a more positive and traditional Judeo-Christian view. We should note, though, that Stark is looking at *conventional* religion, which in the eyes of many may not be religion at its best. He does not speak to the question of whether positive, creative, but statistically deviant, religion is associated with emotionally deviant behavior. In a related paper, Knudten and Knudten survey the available research having to do with religion and crime, assuming for our purposes that crime may be thought of as an index of maladjustment. Their conclusions are probably less than surprising: little is known, and much research is needed.

Another belief that has had some influence is that of Anton Boisen, who was convinced that certain kinds of schizophrenic experiences and religious conversions are both problem-solving efforts. They are "attempts to face and deal with the abiding issues of life, attempts at reorganization which tend either to make or break" (Boisen, 1936). They have a common situation: inner conflict, accompanied by the sense of ultimate loyalties and unattained possibilities that Boisen saw as being religious. If the attempted personality reorganization is successful, it may be considered to be a religious experience; if not, it is thought of as psychosis.

This thesis has never had an adequate empirical test, but I believe that it remains in the background of the next study in this group. Lowe and Braaten elected not to compare normals and nonnormals, but to look more closely at the nature of the religious concern that is present in a hospitalized group in order to seek out differences between subgroups in that sample. The largest difference they found was related to length of hospitalization, and it is consistent with studies they mention and another by Lindenthal et al. (1970), which concluded that people in crisis situations tend to turn away from social sources of help toward those that are more individual, such as prayer.

Hood's article picks up on the observations, to which I have alluded, that some religious leaders in the Judeo-Christian tradition (such as Saul, Ezekiel, Paul of Tarsus, Fox, Bunyan) have exhibited psychotic behavior and that mystical experiences and psychotic episodes may have common elements. Specifically, he examines the question of whether or not mystical experiences are associated with some kind of emotional vulnerability. Although no final answer on this is yet available, and his results indicate the need for careful concept definition, the article supports the position that intense religious experiences are positively associated with psychological strength instead.

The last two articles come out of the Christian Church's concern for personal wholeness and some of the methods it has adopted toward that end. The newly emerged speciality of pastoral counseling is one of the largest single applied areas of the psychology of religion. Partly because of the practical bent of those in it, not much empirical research has appeared, although a lot of essays have been written (Tisdale, 1967d). My article takes a short look at some of the possible effects of pastoral counseling and is included here, not because of its astonishing conclusions (they aren't), but because it opens up an empirical window on this area for the first time. In a departure from the more usual studies in this collection, the concluding article by Oden traces the historical resemblances between the encounter movement of today and earlier Jewish and Christian pietistic traditions. This suggests at least one point of contact between religious experience and humanistic approaches to healing and growth.

20

Psychopathology and Religious Commitment*

Rodney Stark

It has long been charged that religiousness either is pathological per se or stems from pathological states of mind. Freud (1928) argued that religion is a kind of universal obsessional neurosis, if not an outright delusion. William James (1902) also believed much religiousness had a psychopathological origin, although, unlike Freud, he considered this a blessing in disguise. Such views remain common among social scientists. Nevertheless, the rapid rise of the pastoral psychology movement and various religion-and-mental-health groups is predicated on the notion that religiousness can relieve the problems of the mentally ill: that religious commitment is a source of psychological health, not the consequence of psychopathology. Obviously, these two positions are contradictory.

In this paper I shall try to sort out what is at issue on both theoretical and logical grounds and then seek empirical verification of the following hypothesis: *The various mental conditions referred to by such terms as* psychopathology *or being* mentally ill *or ill-*

*The unedited version of this article appeared originally in *The Review of Religious Research*, 1971, 12 : 165-76. Copyright 1971 by the Religious Research Association. Reprinted by permission.

adjusted *are negatively related to conventional forms of religious commitment.*

The best-known assertions on this question and much of the evidence bears on the psychopathological basis of religious innovation. Many scholars have scrutinized the lives of founders of religions, saints, famous mystics, and the like, and have argued that deep-seated mental pathologies could be detected in many, if not most, of them. However, this could be true without having any bearing on the general basis of religiousness. The question of why a man believes *he* has been chosen by divinity for special mystical experiences or for bringing revelations to mankind is logically distinct from the question of why *other men accept* his message as true, his authority as divinely sanctioned, or his visions as real. Consequently, even if one could show that all great religious innovators were mad, that would not necessarily tell us anything about why their *followers* followed. Indeed, as will be discussed shortly, there are strong logical grounds for doubting that mental pathologies *could* be a major source of religious adherence.

A second basis on which a connection between mental illness and religious commitment has been assumed is that religious imagery and preoccupations are common among persons in asylums (Strunk, 1959). But these arguments are uniformly faulty. The incidence of religiousness among psychotics *without a comparison with the incidence among nonpsychotics* tells us nothing. If religiousness is common in a given culture, one would also expect to find it common in the insane asylums of that culture. Indeed, the majority of mental patients in America are probably Democrats, but this has led very few to consider party choice as a source or consequence of insanity.

The most critical objection to attributing religiousness to psychopathology is that pathological conditions *logically* cannot account for the predominant behavior of stable social groups. If normal behavior (that is, typical and nondisruptive behavior) is to be explained by postulating an underlying pathological condition, then the terms *pathological* and *normal* have no useful meaning. By definition, pathologies (abnormalities) cannot be sufficiently common to account for normalities.

Nevertheless, even if it is illogical to attribute the bulk of religious commitment to mental illness or abnormality, it remains possible that for persons with mental problems the churches take on a special salience: that engrossment in faith can help comfort the neurotic and psychotic. If this were true, then one would expect to find empirically that persons with poorer mental health were prone to religious commitment and thus that a positive correlation obtained between psychopathology and religious commitment. But on theoretical grounds, even this seems unlikely.

In our society, religiousness is above all *conventional*, both as a viewpoint and as a multifaceted mode of behavior. Yet, the distinguishing feature of the mentally ill (or less than healthy) is their estrangement from and/or inability to utilize conventional means for finding meaning, purpose, and rewards. For example, family life is a primary conventional means for gaining security, identity, affection, engrossment, and the like. But overwhelming evidence shows that persons with poor mental health, rather than being overly engrossed in family life, are disproportionately unmarried, divorced, childless, and otherwise outside the bonds of this conventional commitment (Srole et al., 1962). Their deviant marital and family status is at once a symptom and a source of their mental abnormalities. More important, this is but one of many negative correlations between mental ill health and conventional sources of rewards and compensations. Consequently, far from expecting that psychological abnormalities typically will motivate people toward increased religious commitment, we must expect that, as is the case with other conventional activities and institutions, psychopathology will motivate toward (and perhaps partly stem from) religious isolation, estrangement, and apathy.

To put the central argument another way, it is extremely important to distinguish between what could best be called conventional religious commitment and extremist or pathological forms of commitment. The kind of religiousness with which this paper is concerned is that of the greatest social relevance, the conventional. It is a form of religiousness that is common in our society. But the form of religiousness most often examined in support of psychopathological theories is extreme, unusual, and sometimes pathological per se.

Morbid fears of Satan, convictions that one has received a new revelation for mankind, or obsessions with personal holiness are not the kind of religiousness social scientists usually try to explain. But through a failure to distinguish between conventional and extreme forms of religiousness, the theories and investigations of the extreme are commonly generalized to the conventional. I doubt that this is warranted. The empirical investigation that follows will assess this doubt.

There are perhaps no more elusive and value-laden concepts in social science than mental illness, insanity, neurosis, inadequacy, and other terms referring to various forms and degrees of psychopathology. It does not seem fruitful to approach here the mysteries or disputes about what ought to be meant by these terms. As an alternative, I shall employ a variety of definitions and measures.

The first of these is the most severe measure of psychopathology on which relevant data were available: psychiatric judgments that persons are seriously in need of intensive treatment because of "mental" impairment (most of these persons have records of prior psychiatric hospitalization). Then I shall turn to national survey data and examine several indices, one intended to measure psychic inadequacy and the other neurotic distrust. Finally, the investigation will take up what I judge to be the mildest measure of psychopathology available in these data: authoritarianism as measured by the F scale.

The main reason for adopting this multiple approach is to assess the generalizability of effects across a mild-to-serious spectrum of psychopathology. I hope thus to satisfy those who would judge survey measures as not isolating sufficiently serious impairment to produce meaningful findings, as well as those who would dismiss findings based only on serious impairment as inapplicable to milder forms of psychopathology.

Of the studies examined, only one group seems reliable, if only tangentially relevant. A number of studies have found that, among elderly persons, there is a positive correlation between good psychological adjustment and religious commitment (Moberg, 1965c). In summary, the state of the empirical literature leaves open the question of how psychopathology is related to conventional religious commitment in the general population. I now turn to empirical data to try to answer this question.

RELIGION AND MENTAL ILLNESS:
THE SAN MATEO COUNTY STUDY

In the summer of 1966, the Survey Research Center of the University of California, Berkeley, undertook a study for the San Mateo County Mental Health Department based on a comparison of 100 patients randomly selected from the rolls of the North County Outpatient Mental Health Clinic and 100 persons selected by stratified random techniques from the same area as served by the clinic. The samples were matched on age, sex, marital status, and education. Included in the interviews conducted with both groups were several questions on religious commitment. Thus the data provide a basis for testing the hypothesis that mental illness is negatively associated with religious commitment.

Table 1 presents the findings. On all measures of religious commitment, the persons diagnosed as mentally ill (in treatment at an outpatient clinic) are significantly *less* religiously committed than are persons chosen from the general population. For example, while only 3 percent of the control group said they had no religious affiliation, 16 percent of the patient sample claimed no affiliation. The control group reveals the level of nonaffiliation typically found in survey studies of the general population, while the psychiatric patients are five times as likely to be nonaffiliated. Similar differences exist on not belonging to a church congregation (while nearly everyone in America claims a *denomination,* only about half claim to belong to a *congregation*) and on church attendance. Of course, all these are measures of institutional or ritual participation, but that is not the case with the importance one places on religion in his life. Table 1 shows that here, too, the controls exhibit more commitment than do the patients.

In conclusion, these data support the hypothesis that mental illness and religious commitment are negatively related.

Table 1

Differences in Religious Commitment between a
Sample of 100 Mentally Ill Persons and a
Matched Control Group

	Mentally Ill	Matched Controls
Percent who claim no religious affiliation	16**	3**
Percent who say religion is "not important at all" to them	16**	4**
Percent who do *not* belong to a church congregation	54*	40*
Percent who attend church:		
Once a month or more	47	57
At least several times a year	24	32
Once a year or less	8	6
Never	21**	5**

*significantly different at .05 level
**significantly different at .01 level

RELIGION AND PSYCHIC INADEQUACY

It could be argued that, while seriously disturbed persons are less religious than are normal persons, this is a special case. It could still be true that psychopathologies produce religious commitment within the population of persons well enough to stay out of mental hospitals and clinics. I have earlier rejected this position on logical and theoretical grounds. Now it will be tested empirically.

From items included in a national survey of Northern whites, an index was constructed to measure psychic inadequacy. The items are typical of those widely used in survey studies of mental health: for example, "I worry a lot," "I often feel quite lonely," "I tend to go to pieces in a crisis." Agreement with such items seems a reasonable indicator that the person believes himself unable to cope adequately with others and with his day-to-day life. Five such items were used to construct the index, and scores were dichotomized so that persons were classified as being high on psychic inadequacy if they agreed with three or more of the items.

Table 2 shows the relationship between psychic inadequacy and a three-item measure of religious orthodoxy. In *all* denominational groups, the relationship is *negative*. Persons scoring high on psychic inadequacy are less likely to be high on religious orthodoxy than are persons scoring low on psychic inadequacy. Rather than turning to orthodoxy for comfort against their feelings of inadequacy and inability to deal with life, such people seem less likely to be orthodox, as hypothesized. It must be admitted that the time order is indeterminate here as elsewhere in these data (i.e., whether psychological health is product or source of religious commitment). However, the widespread belief that psychopathology is a source of religious commitment requires a positive association between the two. Finding that the sign of the association is the opposite of that predicted by such theories deals them a fatal blow.

Table 2

Percent of Psychic Inadequacy High on Orthodoxy Index

	Psychic Inadequacy	
	Low	High
Liberal Protestants	9	0*
Moderate Protestants	23	13
Conservative Protestants	43	25
Roman Catholics	28	19

*Too few cases for a stable percentage, presented for descriptive interest only.

Table 3 shows that the same finding obtains when religious commitment is measured by church attendance. Except among persons in moderate Protestant bodies, where there is absolutely no difference, those high on psychic inadequacy are less likely to be frequent church attenders than are those who are more adequate. Thus, both religious participation and belief are negatively related to this measure of psychopathology. Here, as elsewhere in this study, controls for sex, age, and social class did not affect the reported relationships.

Table 3

Percent of Psychic Inadequacy Groups
Who Attend Church Weekly

| | Psychic Inadequacy | |
	Low	High
Liberal Protestants	31	25*
Moderate Protestants	26	26
Conservative Protestants	47	13
Roman Catholics	72	65

*Too few cases for stable percentages, presented for descriptive interest only.

RELIGION AND NEUROTIC DISTRUST

I turn now to a slightly less severe measure of psychopathology. Three items from the interviews were combined to form an index of neurotic distrust. All these assess whether or not the person admits being abnormally suspicious and distrustful of others. Presumably, such distrust is symptomatic of a pathological incapacity to maintain normal patterns of interaction or even contact with others.

Tables 4 and 5 replicate the findings for psychic inadequacy. The higher a person's score on neurotic distrust, the less likely he is to be high on religious orthodoxy or to be a weekly church attender, regardless of denominational group. (The one exception is no difference on church attendance among liberal Protestants.)

Table 4

Percent of Neurotic Distrust Groups
High on Orthodoxy Index

	Neurotic Distrust	
	Low	High
Liberal Protestants	10	6
Moderate Protestants	22	18
Conservative Protestants	44	31
Roman Catholics	30	16

Table 5

Percent of Neurotic Distrust Groups
Who Attend Church Weekly

	Neurotic Distrust	
	Low	High
Liberal Protestants	31	31
Moderate Protestants	30	21
Conservative Protestants	46	33
Roman Catholics	72	68

To sum up thus far: whether psychopathology is measured by clinical diagnosis of severe impairment or by more inclusive and less severe survey indices, there is a negative relationship between psychopathology and religious commitment. Clearly, then, insofar as pathologically based theories of commitment have been generalized to ordinary forms of religious commitment and to the general population, to adherents rather than only to innovators or professionals, these theories are false. Let us see how far these findings can be generalized by investigating the effect of a relatively mild form of what is commonly regarded as psychopathological: authoritarianism.

RELIGION AND AUTHORITARIANISM

Since the publication of *The Authoritarian Personality* (Adorno et al, 1950), the concept of authoritarianism—and the related concepts of open-mindedness, tough-mindedness, and punitiveness—have become among the most heavily worked in social science. The research bibliography on authoritarianism now comprises hundreds of entries, and the concept has been used to explain such diverse events as political behavior, the hierarchical structure of the Roman Catholic Church, refusal to participate in survey studies, and errors in visual perception. But, even beyond its role in actual research, authoritarianism has become a major term in social science speculation and a catchall explanation in informal discussions among social scientists. Inevitably, such popularity has led to considerable abuse.

As developed by its originators, authoritarianism—and the famous F scale used to measure it—refers to rigidity in the personality structure of individuals: an inability to tolerate ambiguity or ambivalence. Furthermore, the concept is based on a psychodynamic theory of human socialization. This kind of personality structure is thought to be laid down in early childhood training and experience and to become a basic feature of the psychic economy, which the authors characterized as authoritarian or fascistic (thus the name of their empirical scale: Fascism or the F scale).

Perhaps partly because the word *fascist* cannot be taken neutrally, but drips with political and moral connotations, the concept of authoritarianism not only became popular for research but became an important part of the private, pejorative lexicon of social scientists. Thus, it has been all too readily applied to persons holding political, religious, or philosophical views to which particular social scientists were opposed.

One of the enduring abuses in social science is the tendency for its practitioners' private discourse or public speculations to enter into the scholarly canons without recourse to research or even regard for conflicting research evidence. Through widespread repetition, things come to be taken as "well known," and are believed, that in fact have never been properly tested, and some may even have been tested and found wanting. This is especially likely when these assumptions are congruent with one's prejudices.

The widespread belief that there is a strong positive relationship between religious orthodoxy and authoritarianism appears to be a prominent instance of this tendency to transform suspicions and speculations into certainties.

When questioned, all but one of a dozen colleagues of mine thought that an empirical relationship between religious orthodoxy and the F scale had been presented in *The Authoritarian Personality*. Had the author himself been asked this same question several years ago, he would very probably have said such data had been presented. In actual fact, no such table appears in the book, and the only discussion of the possibility of such a relationship appears in sections based on individual clinical case studies. (Some relationships between religious commitment and ethnocentrism were presented, which may partly account for the later confusion.) Furthermore, the various authors of these sections were very cautious about committing themselves regarding whether or not such a relationship would obtain empirically.

In the twenty-one years since the original publication, a handful of inferior attempts have been made to test this hypothesis. Despite their inadequacy, the weight of the findings is that *there is no relationship between authoritarianism and various forms of conventional religious commitment*. If these findings are dismissed for their manifest shortcomings, then we are back where the original authors left us, with no evidence one way or the other, and the question is open. Yet, through the passage of time, the tentative suspicions of the original authors have become a virtual article of faith. Indeed, one of these original authors now shares this certitude. In a recent review article (Levinson, 1967), he argues that the uncontrolled factor of authoritarianism probably accounts for the relationship reported between certain religious convictions and anti-Semitism (Glock and Stark, 1966). If it were the case that authoritarianism is not related to religious orthodoxy (or is negatively related to it), then his argument would be totally irrelevant. However, Levinson really doesn't consider that such a thing is possible, nor would many other social scientists.

To put it plainly, many social scientists are inclined to regard conservative religious beliefs as abnormal. Because they reject the truth of such beliefs, they find it difficult to imagine that a truly normal person could believe them. By the same assumption, they doubt that the mere fact that a person was raised in a subculture where such beliefs are typical can importantly account for his acceptance of these beliefs. Instead, they are inclined to argue that growing up in such a subculture first disfigures the personality in basic ways, and the beliefs then are adopted for the role that they play in appeasing these inner needs.

Levinson's disagreement with my earlier interpretations stems from more than a general tendency to regard religious beliefs as abnormal. It is part of a widespread conflict in social science between cognitive and emotive theories of behavior. Cognitive theories are inclined to take seriously the role played by the beliefs people hold and to regard beliefs as in large measure *learned* by the individual through interaction with others. Emotive theories are inclined to treat beliefs and attitudes as epiphenomenal, as the products of underlying psychodynamic processes.

Since the initial publication of *The Authoritarian Personality*, which based its central interpretations on psychoanalytic-emotive explanations, it has been much criticized on the ground that scales such as the F scale are essentially measures of cognitive sophistication. Indeed, there is now some important evidence against the notion that F represents a deep-seated psychological phenomenon originating in childhood training (Selznick and Steinberg, 1969). Such a reinterpretation of authoritarianism removes it from the class of psychopathological concepts and places it with the cognitive, along with other kinds of beliefs, knowledge, and convictions. While I am impressed by the evidence on which this reinterpretation is based, for the purposes of this investigation I have chosen to take the original authors at their word. Because of the widespread assumption that authoritarianism is a major source of religious commitment, and because of the psychopathological interpretation given this assumption, it seems important to test it on reliable empirical data. If there is no positive correlation between the F scale and religious commitment, then the question of emotive versus cognitive explanations of this relationship becomes irrelevant.

Unlike the more severe forms of psychopathology investigated earlier, authoritarianism is probably not sufficiently disabling to produce an alienation from religion. Thus, it seems dubious to extend the earlier hypothesis to include F. On the other hand, because it seems doubtful that conventional religiousness is abnormal, and because it is not especially "fanatic," there seems no theoretical basis for predicting a positive relationship. Therefore I am led to hypothesize that *there will be little or no relationship between F and conventional religiousness and that, to the extent that such a relationship does obtain, its sign will be negative.*

In the past decade, at least six empirical studies of the relationship between authoritarianism and religious commitment have been reported. Most display a very low quality of analysis, and all are hampered by being based on extremely odd populations; to call them samples would in most instances deprive that word of all meaning. Nevertheless, excluding one study because the selection of respondents has so patently produced the findings, four of the remaining five reported no relationship between authoritarianism and various forms of religious commitment (Frymier, 1959; Hills, 1959; Jones, 1958; Siegman, 1962). The weight of what evidence they provide supports the hypothesis that there will be either no relationship or a negative one. Since they provide a very low level of data, I shall assume that past research leaves the question unanswered. Thus, the national sample provides an opportunity to find an empirical answer.

Table 6 supports the hypothesis. Among Protestants there is no meaningful relationship between the F scale and religious orthodoxy. Among Roman Catholics there is a relationship, but it is negative. Additional evidence reported elsewhere lends credence to the interpretation that there is something about the way in which modern American Catholicism has stressed democratic ideals and norms of tolerance that accounts for the fact that orthodoxy for Catholics tends to be mildly incompatible with the beliefs contained in the F scale (Glock and Stark, 1966; Stark and Glock, 1968). But the main point of present interest is the fact that the widespread assumption that authoritarianism is positively related to conventional religious orthodoxy is falsified among both Protestants and Catholics.

Table 7 provides further confirmation, showing that the F scale is not positively related to church attendance either. Among liberal and moderate Protestant groups there appears to be no relationship at all. Among conservative Protestants and Roman Catholics a relationship does obtain, but again it is in the wrong direction. Conventional religious commitment is in no way a function of an underlying authoritarian personality.

Table 6

Percent of Authoritarian Groups High on Orthodoxy

	Authoritarianism		
	Low	Medium	High
Liberal Protestants	8	13	12
Moderate Protestants	20	22	22
Conservative Protestants	44	42	40
Roman Catholics	36	28	11

Table 7

Percent of Authoritarian Groups
Who Attend Church Regularly

	Authoritarianism		
	Low	Medium	High
Liberal Protestants	28	34	31
Moderate Protestants	26	25	27
Conservative Protestants	57	39	18
Roman Catholics	75	70	66

To sum up the evidence, it seems amply demonstrated by the variety of measures used that conventional religiousness is not a product of psychopathology. Indeed, psychopathology seems to *impede* the manifestation of conventional religious beliefs and activities. Far from being especially apt to turn to faith in order to seek psychic comforts for their psychopathological afflictions, the neurotic and mentally ill seem to be significantly less likely to exhibit conventional religious commitment. Thus, the generalization from the possible psychopathology of persons who have exhibited extreme forms of religious behavior—mystics, saints, martyrs, innovators, or founders of faiths—is shown to be unwarranted. Here, as on many other matters in social science, we must free ourselves from prejudgments of pathology if we are to make progress in understanding human behavior.

21

Juvenile Delinquency, Crime, and Religion*

*Richard D. Knudten and
Mary S. Knudten*

RELIGION, LAW, AND CRIME

The relations among religion, law, and criminal deviance are complex and oftentimes unclear. While religious ideals are frequently expressed in criminal law, not all laws possess religious significance. In some instances criminal law is more inclusive than religious ethics and in others less so. Traditionally, religion has been held to be influential in preventing deviant and criminal behavior, but empirical proof as to the relation of the two has been generally lacking.

Much of our current concern for criminal deviance is a by-product of the unstated assumptions of our society. Historically, a central element in Puritanism, upon which much of our modern conception of crime and delinquency is based, has been the zeal to guarantee individual salvation as well as that of the community. This view has

*The unedited version of this article appeared originally in *The Review of Religious Research*, 1971, 12: 130-52. Copyright 1971 by the Religious Research Association. Reprinted by permission.

continued to the present time. The delinquency of children and criminality of adults were held to be products of community failure and neglect. Later generations modified this view somewhat by their emphasis upon the social gospel, in which the teachings of Jesus were used to encourage humanitarian enterprises. The great revivals, beginning about 1800, stimulated the lower socioeconomic groups to express the equalitarian ideals of the American Revolution in religious terms. At the same time, religious ideals were utilized to inhibit change and to establish a conservative control that resulted in nineteenth-century turmoil among laymen and clergy. Many of the continuing arguments over capital punishment, objectives of discipline, and conceptions of the criminal offender reflect this tension.

But what is the function of religion in maintaining social control? The role of the churches in Great Britain in maintaining public order was examined in a study of the police by the Church Assembly Board for Social Responsibility (1967). As more areas of personal and social life are affected by public law, there is a corresponding increase in the number of people brought into contact with the police through the criminal code, and this, it concluded, has implications for the church and its program. If laws do not carry general public consent and are not uniformly enforceable, police-community relations frequently deteriorate. The necessity for maintaining law and order is not simply a police responsibility but rests with the community. As a result, churches, the report noted, must carry some responsibility for the education of the public concerning the role and function of the police in modern society. Police thinking and organization must be influenced by the special insights into social life that the Christian faith provides.

However, not all religious insights are positive. For example, some religious sects that consist of groups of fanatical "true believers" commonly develop a high degree of social solidarity and rarely engage in "normal" criminality in the form of theft, sex offenses, or crimes of violence. Such sect aggressiveness is most commonly directed against the state and is expressed criminally in the refusal to perform military service or to provide religiously unacceptable medical aid for children. While past research confirms that many crimes are prevented by membership in a religious sect, it also indicates that others may be caused by it (Middendorf, 1965; Poblete and O'Dea, 1960).

Even general ethics, highly removed from sect solidarity, may have criminal ramifications that appear to be based upon religious precepts when in fact they are not. The relationship of religion to civil rights militancy, for example, is imprecise and ambiguous. In some instances, religion has been a stimulant to change; in others, an opiate (Marx, 1967). And yet there are other dimensions to the problem of delinquency, crime, and religion. The rise of a drug subculture has some overtones for religion and some religious overtones. Goff (1964) believes that, while the church can help to give a meaningful philosophy of life to a narcotics addict, few clergymen in religious institutions have a sympathetic understanding of the problem.

RELIGIOUS RESEARCH IN
JUVENILE DELINQUENCY

In their 1926 study of right and wrong with a sample of 8,150 pupils in public and private schools in several communities, Hartshorne and May (1928) discovered that religious behavior is not a unified character trait that can be related directly or simply to delinquency. Students' knowledge about the Bible or their moral precepts were generally inadequate to control human behavior. Deceit in children, they noted, is nearly as prevalent among those enrolled in Sunday schools as among those not enrolled. Neither regularity in Sunday school attendance nor length of time in such participation appeared to influence the juvenile's tendency to deceive. The influence of the family was seen as the principal determinant of the values of the child; the impact of the school and church seemed less significant. Thirty years later, The Religious News Service (1957) reported that 21 of 126 youth who came before the Elkhart, Indiana, Juvenile Court in 1956 maintained perfect attendance at Sunday school and church; 30 indicated no attendance at religious functions; while 75 revealed uneven attendance practices. Only 35 percent came from broken homes. The implications of the report were that attendance records are not a measure of the effectiveness of parish programs and that delinquency cannot be treated by the simple injunction of going to church.

In a Detroit study, Wattenburg (1950) attempted to relate attendance to recidivism. Of 2,137 delinquent boys who were interviewed by the Detroit police after complaints of behavior had been recorded, 4 percent attended church regularly, 25 percent occasionally, 16 percent seldom, 14 percent never, and 1 percent gave no information. However, of the recidivists, 65 percent attended regularly or occasionally as compared to 71 percent of the nonrecidivist population in the study. In a comparison of 500 correctional schools and 500 nondelinquent boys by Sheldon and Eleanor Glueck (1950), 39 percent of the delinquents attended church regularly, 54 percent occasionally and 7 percent never. Among nondelinquents, the corresponding percentages were 67, 29, and 4. Dominic (1954) found that only 2 percent of the delinquent girls in her study attended church with some regularity.

Diaz (1952) discovered in a study of 950 school girls that delinquents have more favorable attitudes to religious issues than nondelinquents and that the training "did not contribute to the subject's ability to apply the principles of moral law to life situations." Based upon data secured from twenty-seven penitentiaries and nineteen reform schools, Falk (1961) concluded that 71.8 percent of the measured population claimed membership in some organized religion as contrasted with 64.6 percent of the total population of the United States. Sinclair (1964) uncovered significant differences in religious attitudes between two groups of 40 girls selected from local churches and the Long Lane School, a state school for legal custody of girls who exemplified habitual antisocial behavior. Differences in attitudes were also found between white and black respondents. The attitudes of the institutionalized girls appeared to be more like those of the girls from the neighborhood black churches than those of the girls coming from the white churches (Webb and Webb, 1957a).

Roberts (1953) discovered in a questionnaire given to 150 delinquents at the Gumpert School for Girls near Pittsburgh and the Pennsylvania Training School at Morganza that approximately one-half of the girls' parents were church members but most were inactive; religious training in their homes was very limited and usually confined to a few perfunctory observances; their religious lives were ideationally strong but functionally weak, making their behavior inconsistent; religion was a weak motivating force; frustration, rebellion, and confusion were produced by unwholesome family and community situations; from two-thirds to three-quarters of those institutionalized could have been saved from this commitment or behavior leading to commitment if the churches had provided some assistance; and less than 10 percent needed expert professional assistance to overcome their emotional and physical problems. The churches, he concluded, should develop a more realistic and creative type of Christian education that relates to the child's emotional experience, create a church-and-home cooperative program, provide more church-sponsored activities for children and stronger inducements for children to attend, and offer an effective counseling service for those in need.

Goldschneider and Simpson (1967) classified 58 percent of 13,836 Los Angeles delinquents as Protestant, 35 percent Roman Catholic, 3 percent Jewish and 3 percent other. At the time, the Los Angeles population included an estimated 22 percent Catholic and 7 percent Jewish composition. As a result of their study, the authors concluded that the organized religion to which one adheres is a good indicator of family stability and community. Gannon (1967b) measured the religious beliefs, experience, and commitments of delinquent youth and found that the delinquents' scores on the Thurstone scale revealed they had a slight but marginal commitment to religious beliefs and values and a high level of basic theological orthodoxy regarding Catholic doctrine. Consequently, he concluded, these youth had a "commitment by default" to religion.

Alberts (1963) completed a study of ministers' attitudes toward juvenile delinquency through an examination of attitudes of 92 Protestant ministers in the Boston area who had been nominally associated with juvenile offenders brought before the Boston area juvenile court in 1957-58. Using the authoritarianism (F) scale, traditional family ideology scale, and original juvenile delinquency attitude scale, he found that a minister's emotional disposition, more than his abstract theological beliefs, generally determined the nature, extent, and effectiveness of his approach to juvenile delinquency.

Gerkin (1955) argues that delinquents' homes are rejecting, rigid, authoritarian, inconsistent, and overprotective. While the clergyman may offer parents and children some aid in times of crisis, he is usually called only when the problem becomes acute. An effective minister, however, will utilize such situations to help the people examine the deeper meanings of their relationship to each other and to God and to verbalize and understand their feelings about what has happened in the situation.

RELIGIOUS RESEARCH AND
ADULT CRIMINALITY

In an early study, Clemmer (1940) noted that 51 percent of 2,343 male prisoners examined declared that they had no religious preference. Of those who claimed some religious preference, 308 (13 percent) were Roman Catholic, 3 were Jewish, and the remaining represented twenty-two Protestant denominations. While Baptists and Catholics had the highest commitment rate of those institutionalized within prisons, two-thirds of the membership of these churches in 1949 came from the lower class (Smith, 1949). A report of the Florida Division of Corrections disclosed in 1966 that, of the 3,337 admitted to Florida prisons in 1965-66, 52 percent listed a Baptist preference, 14 percent Catholic, 24 percent some other Christian denomination, 2 percent another religion, and 5 percent no preference.

Because of the age of these studies and their limited samples, it seems clear that *knowledge concerning the relationship of religion to adult crime and/or imprisonment is incomplete.* An inmate's citation of a denominational preference does not necessarily imply that he is affiliated with the group, although he may have attended specific church functions occasionally or be inclined potentially in that direction. It is also possible that he is simply naming the denomination he believes the parole board tends to sanction. Whatever the relationships, however, it is obvious that the earlier conception of imprisonment as a time to bring about the spiritual renovation of the prisoner has lost most of its impact. Although imprisonment has been viewed as a means by which prisoners may work out their penance on earth and evaluate the folly of their deeds, modern prison philosophy suggests that this conception of imprisonment as a means of expiation of sin is no longer viable.

The research on religious factors in the situations of misdemeanant offenders in four metropolitan counties of Georgia by Pittard and Payne (1970) in the years 1965 to 1967 disclosed that those involved in misdemeanant convictions are predominantly, although not entirely, from the lower-than-average rates of religious group affiliation compared with rates for the area as a whole. Nearly 60 percent of the 503 interviewed belonged to Protestant groups, 36.6 percent had no religious affiliation, and 2.4 percent were Catholic. There were no Jewish respondents. Protestants were predominantly Baptist, Methodist, and sect members. The study disclosed that most of the convicted misdemeanants had only minimal or no contact with a minister, church member, or other religious functionary while growing up or even during their current trouble.

McCleery (1961) conducted an examination of incorrigible inmates within two prisons. Incorrigibles, he concluded, defined crime as a sinful and immoral act prohibited by the Bible; however, the emphasis of their definition was upon the elements of deliberation and intent rather than upon the act itself. While these men believed themselves to be more religious than most persons, openly expressing a faith in God, many of them were opposed to the institutional church and its ministry. Consequently, they were openly skeptical of the motives of inmates who attended services and/or took part in other religious activities. Similar tendencies were found in an unpublished study by one of these authors among 640 inmates at an Indiana maximum security prison.

THE CLERGY AND DELINQUENCY CRIME

The role of the chaplain has received limited attention over the years. What work has been done has been largely subjective or topical. Kuether (1951), for example, notes that, with the possible exception of the physician, the chaplain is the first prison staff member to demonstrate his interest in a prison inmate. Prison chaplains sought gifts, books, and recreational equipment for inmates, worked with prisoners' families, and developed prison schools long before standardized treatment incorporated such procedures into its program. However, the chaplain's function has now become institutionalized, as witnessed in the definition of the place of religion in a penal system in Principle 17 of the *Declaration of Principles* of the American Correctional Association (1960):

Religion represents a rich resource in the moral and spiritual regeneration of mankind. Especially trained chaplains, religious instruction and counseling, together with adequate facilities for group worship of the inmate's own choice are essential elements in the program of a correctional association.

The conception and function of the chaplain vary. He may be a jack-of-all-trades operative who serves as a court of last resort but who joins guards on active duty in times of emergency; or he may be a psychiatric worker and theologian who has become a well-accepted member of a treatment team. Other roles exist between these two extremes (Kannwisher, 1957; Maxey, 1964). In any case, Morris (1961) believes that the selectness of the prison chaplain's congregation makes it ultimately necessary for him to have the ability to deal with a large number of maladjusted personalities.

Robert and Muriel Webb (1957b) urge that clergymen serve as chaplains in detention homes and correctional schools and that lay members become volunteers to work with delinquents so that religious values may have a greater penetration into the lives of delinquent youth. The church's primary contribution to delinquency and crime control, they argue, is its universal belief in the dignity and worth of the individual person. But Eshelman (1968) notes that the scope and character of the prison ministry is a specialty outside the mainstream of established religions. The mainline churches cater to suburbanites and accommodate their message to the affluent in order to survive. Interest in prison inmates emanates most frequently from the unpretentious churches that perceive that the crime problem is a religious problem.

Kandle and Cassler (1968) provide a guide for pastoral care in correctional institutions. They indicate steps necessary to establish a program for spiritual renewal and prisoner rehabilitation and outline problems related to prison visits, counseling, comforting the family, and helping the released prisoner back into the community and church. They also probe the prisoner's private world of doubt, fear, resentment, and loneliness and his life within the prison community. French (1964) emphasizes the need for honesty and a noncondemnatory attitude if a clergyman is to minister effectively to the delinquent, while Burns (1961) suggests that, if clergymen are to minister effectively to parents and children facing crisis situations, they must understand both the objective facts of the case and the inner world of the people involved.

However, the role and function of the chaplain are filled with many tensions. Canadian correctional chaplaincy programs have recently been in crisis due to the divisions within the religious world and the dissociation of church and state in matters pertaining to correctional philosophy and practice. Religious groups have given corrections infrequent glimpses of their religious insights regarding offenders. The religious emphasis upon the individual and his redemption has been conceived as a primary instrument for the protection of society. Consequently, West (1968) maintains, religious bodies must more forcefully relate their philosophy of life to the correctional process. The first step in accomplishing this must be the return of the chaplaincy to the church. The chaplain should not be a civil servant but must be responsible to his religious body. In turn, his group must accept the chaplain and become responsible for his actions. Whatever tensions arise as a result of this process may bring about healthy changes in the correctional process in the long run.

Much of the chaplain's value is dependent upon the confidentiality of his clerical role. Although forty-four states and the District of Columbia have statutes recognizing the privileged nature of communications with clergymen (Kuhlmann, 1968), the wording of these statutes and the cases construing them leave clergymen vulnerable in many situations. In order to overcome such limitations, Kuhlmann suggests a new statute together with practical suggestions and comments from many clergymen and lawyers who are sensitive to the problems of this area.

RELIGIOUS RESEARCH IN CORRECTIONS

Research into the area of religion and corrections is largely nonempirical and highly subjective. Barnes and Teeters (1959) recognized that, in the past, the influence of religion in corrections often took the form of the gathering of food and clothing for jail inmates by such organizations as the Philadelphia Society for the Relief of Distressed Prisoners. Religious concern also led the Quakers to participate in prison rehabilitation programs. An examination of the Quaker contribution to penological history is presented by Van Etten (1953), who notes that much of their concern was undoubtedly stimulated by their own experiences in English incarceration prior to their immigration to America. George Fox, William Penn, and Elizabeth Fry, outstanding penal reformers, all lived or worked intensively in prison surroundings at one time or another.

The Salvation Army, as well, worked in correctional institutions after 1885, providing services for both the released prisoner and the inmate's family. The Volunteers of America, founded by Maud Booth after an 1896 visit to Sing Sing Prison, also sponsored prison visitations, preparole investigations, job placement, and other services (McMahon, 1963). However, Johnson (1968) suggests that nineteenth-century efforts to legislate morality have ultimately impeded progress toward the development of a therapeutic correctional ideology and that the movement of the churches to the suburbs has left the urban community without the counterbalancing support of organized religion in deteriorating areas. This assumption, however, is questionable inasmuch as most major metropolitan areas have strong denominational and interdenominational programs in the inner city (Pittard and Payne, 1970).

Kirkpatrick (1965) examined the function of the church in corrections. Coordination of community and church correctional services, he concluded, is ultimately desirable for superior results. While the church may be unrealistic in regard to the level of the prisoner's motivation and his capacity for change, the experiences of the John Howard and Elizabeth Fry societies, two aftercare agencies, give some insight into what behavioral changes may be accomplished. Consequently, all persons engaged in the criminal-correctional process must appreciate the role of the family, the strength of religion and prayer, and the meaning of God in the rehabilitation process. Potentially, the church has a special capacity for reforming the values of the prisoner and his family. James (1967) argues that religion has the right and duty to speak in the field of corrections, since it is vitally concerned with man, his origin and destiny, and the ethics of the means of achieving his destiny. Christians must strive to interpret their theological understanding of the goal of man to the members of society at large and to those individuals isolated from society and in correctional institutions.

Regimbal (1964) examined criminology and crime among Roman Catholics and probed the position of religion in the psychological treatment and rehabilitation of the offenders. A second study of the religious history of fifty-nine Catholic boys disclosed that Catholic males had been significantly undertrained in the practice of religion. Consequently, their religious situation, Conner (1960) believes, must be taken into consideration in seeking causes and solutions to the problem of juvenile delinquency. Gannon (1967a) has presented a more empirical examination of the effects of Catholic religious instruction on male adolescents at the Illinois State Training School for Boys. His expectations of a slight increase in religious commitment and little substantial change in doctrinal or ethical orthodoxy were verified, but his hypothesis projecting little change in related attitudes and behavior was not substantiated. Overall, the data revealed a "neat compartmentalization" between the values the group expressed and those lived by. However, Gannon believes that it is possible that the apparent compartmentalization may indicate a state of conflicting attractions in addition to an inability of the delinquents either to conceptualize or to verbalize the conflict.

A report from Florida State University (Department of Criminology, 1965) indicates that the needs of offenders can be broken down into three types: (1) physical, (2) social, and (3) spiritual. Each, the report suggests, should be included within a rehabilitation program. Consequently, volunteer and religious agency services should be incorporated within juvenile court procedures so that they may give advice as to what resources are available and should be brought to bear on an appropriate problem. The dependence upon individualization of treatment by the probation officer fails to take into account the client's needs for group reintegration, which a volunteer or a religious agency may often offer. However, the use of voluntary agencies is dependent on the probation officer's ability to know how, where, and when to use such services.

A follow-up report on the Cambridge-Somerville youth study (McCord and McCord, 1959) disclosed that religion formed an important part of the treatment program for previously delinquent youth. Boys and their families were encouraged to attend church; ministers and priests were alerted to their problems. The assistance given by religious authorities, however, seemed to be more in the counseling and general support field than in the area of value changes.

Rector (1966) believes that the church can serve as a better bridge to the community than any other institution. Therefore, it should join with other institutions in developing legislation that expunges offenders' records and legally forgives them; at the same time, the church should also educate its own members regarding the doctrine of forgiveness. Through such activity, the church fulfills its traditional function of serving man, especially the oppressed. However, the question becomes confusing when one recognizes that prisoners come disproportionately from lower-class denominations and sects of the oppressed (Krasner, 1961; Myers, 1957; Zinn, 1959).

Religious freedom of a sect group in a prison community is discussed by Frankino (1965), who examined the attempts of the Black Muslims to secure the right to exist as a religious body within the prison. While the courts have generally upheld the principles that a prison community is not a free society and that prison management must have wide discretionary powers, the prisoners' constitutional right to religious freedom must also be upheld. This right, however, is subject to the rules and regulations necessary for the safety of prisoners and the orderly functioning of the institution.

PREVENTION AND RELIGIOUS RESEARCH

As in the area of religion and correction, minimal empirical work has been done in the field of religion and prevention. Nussey (1963) sees the task of religion in delinquency and crime prevention to be the maintenance and practice of ethical principles through spreading the Gospel and converting evil forces within society. On the other hand, Green (1960) suspects that the advent of modern science and the translation of scientific theory into technology has stripped the supernatural realm of much of its power, making the conversion idea somewhat impractical if not outright impotent. Nevertheless, religion can help prevent crime and delinquency if it offers values, goals, understanding, and hope to potential and actual offenders.

As an institution, the church can offer the offender material support, employment help, education, counseling, recreation, and worship (Hargraves, 1959). However, it often has failed the offender by being clannish, rigid, and uninterested in community needs. Better communication and closer cooperation must develop between the church, corrections, and prevention. Bloch and Flynn (1956) maintain that, unless religious experiences are reinforced by primary associations, home atmosphere, school experience, and community contacts, they remain largely on an impersonal level with little or no direct relevance to the kinds of moral choices the individual must make.

The attempt to measure the influence of religion as a crime and delinquency preventive is faced with many difficulties (Smith, 1951). The wide variations that exist among various groups concerning a belief in the hereafter, identification with the supernatural, elements in a code of ethics, members' ideals, rates of church membership or church attendance, attitudes toward doctrine, and variations between stated beliefs and personal commitments influence any attempt to measure the relation between religion and delinquency and/or crime (Barnes and Teeters, 1959). While the greatest deterrents to delinquency may be sanctions and internalized moral standards, moral education has generally been overlooked in the attempt to control juvenile delinquency. Duvall (1961) holds that delinquency has too long been given a "sickness-victim" explanation or has been held to be an emotional disturbance, when actually the problem is largely one of moral standards. McCann (1956) questions whether it is wise to inspire a religious attack on delinquency directed at intensification of the moral sanction when much of the delinquent's problem is related to a poorly integrated superego.

An investigation of the Tenderloin area by the inner-city Methodist churches of San Francisco recommended increased church involvement with troubled youth; street workers functioning on a person-to-person basis; establishment of a health clinic and social center; legal aid through the Citizens Alert Program and through a legal aid center; establishment of a community house-halfway house; and high school classes for dropouts (Hansen, Bird, Forrester, and Des Marais, 1966). Such programs aimed at prevention cost money and necessitate changes in the churches' traditional conception of their function. Gannon (1967a) believes that religious values will have a controlling influence only if strongly supported by other factors more immediately crucial to delinquency, especially in the family and peer group. If religion does exert influence, he contends, it does so on an experiential and not an ideological level.

In a paper included within the President's Commission Task Force Report on Juvenile Delinquency and Youth Crime, Fitzpatrick (1967) noted the potential preventative value of the East Harlem Protestant Parish in New York City; Our Lady's Youth Center in El Paso, Texas; Centro Catolico Puertorriqueno in Jersey City, N.J.; Damascus Christian Church in the Bronx, N.Y.; the Jewish Board of Guardians Program in New York; and the Nativity Mission Center in New York City. However, even these programs, he suggests, depend upon ethnic or racial strength and the solidarity of the community. Kvaraceus (1954) similarly sees that churches have cooperated with character-building agencies for an integrated attack on delinquency through such organizations as the Christian Endeavor Society and the Catholic Youth Organization. Through such attempts, churches have tried to bridge the gap between the sacred and the real.

However, despite such promising programs, one of the reasons why American religious institutions cannot more fully prevent delinquency and crime is that differential integration of personality patterns prevents the total or even major acceptance of such systems by habitual criminals. Personality integration can be achieved only in groups and through common experiences. Consequently, if religious organizations provide opportunities for meaningful group experiences, the integration of the personality may be achieved and the teachings of that institution may become a vital force in the maintenance of personality. However, it is also possible that such teachings may become meaningless and the commitment toward religion may become only a formal outward shell if its emphases are otherwise unrelated to the lives of individuals or the wider integration of the group (Falk, 1961).

SUMMARY AND CONCLUSIONS

A review of the literature pertaining to juvenile delinquency, crime, and religion points out the need for research in all spheres of this field. Empirical research is especially lacking in the areas of religion and juvenile delinquency, religion and crime, religion and corrections, and the role of religion in prevention.

The authors conclude the following:

1. Most research done in the area to date is insignificant scientifical-ly. The overemphasis upon historical and descriptive analysis indicates that our knowledge concerning the importance or unim-portance of religion in the delinquency- and crime-creating pro-cess, with few exceptions, is not open to scientific levels of "proof."

2. The lack of accurate statistics concerning religion hinders the evaluative process. In addition, because of the American attitude of separation of church and state, a large number of empirical projects cannot be inclusive research studies but must depend upon volunteer participants. Rarely have studies even been attempted on those who refuse to participate in an operational project.

3. No unified research into the field has been attempted by a series of collaborating investigators. Most evaluations have been attempted individually without a wide dissemination of data. In fact, it is clear that few investigators have even been interested in the problem of religion and deviance generally.

4. At the core of any attempt to measure the religious variable and delinquency-crime is the problem of measuring religiosity and the need to consider religious values, beliefs, and influence as only one element of the delinquent- and criminal-producing pro-cess. This limitation, however, is gradually being overcome with the introduction of several empirical studies of religion among the clergy, the laity, and the unchurched by persons with widely various perspectives — for example, Stark, Glock, Hadden, Demerath, and Kersten.

5. The need for controlled experimental research is especially great. However, it is also the hardest to complete. The simple securing of access to a delinquent-criminal sample often takes months of cultivation. Frequently, institutional problems will undermine the best-laid hypotheses and methods of the researcher.

6. Until some clear hypotheses are suggested, adequate research will not be carried out. Most research is on the ad hoc level. Some attempts at the development of testable hypotheses must be made if future research is to move from this type of ad hoc description to a consistent and unified understanding of these

phenomena. Only then can a theory of the middle range pertaining to these concerns be formulated.

7. What is known about delinquency, crime, and religion is as follows: the relationship of religion and deviant behavior is obscure; early studies by Lombroso and Bonger, among others, can only be accepted as quasi-scientific attempts to measure the problem; wide debate exists as to whether religious principles are distinctive and can be measured discretely from other values; little is known about the role of the clergy or chaplaincy in the correctional process; and research into the proper function of religion in prevention of crime and delinquency is nonexistent.

The past is prologue; the future of research in this area lies ahead.

22

Differences in Religious Attitudes in Mental Illness*

C. Marshall Lowe and
Roger O. Braaten

There is agreement from a variety of sources that heightened religious concern and conflict characterize patients in psychiatric hospitals. One such source is personality theory. Freudian psychoanalysis has related psychopathology to religion by regarding religion as a projection of unconscious needs. Freud regarded religion as an attempt to gain control over the sensory world by means of the wish world. More particularly, Freud saw in religion an attempt to displace one's dependence upon the father. While Freud himself did not systematically develop the place that religious delusion occupies in schizophrenia, other psychoanalysts have felt that excessive religiosity is a hallmark of the paranoid schizophrenic's substitution of the primary process for a secondary process.

Clinical evidence also relates heightened religious concern to

*The unedited version of this article appeared originally in *The Journal for the Scientific Study of Religion*, 1966, 5: 435-45. Copyright 1966 by the Society for the Scientific Study of Religion. Reprinted by permission.

279

mental illness. Anton Boisen (1960), describing his own religious experience in a psychotic state, comes to the conclusion that religious delusion can be therapeutic. While he also sees the excessive religious concern of the paranoid as being a distortion of reality, Boisen regards it as a desperate attempt to find a necessary part of reality that has hitherto eluded the person because of unresolved unconscious conflict. Instead of seeing heightened religious concern as an attempt to deny responsibility by projecting dependency needs upon a paternalistic deity, Boisen sees in this process the attempt of the person to gain independence by calling upon irrational and hitherto unconscious thought processes to help break the tug-of-war that is within him.

While both psychoanalytic personality theory and clinical evidence relate heightened religiosity to disordered personality states, there has been little work of an empirical nature to test such a hypothesis in a clinical setting. Two studies that have compared psychiatric patients with normals have both cast doubt upon the belief that increased religiosity occurs in mental illness. Armstrong, Larsen, and Mourer (1962) compared the religious attitudes and practices of psychiatric patients and normals and found that patients were significantly less interested in religion than normals. Reifsnyder and Campbell (1960) compared newly admitted male psychiatric patients with a normal group consisting of male Protestant church members. Their results confirm those found by Armstrong, Larsen, and Mourer.

Previous studies leave certain questions unanswered. First of all, the problem has not been settled as to whether psychiatric patients and normals differ because of mental illness as such or because of some other difference that also exists between the two groups. For example, in both the Armstrong, Larsen, and Mourer study and the Reifsnyder and Campbell study, there are pronounced differences in educational level between the two groups, so that the differences that were found may be due to differences in education. Secondly, previous studies have been based mainly upon attitude scales that have measured the direction but not the intensity of religious belief. They have thus quite adequately tapped the cognitive dimension of religion but have tended to neglect the affective and conative aspects. Finally, the emphasis in previous studies has been on considering how patients in general differ from normals in general. Since psychiatric patients perhaps differ more among themselves than they differ from normals, it is important to know what intragroup differences exist.

Since previous studies have used normals as a comparison either with other normals or with psychiatric patients, the purpose of the present study is to measure religious attitudes of nonnormals, i.e., persons in that end of the adjustment continuum that is characterized by psychiatric hospitalization. In addition, the approach of this study differs in that it uses a comparatively small number of attitude items administered to a larger patient sample. A large sample was used so that it could be subdivided to enable the elimination of extraneous variables should patient group differences be found on more than one pertinent characteristic at the same time. Finally, this study attempts to develop a more functional approach by including in the attitude scale items dealing with motives and emotions as well as with beliefs.

METHOD

THE RELIGIOUS ATTITUDE INVENTORY

The religious attitude inventory used in this study consists of twenty-seven items. Of these, eighteen were felt to bear a possible cause or effect relationship with psychiatric illness. In addition to these eighteen items, four items concerning knowledge of the Bible and five items concerning degree of religious background were included. The latter provided a control for the effect of the prehospital religious experience of the subjects.

Each question necessitated a forced choice of different alternatives. Where possible, the answers were placed on a five-point continuum with approximately equal intervals between each. In some questions, however, the subject was required to pick out the best answer from among five to eight discrete alternatives, such as in choosing his best idea of God. Questions dealing with religious background and the question dealing with exceptional religious experience could be answered yes or no. Finally, questions dealing with religious knowledge were placed in multiple-choice format.

SUBJECTS

All patients on the psychiatric wards of the Brecksville VA Hospital were asked to fill out the attitude questionnaire. Patients on medical, neurological, and geriatric wards were not tested. Out of an average psychiatric ward population of 685, there were 508 scorable questionnaires completed. Approximately 10 percent of the total sample was missed because of repeated absence from the ward when the questionnaire was administered. The balance was about equally divided between those who refused because of the personal nature of the questions and those who were unable to comprehend the instructions. While this last group included a handful of confused and grossly delusional patients, it comprised for the most part patients who were severely retarded and regressed.

RESULTS

The results disprove several traditional beliefs of the psychiatric folklore. A number of items that, according to several theories, should distinguish among different types of patients do not. On other items, certain clear-cut differences emerge that would not have been predicted on the basis of traditional views of religious experience in psychotics. While the items of the questionnaire are concrete and cannot be combined into scales, questions of similar content will be grouped together for the purpose of presenting results.

DEGREE OF INVOLVEMENT IN RELIGIOUS ACTIVITIES

Although it has commonly been thought that paranoid patients are often hyperreligious, there is no confirmation of the view that paranoid schizophrenics differ from other patients in terms of frequency of church attendance, Bible reading, or prayer. There is in fact no statistically significant difference on self-reports of any of these three activities among diagnostic groups or between committed vs. voluntary patients, closed vs. open wards, or groups with different lengths of prior hospitalization. To the extent that patients and normals differ on the amount of religious participation they report, patients seem to exhibit less participation than do people in the community. Gallup (1964) asked the general community similarly worded questions in regard to prayer and church attendance, and these practices were reported in greater frequency by the public than by the patients in this study.

RELIGIOUS ATTITUDES

Five items in the scale tap religious attitudes that differ both quantitatively and qualitatively. All but one of these items are significantly related to one or more of the patient characteristics.

Religious attitudes can be judged quantitatively in terms of how certain one is of the existence of God and how close one feels to God. Typically, admitted disbelief in God is a rather deviant response among the general public. And so in the present study, the modal response was certainty of the existence of God. However, there is noticeably decreasing certainty the longer the patient has been institutionalized, dropping from 81 percent for those hospitalized less than seven years to 64 percent for those hospitalized seven years or more. The differences are statistically significant.

Related to degree of belief in God is how close one feels to God. While three-quarters of the total group of patients were certain of God's existence, only one-half felt "he is here with me," as opposed to being "available if needed," "far distant," or "nowhere." While answers to this item were not related to length of hospitalization, the sicker patients, in terms of both diagnosis (psychotic rather than neurotic) and closed ward status, had a slight tendency to feel God further removed from them.

There are also qualitative differences in religious attitudes among patients. In finishing the statement, "Religion is valuable because . . .," shorter term patients chose the answer, "It gives aim and purpose in life," while longer term patients selected with greater frequency, "It is comforting in trouble" and "It helps us improve ourselves."

A related question is, "What is your idea of God?" Here the statistically significant differences are between different diagnostic groups. The most commonly chosen answer to this question was "Heavenly Father." Paranoid schizophrenics, however, selected this answer less frequently than other diagnostic groups, choosing instead the more impersonal idea of "Creator." Since, according to the psychoanalytic theory of development, the paranoid has had difficulty in identifying with his own father, one might hypothesize that such a failure in identification makes it difficult for the paranoid to perceive God as his Heavenly Father.

Neurotics on this item had a greater tendency to choose "Final Judge" as their best idea of God. This choice can be interpreted as a projection of the fact that anxiety neurotics in this particular clinical population tended to feel greater guilt than other diagnostic groups and to feel it more often.

NATURE OF RELIGIOUS EXPERIENCE

Five questions were included in the questionnaire to deal with different types of religious feelings. Since the paranoid schizophrenic is regarded as often manifesting "excessive religiosity" (American Psychiatric Association, 1952), the question, "Have you had an exceptional religious experience when God has seemed especially real to you?" was included to tap hallucinatory or delusional experiences involving religion. Responses to this item were not related, however, to any of the patient characteristics, suggesting that if unusual numbers of paranoids or other types of schizophrenics have had such experiences, many of them are not now aware of it.

Other questions deal with the types of religious feelings experienced in going to church, reading the Bible, and praying. There is some suggestion that the religious experience of the less institutionalized patient has a more pragmatic orientation than that of the more chronic patient. While newly admitted patients say they pray when they have problems, prayer in the more chronic patient is related to a more pervasive unhappiness. So also, longer-term patients indicate more of a tendency to read the Bible primarily for its literary value.

It is doubtful that there are interpretable differences in religious experience related to any other patient characteristics. Schizophrenic patients tend to feel sad or afraid on going to church, while voluntary patients more often feel afraid. Since the significance level for these comparisons is only at the .05 level, these findings may be an artifact of the large number of comparisons made.

ATTITUDE TOWARD SELF AND OTHERS

Two questions deal with the perception of God's attitude toward self, and two more items with one's own attitude toward self and others. The item "God forgives my sins" was included for the purpose of eliciting intense guilt feelings, which are commonly regarded as associated with both neurotic and psychotic types of depressions. Neither diagnosis nor any other patient characteristic, however, was related to any particular answer on the item.

On the other hand, a second item that deals with acceptance by God ("God loves me") did discriminate among groups differing in length of hospitalization and to a minor extent between open- and closed-ward patients, with shorter-term and open-ward patients feeling more loved by God ($p<.05$).

Items dealing with self-acceptance and acceptance of others are grouped with items dealing with acceptance by God because it was hypothesized that acceptance by God would be related to acceptance of self and acceptance of others. A comparison of responses to the three items does reveal that there is a significant relationship between love by God and love both of self and for others, although there was not a significant relationship directly between love of self and love of others. It is consistent with such an interrelationship that long-term patients, feeling rejected by God, also deem loving their neighbor as less important than loving themselves. There were, however, no consistent relationships between attitude toward self and any of the patient variables.

While caring about one's neighbor and feeling loved by God are connected to each other and to length of hospitalization, it is not clear in what direction causal connections lie. It seems likely that factors associated with long-term hospitalization cause feelings of rejection by God and lack of concern about one's neighbor, and not the other way around. But the relationship between feeling loved by God, on the one hand, and loving oneself and caring for one's neighbor, on the other hand, could be due to a tendency to so make God in man's own image that one projects one's own attitudes on God. Or, contrariwise, attitudes toward self and others might be derived from one's perceptions of God's attitude toward man. The latter interpretation would, of course, be in accord with the position of Johannine theology that we love because God first loved us.

DEPENDENCE UPON GOD

A final item in the inventory deals with dependence upon God.

The view has been traditionally held in psychiatry that patients who express a great amount of dependence upon God carry a poor prognosis for leaving the institution, since dependence upon God is seen as a way of avoiding the adult responsibility of taking care of oneself. The results, however, indicate that the opposite is true. It is the shorter-term patient who expresses a greater degree of dependence in terms of considering God's help to be essential in his life. Since length of hospitalization is associated with diagnosis, it is not surprising that neurotics and patients with affective disorders should also place a greater reliance upon God. However, since this difference is significant at only the .05 level, it seems to be secondary to length of hospitalization. Finally, since voluntary patients are generally aware of their need for help more than patients who come to the hospital involuntarily by court commitment, it is not surprising that voluntary patients feel God's help to be more essential than committed patients do.

CONTAMINATING VARIABLES

The possibility was raised in discussing previous studies of the relationship between religious attitudes and psychiatric hospitalization that the differences found between patients and normals were due, not to factors associated directly with psychiatric hospitalization, but to other variables related to differences among patients. These might include such demographic variables as education, occupation, and age, or such religious variables as religious background and degree of religious knowledge.

To make certain that the differences in answers to the inventory were due to the patient characteristics themselves and not to extraneous variables related to patient characteristics, the three demographic variables— age, education, and occupational level— and three religious variables— degree of religious knowledge, degree of religious background, and denomination (Protestant or Catholic)— were compared with the four patient characteristics studied in this investigation.

None of the three contaminating religious variables is associated with the patient characteristics used in this study. Education is likewise unrelated. Age is positively related to length of prior hospitalization and is related also to diagnosis, neurotics being younger and chronic undifferentiated schizophrenics being older. Neurotics also are at a higher level occupationally than other types of patients.

To make certain that response differences found in this study are associated with diagnosis and not with age or occupation, and with length of hospitalization and not with age, chi-squares were done between age and occupation on items on which there were important differences in answers among different types of patients (i.e., where the level of confidence was .01 or higher). Both age and occupation were unrelated to answers on all but one item, indicating that for these other items the patient characteristics are directly related to the differences in responses. One item stem ("Religion is valuable because . . . ") was found to be related to age in the same way that length of hospitalization is, older patients finding religion more comforting in trouble. To determine if age was indeed responsible for differences in responses by patients of different length of hospitalization on this item, separate chi-squares were computed on the item for length of hospitalization for both older and younger patients. There remained a high level of significance (p<.001). Further, no differences were found in the proportions of the answers to this stem for younger and older patients with the same length of hospitalization. Thus both age and length of hospitalization are related to the responses for why religion is valuable.

DISCUSSION

The results have been presented in terms of groups of items that are similar to one another in content. However, the results can also be discussed in summary form in terms of each patient characteristic.

There are only minor differences between the responses of open- versus closed-ward patients. Two items are related to this patient characteristic at only the .05 level of confidence, open-ward patients feeling that God is closer to them and that he is more loving of them. Since open- and closed-ward patients can be presumed to differ from one another as to degree of reality contact, it can be inferred that the current level of psychological functioning is not particularly relevant to the religious beliefs a patient holds.

The only important difference between committed and voluntary patients is in regard to dependence upon God, the voluntary patient admitting a greater need for dependence. While closed-ward status is presumed to reflect the current functioning of the patient, probate court commitment probably reflects an original highly disturbed state. But again there is no general difference in responses associated with this characteristic.

The admission diagnosis is also descriptive of the original severity of the illness. Here there are two clear-cut differences in regard to the patient's idea of God. The neurotic is more likely to regard God as Final Judge, while the paranoid is less likely to regard God as Heavenly Father. Two other differences are significant at only the .05 level of confidence, neurotics feeling closer to God and at the same time feeling a greater need for God's help.

Of the four patient characteristics, the most significant differences were found to be related to length of hospitalization. Of the eighteen comparisons, two are significantly related to length of hospitalization at the .001 level, three at the .01 level, and two at the .05 level. These differences fall into a pattern. Patients who have spent many years in a hospital show progressively more uncertainty that God exists, feel more unloved by God, and feel that God is of less help to them in their lives. At the same time, they show less concern with God and more concern over their own selves. While newly admitted patients see religion as being valuable because it gives aim and purpose in living, patients who have been hospitalized eight years or more differ from them in seeing religion as being valuable in terms of helping them to improve themselves. Further, they show progressively less concern with loving their neighbor as themselves. Finally, the religious behavior of newly admitted patients may be more instrumental than that of longer-term patients. While newly admitted patients pray when they have problems, prayer in the more chronic patient is related to a more pervasive general unhappiness. So also, longer-term patients indicated more of a tendency to read the Bible primarily for its literary value.

While the results show that prolonged hospitalization is the one patient characteristic most closely related to different aspects of religious experience, they do not, of course, indicate why there is a relationship. It is, however, possible to draw a parallel between the religious life of the long-term patient and other aspects of his personality. Long-term schizophrenics are often described as being emotionally flattened or "burned out," the patient appearing to have learned to be indifferent to what had at one time been intense needs. So in his religious life, a patient who had once known acute religious tension may seek release in indifference as he becomes chronic. Longer-term patients are also considered as regressing from a mature and independent mode of life to a simpler and more childlike dependence upon the institution. While such a patient shows a lessened dependence upon God, he does show a generally less mature orientation towards religion. Finally, the chronic patient is described psychiatrically as being autistic, losing interest in the public world of others and turning inwards toward a private way of life. Again, this isolation finds its parallel in this study in a lessened interest both in horizontal relationships with fellowmen and in a vertical relationship to God.

The conclusion can therefore be reached that religious interest among patients is an expression of social interest, rather than a substitute for it. Or, looked at another way, the patient who lacks the spontaneity to make attachments to social objects in his environment will also be unable to develop an emotionally charged interest in religion.

If a decline in religious interest and a decline in personality organization parallel each other, there is also a relationship as to course of treatment. What one prescribes for cure depends, of course, upon what one diagnoses as cause. The more traditional view is that the downward course of adjustment in the chronic schizophrenic is due to organic changes. This view was developed by Kraepelin, who by the term *dementia praecox* denoted a disease that produced an inevitable and all-pervasive decline in general functioning. According to this view, the reawakening of a normal religious interest could result only from organic improvement resulting from the application of new physiological discoveries.

A newer view, however, seems to be gaining popularity. It regards schizophrenia as more social in nature. While proponents of this view may or may not believe that schizophrenia has an organic understratum, they regard the regression and emotional flattening of the chronic schizophrenic as being due, at least partially, to an institutional life where the patient becomes increasingly emotionally deprived and socially isolated. He is seen thus as being regimented to a ward routine until he reaches the point where he can express his individuality only by turning towards himself.

Those concerned with the social aspect of schizophrenia have stressed the therapeutic necessity for treating the environment in which the patient lives. The term *therapeutic community* has been used to describe a social context that seeks to reverse the process of institutionalization by making the mental hospital an "emotional hothouse" where social and psychological growth is facilitated by the accepting attitudes of all who surround the patient.

In view of the close parallel between the sociopsychological and the religious aspects of personality, it may be concluded that there is a definite relationship between the work of the religious community and the therapeutic concern of everyone else who deals therapeutically with the patient. There thus seems to be an interdependence of effort among all who come into close contact with the psychiatric patient.

It must, however, be recognized that much more must be learned about how and why religion in its various aspects is related to psychopathology. This study has been concerned only with modal gross characteristics of a large number of patients suffering from generally chronic psychiatric disabilities. Further research needs to be done with those types of psychiatric cases that are seldom seen in longer-term mental hospitals. Among such cases, the type of experience reported by Boisen may be much more frequent. Research is also needed into why and how patients within the different gross categories used in this study differ in their religious orientation. Such research should focus specifically on the relationship between religious interest and both social adjustment and unconscious thought processes. Finally, somewhat longer scales that can more comprehensively measure the different aspects of religious interest are needed so that an analysis of the relationship between psychiatric illness and religious interest can be extended from the group to the individual case.

23

Psychological Strength and the Report of Intense Religious Experience*

Ralph W. Hood, Jr.

The relationship between psychological health and religion continues to stimulate controversy despite the fact noted by several investigators that these variables are too global in their own right to yield simple predictive relationships. However, in the more restricted areas of intense religious experience and psychological strength, meaningful empirical predictions can be made based upon two major contending perspectives.

Psychoanalytic investigators appear to be especially prone to view intense religious experience in reductionistic terms. In *Civilization and Its Discontents*, Freud (1929) explicitly accepted the validity of an "oceanic feeling" that many place at the basis of a religious mystical experience. However, he argued that this feeling is charac-

*The unedited version of this article appeared originally in *The Journal for the Scientific Study of Religion*, 1974, *13*: 65-71. Copyright 1974 by the Society for the Scientific Study of Religion. Reprinted by permission.

teristic of a primary ego state and is only later associated with religious ideologies, which he more fully treated elsewhere as outright instances of psychopathology. Recently, psychoanalytically oriented investigators have emphasized this view, arguing that mystical and other intense religious experiences are regressions to earlier ego states (Allison, 1966; Arieti, 1967; Owens, 1972; Prince and Savage, 1972). One implication of this perspective is that persons with relatively weak ego strength are likely to be susceptible to intense personal religious experiences.

The psychoanalytic view is countered by an emerging interest in positive aspects of intense experiential states previously labeled "pathological." This includes interest in the positive "religious" potential of drug-induced states of consciousness (Leary, 1964; Masters and Houston, 1966; Pahnke and Richards, 1966) and is expressed even more specifically in the direct assertions of Laski (1961) and Maslow (1964) regarding a positive correspondence between healthy psychological development and "ecstatic" or "peak" experiences (cf. Tisdale, above, chapter 19). Thus, unlike the psychoanalytic investigators, these researchers tend to argue that intense experiential states such as mysticism are more likely to be characteristic of persons with relatively strong ego development and high levels of psychological adequacy.

Rather than continuing the argument at the purely conceptual level, the present studies were undertaken to determine the empirical relationship between psychological strength and intense religious experience, utilizing measures of both these concepts in an empirical setting capable of providing quantifiable data with respect to relevant relationships. Two studies are reported, both of which utilized Hood's (1970) Religious Experience Episodes Measure (REEM) to measure intense religious experience. In the first study, psychological strength was measured by Barron's (1953) Ego Strength Scale, while in the second study psychological strength was measured by Stark's (1971 and above, chapter 20) Index of Psychic Inadequacy. Since Barron's Ego Strength Scale reflects psychodynamic principles compatible with psychoanalytic theory, it was predicted that ego strength as measured by this scale would correlate *negatively* with the report of religious experience as measured by REEM. However,

since Stark's Index of Psychic Inadequacy is nondynamically oriented and is more compatible with conventional notions of psychological strength, it was predicted that ego strength as measured by this
index would correlate *positively* with religious experience as measured by the REEM.

PROCEDURE

The materials for these studies consisted of two independent operationalized measures of psychological strength and one operationalized measure of intense personal religious experience.

MEASURE OF RELIGIOUS EXPERIENCE

Hood's Religious Experience Episodes Measure (REEM) was
used in both studies to measure reported religious experience. This
instrument consists of fifteen descriptions of religious experiences
culled and edited from James (1902). Subjects indicate, using a five-
point scale, the degree to which they have had an experience similar
to the one described in the REEM.

MEASURES OF PSYCHOLOGICAL STRENGTH

Barron's Ego Strength Scale (Es) was used in the first study to
measure psychological strength. This scale consists of eight subscales composed of sixty-eight items selected directly from the large
item pool of the Minnesota Multiphasic Personality Inventory
(MMPI). One subscale has six items measuring attitude toward religion. These items essentially refer to such fundamentalist beliefs as
"Christ performed miracles such as changing water into wine" and
to frequency of prayer and church attendance. Other items in the total
Es scale do not specifically refer to religion but measure such phenomena as phobias, general physical functioning, and sense of reality. Reliability and validity data are based upon the total Es scale,
which is presumed to be a measure of a general capacity for personality integration or ego strength.

Stark's Index of Psychic Inadequacy was used in the second study
as a measure of psychological strength. This index consists of six
items, none of which specifically refer to religion. This index is

scored by noting subjects' agreement with such statements as "I tend to go to pieces in a crisis" or "I worry a lot." Thus, this index is not psychodynamically oriented and permits the two-fold classification of subjects into low and high psychological strength. It has been successfully utilized to distinguish among patterns of conventional religious commitment.

SUBJECTS

All subjects were volunteer freshmen and sophomore psychology students who identified themselves as at least nominally religiously committed. Eighty-two subjects participated in the first study and were administered both the REEM and the Es scale while 114 subjects participated in the second study and were administered both the REEM and the Index of Psychic Inadequacy. In both studies, scales were administered in group settings and randomly counterbalanced. No subjects participated in both studies, and in all cases subject anonymity was assured. Appropriate caution in generalizing results from such limited sampling procedures is necessary.

RESULTS

FIRST STUDY

The range of scores for the eighty-two subjects on the Es scale was 21 to 59, with a mean of 42.0 and a standard deviation of 8.2. These values are compatible with normative data reported by Barron (1953) and by Butcher (1969) for normal subjects. These same Ss yielded a mean response on the REEM of 33.7, with a standard deviation of 10.2.

Results indicate that, insofar as total Es scale is concerned, there is a statistically significant negative correlation between ego strength and the report of intense religious experience ($-.31$). However, removing the six-item religious subscale from the Es scale reduces this correlation to insignificance ($-.16$). Furthermore, the REEM is negatively and significantly correlated with the religious subscale of the Es scale ($-.55$), which is not surprising in view of the fact that only one Es item (church attendance) is scored in such a way that positive agreement contributes to total score. Thus, insofar as ego strength is measured independently of religious commitment, there is only a small and statistically insignificant relationship between ego strength and reported religious experience.

SECOND STUDY

The 114 subjects were classified into high psychological strength (N=71) and low psychological strength (N=43) based upon their responses to the Index of Psychic Inadequacy. Since Stark refers to his scale as an Index of Psychic *In*adequacy, one is tempted to use confusing but formally correct terminology such as "low in psychic inadequacy" and "high in psychic inadequacy." In order to avoid such confusion, we have used the simple term psychological strength in referring to subjects classified on the basis of Stark's index. If we were to use Stark's terminology, we would have to refer to high-psychological-strength subjects as "least psychologically inadequate" and low-psychological-strength subjects as "most psychologically inadequate." The means and standard deviations for these two groups on the REEM were as follows: high psychological strength, mean = 40.7, standard deviation = 12.9; low psychological strength, mean = 33.0, standard deviation = 12.9. The difference between these means is significant. Thus, these results indicate that persons high on Stark's measure of psychological strength are more likely to report intense religious experiences than persons low on this measure.

DISCUSSION

Overall these data are suggestive for further research rather than conclusive in their own right. We have seen that the significant negative correlation between total ego strength and religious experience is misleading. When the six religious items are removed from the Es scale, its correlation with the REEM is reduced to statistical insignificance. The crucial empirical point is obvious: assessments of the relationship between religion and psychological strength must be made by independently operationalized measures. Barron's own bias in constructing the Ego Strength Scale was to use fundamentalist religious commitment and intense personal religious experiences as indicative of lack of ego strength. This bias is reflected in the selection and scoring of these particular scale items and by the nature of

MMPI religious items in general. While there may be theoretical grounds for making such a linkage, our own data suggest that they are questionable. Stark himself emphasized that the empirical relationship between religion and forms of psychopathology has *yet* to be ascertained.

The findings using Stark's index provide the advantage of demonstrating a relationship between religious experience and psychological strength using a psychological measure uncontaminated by religious factors. These data provide support for the hypothesis that persons high in psychological strength are more likely to report intense religious experiences than persons low in psychological strength. While the absolute magnitude of this relationship is perhaps not great, it is empirically consistent with our own conceptualizations regarding the nature of intense religious experiences and psychological strength.

Several investigators have emphasized that a crucial characteristic of mystical states is the experience of a loss of a sense of self, especially insofar as this sense of self is felt to be absorbed in a larger whole, however this whole is defined (Laski, 1961; Maslow, 1964; Stace, 1960). This point is crucial, insofar as infantile ego states are presumed to be "mystical" and hence mystical experiences of adults are claimed to be instances of regression. A point overlooked by such theorists is that, insofar as the mystical experience is one of an absorption of a sense of self into a larger whole, infantile states cannot be mystical states per se, since the infant has no sense of self to lose or to be absorbed into a larger whole (Bowlby, 1960; Eissler, 1962). If this point is acknowledged, much of the apparent similarity between mystical states and infantile ego states is eliminated, thus making it difficult to conceptualize the mystical experience as "regressive."

In fact, the alternative view is suggested: that only a strong ego can be relinquished nonpathologically. It is this position that allows one to conceptualize the ability to have an intense experience that is labeled "mystical," "peak," or "ecstatic" as one most likely to be characteristic of a strongly developed ego, or of a psychologically healthy person. This position is consistent with our data and with the work of other investigators. For instance, Maslow (1964) has argued that peak experiences are characteristic of self-actualized persons, while Hood (1970, 1972a, 1973b) has shown that intrinsically oriented persons are more likely to report intense religious experiences than extrinsically oriented persons. Thus, the finding in this study that persons of high psychological strength are more likely to report intense religious experiences than persons of low psychological strength is not without collateral support. The meaning of this relationship must await further research. Certainly it is possible that intense experiential states are a source of psychological strength or perhaps even that psychological strength can only be developed in a setting that is in some sense "religious."

In summary, it would appear that more detailed investigations of intense experiential religious states and possible patterns of pathology are warranted, especially among wide samplings of both the conventionally and nonconventionally religious. It is especially important to avoid prejudgments as to the psychopathology of experiential states if appropriate scientific assessments of these states are to be undertaken. It is by so doing that new conceptualizations and operational measures are perhaps most likely to emerge.

24

Client Changes in
Pastoral Counseling*

John R. Tisdale

INTRODUCTION

The question of whether "secular" psychotherapy is effective has involved the energies of a number of individuals over the years; the question is not yet fully answered, although it appears that it does have the potential to change people—either to improve or make worse. The related question of what changes (if any) take place in individuals who are in pastoral counseling has been attacked only once (Hiltner and Colston, 1961), with somewhat uncertain results. This study is an attempt to explore this latter question with a group of clients in a pastoral counseling center.

METHOD

Sixty-four clients were interviewed within a week following their intake interview with the center. They were contacted again (if possible) following their final sessions. Because of a wide variety of

*The unedited version of this article appeared originally as *Pastoral Institute of the Lehigh Valley Research Report no. 10*, June 1972. Prepared and distributed by the Pastoral Institute of the Lehigh Valley, Bethlehem, Pa.

problems involved in obtaining the "after" interviews, I was able to obtain only twenty-six complete protocols. These form the basic subject matter of this study, but the clients studied are not likely to form a representative group. What differences this might make is not clear, although it probably narrows the range of variation of much of the follow-up data. The sample almost certainly is biased in favor of those whose experiences were generally pleasant (or at least not unpleasant), although initial interview test data showed no differences between those who had follow-up interviews and those who did not. A control group was not used either, which unfortunately also somewhat limits interpretation of the results obtained.

Of the twenty-six subjects, twelve were men and fourteen women; twenty-three were married at the time of their first interview, two were divorced, and one was single. The median age of the group was 34.5 years. Three had not completed a high school education; eleven others had done so, and an additional ten had gone beyond. Half the subjects were Lutherans; in addition, there were four Episcopalians, three Roman Catholics, two Jews, one Baptist, one Moravian, and two claiming no affiliation.

The most usual presenting problem involved a relationship problem with the spouse (thirteen) or with some other member of the family (six). Only seven individuals came in for other reasons; five of the six family groups in the sample came because of problems in the family situation.

As part of the initial interview, the clients were administered the Allport and Ross Extrinsic Religious Values Scale (ERV), the Adjective Check List (ACL), and a twenty-five-item sentence completion blank. These three were also administered in the closing interview, in addition to the Truax Relationship Questionnaire (TRQ), which provides a measure of the client's perception of certain therapist attitudes. Institute case records were consulted for data on the clients' backgrounds, interview content, and number of interviews.

The chief criterion variable was the client's own rating of his improvement during the course of counseling, on a five-point scale. Although there are very real problems connected with the usual choices of any criterion variable (Garfield, Prager, and Bergin, 1971), this was selected both because of the ease with which it could be obtained and because client satisfaction seems to me to be a necessary condition of a "successful" outcome.

RESULTS

The first level of data analysis was the checking of pretherapy and posttherapy measures for all subjects together to see if any systematic changes took place. Both medians and means were computed for all scales of the three instruments. On the two ERV scales and the twenty-five ACL variables that were checked, the only difference that emerged was a drop in the relative number of unfavorable adjectives that subjects assigned to themselves, as measured by the composite rank test.

When the sentence completions had been coded, four sentences showed statistically significant differences between the before and after measurements. Answers to the stem "God's presence . . ." shifted away from answers emphasizing God's omnipresence to rather individualistic ones that fell into an "other" or "miscellaneous" category. Two items having to do with prayer showed shifts also. "As a result of prayer . . ." showed reductions in responses such as "feel better" and those that referred to the individual's felt communication with God and demonstrated a heavier emphasis on feeling stronger or helped. "Prayer is . . ." also showed an increased emphasis on the good or helpful aspect following counseling. The "I need . . ." stem showed a drop in the help/understanding and love categories and an increase in the responses indicating God, faith, or religion and the idiosyncratic "other" category.

The second level of analysis involved checking two sets of outcome variables against specific kinds of data in an attempt to tap differential improvements within the subject group. The subjects' own ratings of how much help they had received were classified into three groups, and the six scores on the Relationship Questionnaire were separated into low, middle, and high criterion groups with approximately 27 percent of the cases in each of the extremes. Using chi-square as the basic analytic tool, these groups were compared with each other and several other variables as well.

One scale on the TRQ, the "concreteness" scale, was related to outcome. Therapist behavior indicating rather specific and clear responses to clients was associated with relatively low levels of client satisfaction with the counseling process, an unexpected result. Two postcounseling ACL scales were related to degree of client satisfaction: the proportion of "favorable" self-descriptive adjectives used was higher in the group reporting "very much" help (median test), while the counseling readiness scale tended to be lower in that group (composite rank test), indicating a greater amount of self-satisfaction in both instances.

When checked against social and background variables, outcome was related only to the researcher's estimate of the subject's improvement based upon a close inspection of the counseling records for each individual. Since there is the possibility of contamination in this measurement, no great significance should be attached to it.

The TRQ scales were checked primarily against the posttherapy sentence completion endings of those four items showing change over the counseling period. No significant relationships between any of the pairs were found. The self-ratings were checked against both the pretherapy and posttherapy endings, and a significant relationship was found with the initial endings to the sentence "As a result of prayer, I. . . ." In general, those who reported that they were aided, helped, made stronger, or felt better as a result of prayer reported either little or very much improvement later in counseling—but not much in between.

DISCUSSION

In general, the lack of clear differences between the subgroups is not very encouraging, although the relative "coarseness" of the measuring instruments may be partly at fault. Two things, however, emerged that should be noted.

The first is that the self-descriptions reflected in two ACL scales did change in relation to degree of improvement and in expected ways. Clients who felt they had benefitted most from therapy also tended to see themselves in a more positive vein and to report less feelings of personal distress than those who reported the least benefit. This is encouraging and suggests that real changes were taking place, at least as measured by different kinds of client self-reports.

Relevant to the other finding that emerged is an earlier assessment (Tisdale, 1970) of responses to the incomplete sentences by a larger group of clients (including these subjects). Several generalizations were made about the religious experience of these people. First, their religion was strongly pragmatic. It was useful, workable, and functional. It achieved specifiable results in their lives and affected their behavior in some observable and significant ways. Religion generally served either to help the individuals maintain normal living and self-control or to gain some freedom from anxiety and increase self-acceptance. This group also, as one might expect, viewed religion positively in terms of both institutional affiliation and devotional practices. Third, God was perceived primarily in terms suggesting benevolence and immanence, although a minority indicated instead the importance of transcendence. Worship was seen essentially as a form of communication, usually from men to a divinity rather than the reverse. Finally, the disturbing, unsettling functions of religion were nearly nonexistent for this group. Whenever religion's function was noted, it almost always was seen as supportive: a source of strength, calm, peace, help. These subjects were, in some ways, reminiscent of Monaghan's (1967) "comfort-seekers" in a fundamentalist church.

What, then, can be said about the changes that occurred in these sentence completions? Three of the four sentences that changed had to do with religious material, and the general trends for all four seemed to be in the direction of more positive and more highly individualized and articulated feelings about God's presence, prayer, and one's own needs. Individuals were composing many more idiosyncratic responses to the items, which reflected their earlier positive orientation but did so in more specialized ways. Not only did those who benefitted from therapy seem to become "more religious," but their religious experience seemed increasingly to reflect and express their individual uniqueness. Although these results must be regarded for now as quite tentative, they are the first empirical suggestion I know of that pastoral counseling does indeed make differences in clients' religious perceptions. This lead should be followed up in the future, probably with open-ended or projective instruments such as were used here.

This study has, then, run into some of the difficulties shared by others investigating similar questions, but it has also uncovered some interesting possibilities for both pastoral counselors and those concerned with religious aspects of any psychotherapy.

25

The New Pietism*

Thomas C. Oden

INTRODUCTION

Important antecedents of current encounter group processes can be found in the life and literature of Protestant and Jewish pietism. The encounter group is a demythologized and secularized form of a style of interpersonal encounter and community that is familiar to historians of Protestant pietism (or of the Jewish Hasidic movement that was parallel to it). Pietism emphasized here-and-now experiencing, intensive small-group encounter, honest confession within a trusting community, experimental mysticism, mutual pastoral care, and the operation of the spirit at the level of nonverbal communication. The purpose of this article is to point out some of the similarities between these two movements.

In doing so, I wish specifically to avoid the reductionist impression that current encounter group processes can be boiled down essentially to what was taking place in the eighteenth-century religious societies. Admitting many differences, I am trying instead to unveil the striking similarities between the two movements and to

*The unedited version of this article appeared originally in *The Journal of Humanistic Psychology*, Spring 1972, pp. 24-41. Copyright 1972 by the Association for Humanistic Psychology. Reprinted by permission.

hypothesize that there may be some discernible flow of influence from the pietistic encounter style to the current encounter style (Mowrer, 1971).

Nor is my intent to debunk encounter groups by revealing their historical origins in such a way as to embarrass group proponents. Rather, I am attempting to support the encounter culture precisely through showing that its historical origins are connected with rich Western religious sources from which it is now estranged (Oden, 1966; 1967; 1969). I am not suggesting that the encounter culture is unimaginative or unoriginal in its borrowings from religious traditions. What I am affirming is that both the classical form of group encounter in pietism and its latter-day manifestations have been in some respects amazingly creative, and that the creative edge of each deserves to be in better touch with the other.

RESISTANCE TO HISTORICAL ANALYSIS

In probing these striking similarities, I am not arguing that modern group leaders have been overtly or even secretly reading the literature of Protestant or Jewish pietism. The fact that most would not wish to be caught dead doing so, however, is of considerable interest. A curious part of the task of historical inquiry is to show why they have preferred *not* to behold their own history, and why they have remained unaware of the subtle and indirect forms in which they have reappropriated and transmuted an available religious tradition. These pietistic patterns were quietly and inertly "in the air" as available social models for the progenitors of current group encounter such as Lewin, Moreno, Rogers, and the NTL innovators. The fact that they were borrowed and applied *unconsciously* rather than consciously is noteworthy, to say the least, especially among professionals so deliberately committed to "making the unconscious conscious."

Why have the otherwise intelligent proponents of the intensive group experience in the twentieth century not recognized their Protestant and Jewish pietistic origins? Quite simply, the tradition of emotive and quasi-fanatical pietism has long been out of favor with those who form the clientele of the encounter culture. In fact, the pietistic tradition is radically in disfavor today among almost everyone, including the seminaries and even the churches and synagogues that pietism has spawned. Pietistic words like "revival" and "religion of the heart" and "conversion" and "testimony" are repulsive to self-consciously modern men. The irony, of course, is that, although the words are no longer acceptable, all of the meanings that those words freighted have been taken back right into the heart of the encounter culture.

A curious form of dissimulation persists in the encounter culture. If you can convince the encounter clientele that the meditation they are doing comes from Eastern religions, and not from the West, you can proceed amiably. If you can apply words like *chakras, satori,* and *karma* to your interpretations, instead of using their ordinary Western equivalents (which actually are more in touch with where the clientele is), you will find ready hearers, even though such terms come from authoritarian traditions that would be ipso facto rejected if they were Western. A group leader probably will be more acceptable if he can persuade participants that the "peak experiences" he is facilitating have nothing to do with Western religion, and if Western, certainly not Protestant, and if Protestant, certainly not Calvinist Puritanism, and if Calvinism, certainly not pietism, against which the participants understand themselves to be most certainly rebelling. The former Episcopal priest Alan Watts can get a hearing if he talks about Zen but not about Christianity. William Schutz is more likely to speak of *Kundalini Yoga* than of "the way to the Supreme Being," or of *chakras* than "centers of body energy."

PIETISM

It is regrettable that we are compelled to use the historian's term *pietism* to describe a movement so creative and variegated, since that term has been so badly abused by a long tradition of religious experience that often bordered on fanaticism and antiintellectualism. Puritanism is doubtless even worse in the encounter vocabulary. The irony, of course, is that it is precisely the pietistic wing of the Puritan Protestant tradition (so strongly influenced by English Calvinist dissent) that is being reappropriated in current encounter groups. We hypothesize that the deepest roots of the encounter movement are in the least likely of all places: more generally in Calvinism than in any other religious tradition, including all Hindu and Buddhist themes combined. In fact, the Zen and Yoga themes that have been so overtly incorporated into the encounter culture have largely been absorbed into a worldview decisively shaped by Puritan Protestant-ism, and in fact the Americanized Zen and Yoga often become unrecognizable to Easterners. It is a curious self-deception to imag-ine that the deeper motivating forces behind the encounter culture come from Eastern religions. This is merely a functional facade for what is actually happening. If and when the actual historical models are carefully clarified, this self-deception will be more and more difficult to sustain (Watts, 1961).

CONVERSION

A prominent feature of all forms of pietism, as well as the current culture, is the concept of a spiritual breakthrough of intense emotive depth that changes behavior radically. The literature of pietism is filled with testimonials of persons who have undergone sudden and radical conversion experiences (e.g., Bodamer, 1961; Dimond, 1926). Typically, after having first described themselves as being crushed by guilt and despair, they then tell how, within a supportive group, they experienced a radical turning point in which they deeply felt the acceptance and grace of God, whereupon a rich flow of gratitude and freedom motivated them to reshape their behavior. This is the center of the pietistic conversion experience, epitomized best by John Wesley's feeling his heart "strangely warmed" when an assurance was given him that Christ "had taken away my sins, even mine."

Compare this with an account written by a member of a basic encounter group, as quoted by Rogers (1970):

> I had really buried under a layer of concrete many feelings I was afraid people were going to laugh at or stomp on which, needless to say, was working all kinds of hell on my family and on me. . . . The real turning point for me was a simple gesture on your part of putting your arm around my shoulder one afternoon when I had made some crack about you not being a member of the group—that no one could cry on your shoulder. In my notes I had written the night before, "There is no man in the world who loves me!" You seemed to be so genuinely concerned that day I was overwhelmed! . . . I *received*

the gesture as one of the first feelings of acceptance—of me, just the dumb way I am, prickles and all—that I had ever experienced. I have felt needed, loving, competent, furious, frantic, anything but just plain *loved*. You can imagine the flood of gratitude, humility, release that swept over me. I wrote with considerable joy, "I actually felt loved." I doubt that I shall soon forget it.

OTHER SIMILARITIES

To clarify similarities between small-group encounter styles of free-church Protestantism and those of the contemporary encounter culture, the ensuing quotations from both traditions are presented in side-by-side columns; and they comprise a sampling of five areas: (1) the small group format, (2) the zealous pursuit of honesty, (3) focus on here-and-now experiencing, (4) the nurture of intimacy, and (5) revival as marathon.

Statements from eighteenth- and nineteenth-century pietistic writings (left column) may be compared with those from the principal leaders of the encounter culture today (right column)—Perls, Rogers, Maslow, Schutz, and others.

Eighteenth- and Nineteenth-Century Religious Group Encounter Styles

Current Encounter Group Styles

1. THE SMALL GROUP FORMAT

Let each member of the class relate his experience with freedom and simplicity. The design of the classes is to ascertain the spiritual state of each member, in order that religious sympathy be excited, mutual regard promoted, mutual encouragement obtained. (Rosser, 1855)

All communication in the group should be as open and honest as it's possible to be . . . learn how to be more open with everyone, including yourself. . . . Talk directly to the person addressed. (Schutz, 1971)

They had no need of being encumbered with many rules, having the best rule of all in their hearts. *No peculiar directions*

This group will meet for many hours and will serve as a kind of laboratory where each individual can increase his understanding of were therefore given to them. . . . Everyone here has an equal liberty of speaking, there being none greater or less than another. . . . I often found the advantage of such a free conversation, and that "in the multitude of counsellors there is safety." (Wesley, 1748/1850)

the forces which influence individual behavior and the performance of groups and organizations. The data for learning will be our own behavior, feelings, and reactions. We begin with *no definite* structure or organization, no agreed-upon procedures, and no specific agenda. It will be up to us to fill the vacuum created by the lack of these familiar elements and to study our group as we evolve. . . . With these few comments, I think we are ready to begin in whatever way you feel will be most helpful. (Seashore, 1968)

I desired a small number . . . to spend an hour with me every Monday morning. My design was, not only to . . . incite them to love one another more, and to watch more carefully over each other, but also to have a select company, to whom I might unbosom myself on all occasions, without reserve. (Wesley, 1748/1850)

The deeper you go the safer it is. If you go deep the group gets close. People begin caring for each other and supporting each other. (Schutz, quoted by Gustaitis, 1969)

They begin to "bear one another's burdens," and naturally to "care for each other." As they had daily a more intimate acquaintance with, so they had a more endearing affection for, each other. (Wesley, 1748/1938)

A climate of mutual trust develops out of this mutual freedom to express real feelings, positive, and negative. (Rogers, 1970)

2. THE ZEALOUS PURSUIT OF HONESTY

Do you desire that every one of us should tell you, from time to time, whatsoever is in his heart

Feedback is most acceptable when the receiver himself has formulated the question which concerning you? Consider! Do you desire we should tell you whatsoever we think, whatsoever we fear, whatsoever we hear concerning you? (Wesley, 1744/1967)

Do you desire to be told of your faults? (Wesley, 1744/1967)

Rules of the Bands: To speak each of us in order, freely and plainly, the true state of our souls, with the faults we have committed in thought, word, or deed, and the temptations we have felt since our last meeting. (Wesley, 1744/1967) Self-examination, severe, thorough, impartial. The class meeting will be productive of but little real, lasting benefit without this. (Rosser, 1855)

Rules of the Bands: It is your desire and design to be, on this and all other occasions, entirely open, so as to speak everything that is in your heart without exception, without disguise and without reserve? Have you nothing you desire to keep secret? (Wesley, 1744/1967)

What known sins have you committed since our last meeting? (Wesley, 1744/1967)

Rules of the Bands: To desire some person among us to speak his

those observing him can answer. It is *solicited*, rather than imposed. (National Training Laboratories, 1968)

Discover your resistances. (Perls, Hefferline, and Goodman, 1951)

The assumption in your groups seems to be, on the contrary, that people are very tough, and not brittle. They can take an awful lot. The best thing to do is get right at them, and not to sneak up on them, or be delicate with them, or try to surround them from the rear. Get right smack into the middle of things right away. I've suggested that a name for this might be "no-crap therapy." It serves to clean out the defenses, the rationalizations, the veils, the evasions and politeness of the world. (Maslow, 1967)

The pursuit of honesty is begun by asking the couples to think of three secrets they have never told their mate and that would be most likely to jeopardize their relationship. During the course of the workshop they tell these secrets. (Schutz, 1971)

I force my groups to be open, to tell me everything. (Schutz, 1971)

Making the rounds, the therapist may feel that a particular theme or own state first, and then to ask the rest, in order, as many and as searching questions as may be, concerning their state, sins and temptations. (Wesley, 1744/1967)

feeling expressed by the patient should be faced vis-a-vis every other person in the group. The patient may have said, "I can't stand anyone in this room." Therapist: "O.K., make the rounds. Say that to each one of us and add some other remark pertaining to your feelings about each person." (Levitsky, 1969)

3. FOCUS ON HERE-AND-NOW EXPERIENCING

Let your expressions be clear and definite, pointed and brief, having reference to your present experience, so that the state of your mind may be easily apprehended. (Newstead, 1843)

Realize [make real] the nowness of your experience. (Perls, 1969)

Beware of resting in past experience. (Newstead, 1843)

Nothing exists except the now. (Perls, quoted by Gustaitis, 1969)

Prayer in the classroom is special, and is concentrated upon some present object, and this explains, to some degree, its power. (Rosser, 1855)

Stay with the here and now as much as possible. (Schutz, 1971)

An ingenuous account of our temptations is the surest way to subdue them. (Rosser, 1855)

The principle of "Can you stay with this feeling?" This technique is invoked at key moments when the patient refers to a feeling or mood or state of mind which is unpleasant and which he has a great urge to dispel. . . . The therapist says, "Can you stay with this feeling?" (Levitsky, 1969)

Do you desire that, in doing this, we should come as close as possible; that we should cut to the quick, and search your heart to the

I and thou; here and now. (Perls, 1969)

bottom? (Wesley, 1744/1967)

Shun the very appearance of affectation. Let your words and your manner be perfectly natural. Do not . . . speak in borrowed nor hackneyed terms, lest it should become a merely formal exercise, and consequently a deceptive one. (Newstead, 1843)

Words are special culprits in the effort to avoid personal confrontation. (Schutz, 1967)

In the evening, I went very unwillingly to a society in Aldersgate Street, where one was reading Luther's preface to the Epistle to the Romans. About a quarter before nine, while he was describing the change which God works in the heart through faith in Christ, I felt my heart strangely warmed. I felt I did trust in Christ, Christ alone, for salvation; and an assurance was given me, that He had taken away my sins, even mine, and saved me from the law of sin and death (Wesley, 1738/1938)

Go to your core—focus, connect to yourself and then to the others with you, and surrender yourself fully to the feeling from your core. (Lewis and Streitfeld, 1970)

4. THE NURTURE OF INTIMACY

Many, many a time, in immediate answer to prayer, in the classroom, so intensely burns the heart with love to God and man, that the whole class is quickened by the subduing and stirring testimony given, and the very classroom seems to be a mansion of glory. (Rosser, 1855)

Participants feel a closeness and intimacy which they have not felt even with their spouses or members of their own family, because they have revealed themselves here more deeply. (Rogers, 1970)

When a happy correspondence between the outward walk and

Where all is known and all accepted . . . further growth

inward piety of believers is discovered, which can be known only by the disclosure of the interior life, we are not only prepared to comfort, but form an intimacy of the holiest nature, a union of the strongest character. (Rosser, 1855)

If we yield to the suggestions that our distresses are the most deplorable, that our sins are so heinous that they ought not to be disclosed, or are so trivial that they need not be confessed . . . or that we should give an unfair and partial account of our true state, . . . and refer in but an obscure manner to whatever in us is disagreeable and unfavorable . . . our testimony in all these cases amounts to nothing more than a hurtful illusion. (Rosser, 1855)

Tell your experience; and tell your conflicts; and tell your comforts. As iron sharpeneth iron, as rubbing of the hands maketh the rest to burn, so let the fruit of the society be mutually sharpening, warming, and influencing. (Rosser, 1855)

We all partake the joy of one; / the common peace we feel: / A peace to worldly minds unknown, / A joy unspeakable. / And if our fellowship below / In Jesus be so sweet, What height of rapture shall we know / When round His throne we meet! [Charles Wesley, hymn, 1747] Brother, is thy heart with mine, as my heart is with thy

becomes possible. . . . To his astonishment, he finds that he is more accepted the more real that he becomes. (Rogers, 1970)

This willingness to take the risk of being one's inner self is certainly one of the steps toward relieving the loneliness that exists in each one of us and putting us in genuine touch with other human beings. A college student expressed this risk very well when he said, "I felt at a loss today in the encounter group. Very naked. Now everyone knows too much about me; at the same time I am more comfortable in the knowledge that I don't have to put on my 'cool.' " (Rogers, 1970)

To discover that a whole group of people finds it much easier to care for the real self than for the external facade is always a moving experience. (Rogers, 1970)

One point at which open encounter and a mystical viewpoint are mutually helpful occurs when an encounter is going very deep. After hostility is worked through and differences acknowledged as people reach the deeper layers of personality, the similarity of all men becomes clearer. We are all in the same struggle but using heart? If it be, give me thy hand. (Charles Wesley, 1742)

different paths with different defenses. The notion that we are all one is given great meaning at these almost mystical moments in the group's life. (Schutz, 1971)

5. REVIVAL AS MARATHON

In this revival originated our camp meetings, and in both these denominations they were every year, and, indeed, have been ever since, more or less. They would erect their camps with logs or frame them, and cover them with clapboards or shingles . . . and here they would collect together from forty to fifty miles around, sometimes further than that. Ten, twenty, and sometimes thirty ministers, of different denominations, would come together and preach night and day, four or five days together: and indeed, I have known these camp-meetings to last three or four weeks, and great good resulted from them. . . . I have seen and heard more than five hundred Christians all shouting aloud the high praises of God at once. (Cartwright, 1856/1956)

The marathon is not unlike a "pressure cooker" in which phony steam boils away and genuine emotions (including negative ones) emerge. The group atmosphere is kept focused every moment on the objectives at hand: to produce *change in orientation* and new ways of dealing with old crucial problems. (Bach, 1966) These experiences led me to the conclusion that the depth that could be reached in a concentrated workshop was so remarkable compared to the other approaches that I have virtually abandoned all other patterns. . . . I've found . . . that one intensive week is equivalent to two or three years of periodic therapy sessions, and that groups are much more effective than individual sessions. (Schutz, 1971)

The fountains of sin need to be broken up. In a true revival, Christians are always brought under such convictions; they see their sins in such a light, that often they find it impossible to maintain a hope of their acceptance. . . . The first step is a deep repentance,

A chronically contracted muscle is in effect saying, "no." . . . Lying on a bed with a firm mattress he is asked to strike the bed repeatedly with his fists and say "no" with each blow in a loud and convincing tone. . . . At this point the group may encourage the subject to "let a breaking down of heart, a getting down into the dust before God, with deep humility, and forsaking sin. (Finney, 1834/1960)

I have been at meetings where the whole congregation would be bathed in tears; and sometimes their cries would be so loud that the preacher's voice could not be heard. Some would be seized with trembling, and in a few moments drop on the floor as if they were dead; while others were embracing each other with streaming eyes, and all were lost in wonder, love and praise. (Lee, 1810)

With regard to these prudential helps we are continually changing one thing after another. [This] is not a weakness or fault, as you imagine, but a peculiar advantage which we enjoy. By this means we declare them all to be merely prudential, not essential, not of divine institution. We prevent, so far as in us lies, their growing formal or dead. We are always open to instruction; willing to be wiser every day than we were before. (Wesley, 1748/1931)

go," to pound with all his strength and yell with all his might. (Ruitenbeek, 1970)

. . . Participants almost unanimously speak of marathons, immediately afterward and a year afterward, as a worthwhile and moving experience. The words "I felt reborn" are often uttered. (Mintz, 1967)

The "open encounter group" implies that the method is always changing and evolving. The groups we run today are run very differently from last year's and next year's groups. (Schutz, 1971)

To juxtapose quotations in this fashion makes the case more concrete and plausible than if one were merely to argue abstractly that similarities of conceptual schemes and procedures exist. It is not to be assumed that there is in every pair of quotations a direct and consistent analogy; but in most cases quotations have been matched with some evident nuance of similarity in such a way that the whole series of quotations will illustrate basic correspondences between the two encounter styles. I hope that this discussion will encourage group facilitators to search more deeply within their own personal and cultural histories in order to gain clearer awareness of how their work shares in a large historical flow of human experience.

For Further Reading

Most of the books in this area that you might want to look at have been mentioned in the introduction to this section. There are two that were not, however, alike only in their brevity and their central topic. The first is Eli Chesen's *Religion May Be Hazardous to Your Health* (New York: Peter H. Wyden, 1972). He seems to want to avoid simply writing a sober (and dull?) scholarly essay on his topic, but not to be simply sensational or controversial. He does avoid being both dull and controversial, but unfortunately he also misses being scholarly. Nevertheless, his volume is worth some examination as an attempt to suggest some possible ill effects of some kinds of religion. On the other hand, Orlo Strunk's *Religion: A Psychological Interpretation* (New York: Abingdon, 1962) is both a readable and serious study of how religion may operate within the perceptual field of the religious person. He concludes with the thesis that religion always serves an integrating function to the individual (as he experiences himself).

Two earlier works are still available. Anton Boisen's *The Exploration of the Inner World* (1936) has been reprinted by the University of Pennsylvania Press (Philadelphia, 1971) in paperback, and so has Freud's *Future of an Illusion* (1928), in a Norton Library edition by W. W. Norton (New York, 1976). Wayne Oates's *Religious Factors in Mental Illness* (New York: Association Press, 1955) is no longer in print, but it does try to relate religion and mental illness. The stimulating *The Crisis in Psychiatry and Religion* (Princeton: Van Nostrand, Reinhold, 1961) by O. H. Mowrer, another look at this general topic, has also gone out of print but may be available in many libraries.

If you wish to learn something about the nature of pastoral counseling, then perhaps Howard Clinebell's *Basic Types of Pastoral Counseling* (Nashville: Abingdon, 1965) is a good place to go. Richard H. Cox's *Religious Systems and Psychotherapy* (Springfield, Ill.: Charles C Thomas, 1973) brings together a wide variety of articles all having to do with ways of viewing the relationships between religion and psychotherapy.

Reference List

Adorno, T. W.; Frenkle-Brunswik, E.; Levinson, D. J.; and Sanford, R. N. *The authoritarian personality.* New York: Harper, 1950.

Alberts, W. E. Ministers' attitudes toward juvenile delinquency. *Journal of Social Psychology*, 1963, *60*, 71-83.

Albrecht, R. E. The meaning of religion to older people—the social aspect. In *Organized religion and the older person*, edited by D. L. Scudder. Gainesville: University of Florida Press, 1958.

Alexander, F. Buddhistic training as an artificial catatonia (The biological meaning of psychic occurrence). *Psychoanalytic Review*, 1931, *13*, 129-45.

Allen, R. O., and Spilka, B. Committed and consensual religion: A specification of religion-prejudice relationships. *Journal for the Scientific Study of Religion*, 1967, *6*, 191-206.

Allison, J. Recent empirical studies of religious conversion experiences. *Pastoral Psychology*, 1966, *17*, 21-33.

Allison, J. Adaptive regression and intense religious experiences. *The Journal of Nervous and Mental Disease*, 1968, *145*, 452-63.

Allport, G. W. *The individual and his religion.* New York: Macmillan, 1950.

Allport, G. W. *The nature of prejudice.* Cambridge, Mass.: Addison-Wesley, 1954.

Allport, G. W. Religion and prejudice. *Crane Review*, 1959, *2*, 1-10.

Allport, G. W. *Personality and social encounter.* Boston: Beacon,

1960.

Allport, G. W. The religious context of prejudice. *Journal for the Scientific Study of Religion*, 1966, *5*, 447-57. (a)

Allport, G. W. Traits revisited. *American Psychologist*, 1966, *21*, 1-10. (b)

Allport, G. W., and Ross, J. M. Personal religious orientation and prejudice. *Journal of Personality and Social Psychology*, 1967, *5*, 432-43.

Allport, G. W., Vernon, P. E., and Lindzey, G. *Study of values: Manual*. 3rd ed. Boston: Houghton Mifflin, 1960.

American Correctional Association. Declaration of principles. Proceedings of the American Correctional Association, 1960.

American Psychiatric Association. *Diagnostic and statistical manual of mental disorders*. Washington, D. C.: American Psychiatric Association, 1952.

Argyle, M. *Religious behaviour*. Glencoe, Ill.: Free Press, 1958.

Arieti, S. *The intrapsychic self*. New York: Basic Books, 1967.

Armstrong, R. G., Larsen, G. L., and Mourer, S. A. Religious attitudes and emotional adjustment. *Journal of Psychological Studies*, 1962, *13*, 35-47.

Bach, G. R. The marathon group: Intensive practice of intimate interaction. *Psychological Reports*, 1966, *18*, 995-1002.

Bahr, H. M. Aging and religious disaffiliation. *Social Forces*, 1970, *49* (Sept.), 59-71.

Bakan, P. The eyes have it. *Psychology today*, April 1971, pp. 64-67, 96.

Barnes, H. E., and Teeters, N. K. *New horizons in criminology*. 3rd ed. Englewood Cliffs, N.J.: Prentice-Hall, 1959.

Barron, F. An ego-strength scale which predicts response to psychotherapy. *Journal of Consulting Psychology*, 1953, *17*, 327-33.

Barron, M. L. The role of religion and religious institutions in treating the milieu of older people. In *Organized religion and the older person*, edited by D. L. Scudder. Gainesville: University of Florida Press, 1958.

Bealer, R. C., and Willets, F. K. The religious interests of American high school youth. *Religious Education*, 1967, *62*, 435-44, 464.

Beard, B. B. Religion at 100. *Modern Maturity*, 1969, *12*, 1-4.

Becker, R. J. Religion and psychological health. In *Research on religious development*, edited by Merton B. Strommen. New York: Hawthorne, 1971.

Bender, I. E. Changes in religious interest: A retest after fifteen years. *Journal of Abnormal and Social Psychology,* 1958, *57,* 41-46.

Bloch, H. A., and Flynn, F. T. *Delinquency.* New York: Random House, 1956.

Bodamer, W. G. Some features of pietistic biography. *Theologische Zeitschrift,* 1961, *17,* 435-37.

Bohrnstedt, G. W. Processes of seeking membership in and recruitment by voluntary social organizations. Doctoral dissertation, University of Wisconsin, 1966.

Bohrnstedt, G. W. Conservatism, authoritarianism, and religiosity of fraternity pledges. *Journal of College Student Personnel,* 1969, *10,* 36-43.

Boisen, A. T. *The exploration of the inner world.* 1936. Reprinted. New York: Harper, Torchbooks, 1952.

Boisen, A. T. *Out of the depths.* New York: Harper, 1960.

Bolton, D. D., and Kammeyer, K. C. W. *The university student.* New Haven: College and University Press, 1967.

Bowlby, J. Grief and mourning in infancy and early childhood. In *The psychoanalytic study of the child,* vol. 15, edited by R. S. Eissler, A. Freud, H. Hartmann, and M. Kriss. New York: International Universities, 1960.

Broderick, C. B. Predicting friendship behavior: A study of the determinants of friendship selection and maintenance in a college population. Doctoral dissertation, Cornell University, 1956.

Brown, D. G., and Lowe, W. L. Religious beliefs and personality characteristics of college students. *Journal of Social Psychology,* 1951, *33,* 103-29.

Brown, L. B. A study of religious belief. *British Journal of Psychology,* 1962, *53,* 259-72.

Brown, L. B. Classification of religious orientation. *Journal for the Scientific Study of Religion,* 1964, *4,* 91-99.

Bryant, M. D. Patterns of religious thinking of university students as related to intelligence. Doctoral dissertation, University of Nebraska, 1958.

Burchard, W. W. Religion at a midwestern university: An interim report. Paper presented at the annual meeting of the Society for the Scientific Study of Religion, 1964.

Burns, C. L. A ministry to delinquents in detention. *Pastoral Psychology,* 1961, *12,* 25-28.

Butcher, J. N. *MMPI: Research developments and clinical applications.* New York: McGraw-Hill, 1969.

Butler, R. N. Viewpoint—an interview with Robert N. Butler. *Geriatrics*, 1964, *26*, 65-75.

Cartwright, P. *Autobiography*. 1856, Reprinted. Nashville: Abingdon, 1956.

Catholic Digest. How important religion is to Americans. *Catholic Digest*, February 1953, pp. 7-12.

Catholic Digest. Effects of college education on religious beliefs and behavior: A preliminary report. Paper presented at the annual meeting of the American Catholic Sociological Society, 1965.

Catholic Digest. Do Americans go to church? *Catholic Digest*, July 1966, pp. 24-32.

Cattell, R. B. *Personality and motivation structure and measurement*. Yonkers-on-Hudson, N.Y.: World Book, 1957.

Chickering, A. W. Institutional differences and student characteristics. *Journal of the American College Health Association*, 1965, *14*, 168-81.

Chickering, A. W., et al. Research and action: Third annual process report. Plainfield, Vt.: Project on Student Development in Small Colleges, 1968.

Church Assembly Board for Social Responsibility. *Police: A social study*. Oxford: Church Army Press, 1967.

Clark, W. H. *Chemical ecstasy: Psychedelic drugs and religion*. New York: Sheed and Ward, 1969.

Clemmer, D. *The prison community*. 1940. Reprinted. New York: Rinehart and Co., 1958.

Cockrum, L. V. Personality traits and interests of theological students. *Religious Education*, 1952, 47, 28-32.

Coe, G. A. *The spiritual life: Studies in the science of religion*. New York: Eaton and Mains, 1900.

Coe, G. A. *The psychology of religion*. Chicago: University of Chicago Press, 1916.

Conner, W. J. The religious history of some delinquent boys. *Guild of Catholic Psychiatrists Bulletin*, 1960, *9*, 181-85.

Couch, A., and Keniston, K. Yeasayers and naysayers: Agreeing response set as a personality variable. *Journal of Abnormal and Social Psychology*, 1960, *60*, 151-74.

Covalt, N. K. The meaning of religion to older people. *Geriatrics*, 1960, *15*, 658-64.

Declaration of principles, revised and approved. Proceedings of the American Correctional Association, New York, 1960.

Deikman, A. J. Experimental meditation. *Journal of Nervous and*

Mental Disease, 1963, *136*, 329-43.

Deikman, A. J. Implications of experimentally induced contemplative meditation. *Journal of Nervous and Mental Disease*, 1966, *142*, 101-16.

Department of Criminology, Florida State University. Using volunteer and religious agencies. *School of Social Welfare*, February 1965, pp. 16-26.

Diaz, C. V. A study of the ability of eleventh grade girls to apply the principles of moral law to actual and hypothetical life situations. Doctoral dissertation, Fordham University, 1952.

Dimond, S. G. *The psychology of the Methodist revival*. New York: Oxford, 1926.

Dittes, J. E. Comment by the editor. *Journal for the Scientific Study of Religion*, 1967, *6*, 190, 220, 235.

Dittes, J. E. Definition as a process of perceptual differentiation. Paper presented at the Conference on Measuring the Religious Variable, Dallas, Texas, 1968.

Dittes, J. E. Psychology of religion. *The handbook of social psychology*, vol. 5, 2d ed., edited by G. Lindzey and E. Aronson. Reading, Mass.: Addison-Wesley, 1969.

Dittes, J. E. Typing the typologies: Some parallels in the career of church-sect and extrinsic-intrinsic. *Journal for the Scientific Study of Religion*, 1971, *10*, 375-83.

Dominic, M. Religion and the juvenile delinquent. *American Catholic Sociological Review*, 1954, *15*, 256-64.

Donelly, H. L. *Measuring certain aspects of faith in God as found in boys and girls fifteen, sixteen, and seventeen years of age*. Philadelphia: Westminster, 1931.

Dunlap, K. *Religion: Its function in human life*. New York: McGraw-Hill, 1956.

Duvall, S. N. Moral education: A general factor in delinquency control. *Pastoral Psychology*, 1961, *12*, 44-47.

Educational Review, Inc. Survey of the political and religious attitudes of American college students. *National Review*, 1963, *15*, 279-301.

Eissler, K. R. On the metapsychology of the preconscious: A tentative contribution to psychoanalytic morphology. In *The psychoanalytic study of the child*, vol. 17, edited by R. S. Eissler, A. Freud, H. Hartmann, and M. Kris. New York: International Universities, 1962.

Elkind, D. The child's conception of his religious denomination: I. The Jewish child. *Journal of Genetic Psychology*, 1961, *99*, 209-25.

Elkind, D. The child's conception of his religious denomination: II. The

Catholic child. *Journal of Genetic Psychology*, 1962, *101*, 185-93.

Elkind, D. The child's conception of his religious denomination: III. The Protestant child. *Journal of Genetic Psychology*, 1963, *103*, 291-304.

Elkind, D., and Elkind, S. F. Varieties of religious experience in young adolescents. *Journal for the Scientific Study of Religion*, 1962, *2*, 102-12.

Erikson, E. H. Wholeness and totality—a psychiatric contribution. In *Totalitarianism*, edited by C. J. Friedrich. Cambridge, Mass.: Harvard University Press, 1954.

Eshelman, B. E. The prison ministry. *Federal Probation*, 1968, *32*, 37-41.

Falk, G. J. Religion, personal integration, and criminality. *Journal of Educational Sociology*, 1961, *35*, 159-61.

Feagin, J. R. Prejudice and religious types: A focused study of Southern fundamentalists. *Journal for the Scientific Study of Religion*, 1964, *4*, 3-13.

Feldman, K. A., and Newcomb, T. M. *The impact of college on students*. 2 vols. San Francisco: Jossey-Bass, 1969.

Ferman, L. A. Religious change on a college campus. *Journal of College Student Personnel*, 1960, *1*, 2-12.

Festinger, L. *A theory of cognitive dissonance*. Evanston: Row Peterson, 1957.

Festinger, L., Riecken, H. W., and Schacter, S. *When prophecy fails*. Minneapolis: University of Minnesota Press, 1956.

Fichtner, J. H. What is a good parishioner? Paper presented at the Conference on Measuring the Religious Variable, Dallas, Texas, 1968.

Finney, C. What a revival of religion is. In *Lectures on revivals of religion*, edited by W. B. McLoughlin. Cambridge, Mass.: Belknap, 1960.

Fitzpatrick, J. P. The role of religion in programs for the prevention and correction of crime and delinquency. In *Task force report: Juvenile delinquency and youth crime*. Washington, D.C.: U.S. Govt. Printing Office, 1967.

Flacks, R. Adaptations of deviants in a college community. Doctoral dissertation, University of Michigan, 1963.

Florida Division of Corrections. *Fifth Biennial Report*. Tallahassee: Florida Division of Corrections, 1966.

Frankino, S. P. The manacles and messenger: A short study in religious freedom in the prison community. *The Catholic University of*

America Law Review, 1965, *15*, 30-66.

French, P. The minister and the delinquent. *Journal of Religion and Health*, 1964, *3*, 271-74.

Freud, S. *Civilization and its discontents*. In *Standard edition of the complete psychological works*, vol. 21, translated and edited by J. Strachey. 1929. Reprint ed. London: Hogarth, 1961.

Freud, S. *The future of an illusion*. In *Standard edition of the complete psychological works*, vol. 21, translated and edited by J. Strachey. 1928. Reprint ed. London: Hogarth, 1961.

Frymier, J. R. Relationship between church attendance and authoritarianism. *Religious Education*, 1959, *54*, 369-71.

Fukuyama, Y. The major dimensions of church membership. Doctoral dissertation, University of Chicago Divinity School, 1960.

Galin, D., and Ornstein, R. W. Lateral specialization of cognitive mode: An EEG study. *Psychophysiology*, 1972, *9*, 412-18.

Gallup, G. Worship practices of public measured. *Cleveland Press*, Feb. 8, 1964.

Gannon, T. M. Religious attitude and behavior changes of institutionalized delinquents. *Sociological Analysis*, 1967, *28*, 215-25. (a)

Gannon, T. M. Religious control and delinquent behavior. *Sociology and Social Research*, 1967, *51*, 418-31. (b)

Garfield, S. L., Prager, R. A., and Bergin, A. E. Evaluation of outcome in psychotherapy. *Journal of Consulting and Clinical Psychology*, 1971, *37*, 307-13.

Gerkin, V. The pastor and parents of delinquent children. *Pastoral Psychology*, 1955, *6*, 8-13.

Gilbert, A. R. Projective cross-examination. *Journal of Psychology*, 1946, *42*, 105-32.

Gilbert, A. R. Self-validation as projective testing. *Journal of Psychology*, 1958, *46*, 203-9.

Gilbert, A. R. The other person: How we "intend" it. *Journal of Psychology*, 1961, *51*, 247-62.

Gilbert, A. R. Toward an automated technique of probing into emotional blocks. *Journal of Psychology*, 1963, *56*, 385-404.

Gill, M. M., and Brenman, M. *Hypnosis and related states: Psychoanalytic studies in regression*. New York: International Universities, 1959.

Glick, O. W., and Jackson, J. M. A longitudinal study of behavior norms and some of their ramifications in a small liberal arts college. Paper presented at the annual meeting of the American Psychological Association, Washington, D. C., 1967.

Glock, C. Y. *Toward a typology of religious orientation*. New York: Columbia University Bureau of Applied Social Research, 1954.

Glock, C. Y. The religious revival in America? In *Religion and the face of America*, edited by Jane Zahn. Berkeley and Los Angeles: University of California Press, 1959.

Glock, C. Y. On the study of religious commitment: Review of recent research bearing on religious and character formation. Supplement to *Religious Education* (Jul.-Aug. 1962). New York: Religious Research Association, 1962.

Glock, C. Y., Ringer, B. R., and Babble, E. R. *To comfort and to challenge*. Berkeley and Los Angeles: University of California Press, 1967.

Glock, C. Y., and Stark, R. *Christian beliefs and anti-Semitism*. New York: Harper and Row, 1966.

Glueck, S., and Glueck, E. *Unraveling juvenile delinquency*. Cambridge, Mass.: Harvard University Press, 1950.

Goddard, E., ed. *A Buddhist bible*. 2nd ed. Thetford, Vt.: Dwight Goddard, 1938.

Goff, D. H. Background paper on narcotic addiction. *Journal of Pastoral Care*, 1964, *18*, 71-76.

Goldman, R. *Religious thinking from childhood to adolescence*. New York: Seabury, 1968.

Goldscheider, C., and Simpson, J. E. Religious affiliation and juvenile delinquency. *Sociological Inquiry*, 1967, *37*, 297-310.

Gordon, J. H. Value differences between freshmen and seniors at a state university. *College Student Survey*, 1967, *1*, 69-70, 92.

Gorsuch, R. L. The conceptualization of God as seen in adjective ratings. *Journal for the Scientific Study of Religion*, 1968, *7*, 56-64.

Green, W. *Sociology*. 3rd ed. New York: McGraw-Hill, 1960.

Gustaitis, R. *Turning on*. New York: New American Library, 1969.

Hall, R. M. Religious beliefs and social values of Syracuse University freshmen and seniors, 1950. Doctoral dissertation, Syracuse University, 1951.

Hammond, P. E. Aging and the ministry. In *Aging and Society*, edited by M. W. Riley, J. W. Riley, Jr., and M. E. Johnson. New York: Russell Sage Foundation, 1969. Vol. 2, *Aging and the professions*.

Hansen, E.; Bird, F.; Forrester, M.; and Des Marais, V. J., Jr. *The white ghetto: Youth and young adults in the Tenderloin area of downtown San Francisco*. San Francisco: Inner-City Methodist Churches of San Francisco, 1966.

Hargraves, J. Preventing juvenile delinquency: The role of the church. *Social Action*, 1959, *26*, 18-25.

Hartmann, H. *Ego psychology and the problem of adaptation.* Translated by D. Rapaport. New York: International Universities, 1958.

Hartshorne, H., and May, M. A. *Studies in the nature of character.* Vol. 1, *Studies in deceit.* New York: Macmillan, 1928.

Hassenger, R. The impact of a value-oriented college on the religious orientations of students with various backgrounds, traits, and college exposures. Doctoral dissertation, University of Chicago, 1965.

Hassenger, R. Catholic college impact on religious orientations. *Sociological Analysis*, 1966, *27*, 67-79.

Havens, J. A study of religious conflict in college students. *Journal of Social Psychology*, 1964, *64*, 77-87.

Heath, D. H. *Growing up in college: Liberal education and maturity.* San Francisco: Jossey-Bass, 1968.

Henderson, L. J. *The fitness of the environment: An inquiry into the biological significance of the properties of matter.* Boston: Beacon, 1958.

Hills, C. G. N. Teacher trainees and authoritarian attitudes. *Australian Journal of Psychology*, 1959, *11*, 171-81.

Hiltner, S., and Colston, L. G. *The context of pastoral counseling.* New York: Abingdon, 1961.

Hilton, T. L., and Korn, J. H. Measured change in personal values. *Educational and Psychological Measurement*, 1964, *241*, 609-22.

Hites, R. W. Change in religious attitudes during four years of college. *Journal of Social Psychology*, 1965, *66*, 51-63.

Hood, R. W., Jr. Religious orientation and the report of religious experience. *Journal for the Scientific Study of Religion*, 1970, *9*, 285-91.

Hood, R. W., Jr. A comparison of the Allport and Feagin scoring procedures for intrinsic-extrinsic religious orientation. *Journal for the Scientific Study of Religion*, 1971, *10*, 370-74.

Hood, R. W., Jr. Normative and motivational determinants of reported religious experience in two Baptist samples. *Review of Religious Research*, 1972, *13*, 192-96. (a)

Hood, R. W., Jr. Religious orientation and the experience of transcendence. Paper presented at the Southeastern Psychological Association, Atlanta, Georgia, 1972. (b)

Hood, R. W., Jr. Forms of religious commitment and intense religious experience. *Review of Religious Research*, 1973, *15*, 29-36. (a)

Hood, R. W., Jr. Religious orientation and the experience of transcendence. *Journal for the Scientific Study of Religion*, 1973, *12*, 441-48.

(b)

Hood, R. W., Jr. Psychological strength and the report of intense religious experience. *Journal for the Scientific Study of Religion*, 1974, *13*, 65-71.

Hunt, M. P., and Metcalf, L. E. *Teaching high school social studies*. New York: Harper and Row, 1968.

Hunt, R. A. A computer procedure for item scale analysis. *Educational and Psychological Measurement*, 1970, *30*, 133-35.

Hunt, R. A., and King, M. B. The intrinsic-extrinsic concept: A review and evaluation. *Journal for the Scientific Study of Religion*, 1971, *10*, 339-56.

Huntley, C. W. Changes in *Study of Values* scores during the four years of college. *Genetic Psychology Monographs*, 1965, *71*, 349-83.

Jacob, P. E. *Changing values in college: An exploratory study of the impact of college teaching*. New York: Harper, 1957.

James, J. T. L. Philosophy, theology, and the correctional process. *Canadian Journal of Corrections*, 1967, *9*, 147-51.

James, W. *Varieties of religious experience*. New York: Longmans, 1902.

Johnson, E. H. *Crime, correction, and society*. Homewood, Ill.: Dorsey, 1968.

Johnson, P. E. *Psychology of religion*. Rev. ed. New York: Abingdon, 1959.

Jones, M. B. Religious values and authoritarian tendency. *Journal of Social Psychology*, 1958, *48*, 83-89.

Kandle, C., and Cassler, H. H. *Ministering to prisoners and their families*. Englewood Cliffs, N.J.: Prentice-Hall, 1968.

Kannwisher, A. E. The role of the Protestant chaplain in correctional institutions. *American Journal of Correction*, 1957, *19*, 29.

Kaplan, A. *The conduct of inquiry*. San Francisco: Chandler, 1964.

Kasamatsu, A., and Hirai, T. Science of Zazen. *Psychologia*, 1963, *6*, 86-91.

Katz, J. A portrait of two classes: The undergraduate students at Berkeley and Stanford from entrance to exit. In *Growth and constraint in college students: A study of the varieties of psychological development*, edited by J. Katz. H.E.W. proj. no. 5-0799. Stanford, Cal.: Stanford University Institute for the Study of Human Problems, 1967.

Katz, J., et al. *No time for youth: Growth and constraint in college students*. San Francisco: Jossey-Bass, 1968.

Keene, J. E. Religious behavior and neuroticism, spontaneity, and world-mindedness. *Sociometry*, 1967, *30*, 137-57.

King, M. B. Measuring the religious variable: Nine proposed dimensions. *Journal for the Scientific Study of Religion*, 1967, *6*, 173-90.

King, M. B., and Hunt, R. A. Measuring the religious variable: Amended findings. *Journal for the Scientific Study of Religion*, 1969, *8*, 321-23.

King, M. B., and Hunt, R. A. *Measuring religious dimensions: Studies of congregational involvement.* S.M.U. Studies in Social Science, no. 1. Dallas: Southern Methodist University Press, 1972.

King, M. B., and Hunt, R. A. Measuring the religious variable: National replication. *Journal for the Scientific Study of Religion*, 1975, *14*, 13-22.

King, S. H. Personality stability: Early findings of the Harvard Student Study. Paper presented at the annual meeting of the American College Personnel Association, 1967.

Kirkpatrick, A. M. The church in corrections. *Canadian Journal of Corrections*, 1965, *7*, 173-77.

Klingelhofer, E. L. Studies of the General Education Program at Sacramento State College. *Technical Bulletin no. 14*. Sacramento: Sacramento State College Student Personnel Services, 1965.

Knowles, D. *The English mystical tradition.* London: Burns and Oates, 1961.

Krasner, W. Hoodlum priest and respectable convicts. *Harper's*, 1961, *222*, 57-62.

Krulee, G. K., O'Keefe, R., and Goldberg, M. Influence of identity processes on student behavior and occupational choice. H.E.W. proj. no. 5-0809. Evanston: Northwestern University Press, 1966.

Kuether, W. Religion and the chaplain. In *Contemporary correction*, edited by P. W. Tappan. New York: McGraw-Hill, 1951.

Kuhlmann, F. L. Communications to clergymen—when are they privileged? *Valparaiso University Law Review*, 1968, *2*, 265-95.

Kvaraceus, W. C. *The community and the delinquent.* Tarrytown-on-Hudson, N.Y.: World Book, 1954.

Laski, M. *Ecstasy: A study of some secular and religious experiences.* London: Cresset, 1961.

Lazerwitz, B. Some factors associated with variations in church attendance. *Social Forces*, 1961, *39*, 301-9.

Lazerwitz, B. Membership in voluntary associations and frequency of church attendance. *Journal for the Scientific Study of Religion*, 1962, *2*, 74-84.

Leary, T. The religious experience: Its production and interpretation. *Psychedelic Review*, 1964, *1*, 324-46.

Lederer, W. Dragons, delinquents, and destiny: An essay on positive superego frustrations. *Psychological Issues*, 1964, *4* (3). Monograph no. 15.

Lee, J. *A short history of the Methodists in the United States of America*. Baltimore: Magill and Cline, 1810.

Lehmann, I. J., and Dressel, P. L. Critical thinking, attitudes, and values in higher education. H.E.W. Coop. Res. proj. no. 590. East Lansing: Michigan State University Press, 1962.

Lenski, G. *The religious factor*. Rev. ed. Garden City, N.Y.: Doubleday, 1963.

Leuba, J. H. A study in the psychology of religious phenomena. *American Journal of Psychology*, 1896, 7, 309-85.

Leuba, J. H. *A psychological study of religion: Its origin, function, and future*. New York: Macmillan, 1912.

Levinson, D. J. Symposium review. *American Sociological Review*, 1967, *32*, 1009-13.

Levitsky, A. The rules and games of gestalt therapy. Mimeographed paper, 1969.

Levy-Agresti, J., and Sperry, R. Differential perceptual capacities in major and minor hemispheres. *Proceedings of the National Academy of Sciences*, 1968, *61*, 1151.

Lewis, H. R., and Streitfeld, A. S. *Growth games*. New York: Harcourt, Brace, Jovanovich, 1970.

Ligon, E. M., and O'Brien, M. The method of characteristic differences. *Religious Education*, 1954, *49*, 284-90.

Lindenthal, J. J.; Myers, J. K.; Pepper, M. P.; and Stern, M. S. Mental status and religious behavior. *Journal for the Scientific Study of Religion*, 1970, *9*, 143-49.

Lindzey, G., and Urdan, J. A. Personality and social choice. *Sociometry*, 1954, *17*, 47-63.

Loewald, H. W. Ego and reality. *International Journal of Psychoanalysis*, 1951, *32*, 10-18.

Long, D., Elkind, D., and Spilka, B. The child's conception of prayer. *Journal for the Scientific Study of Religion*, 1967, *6*, 101-9.

Loukes, H. *Teenage religion*. London: SCM Press, 1961.

Lozoff, M. M. Personality differences and residential choice. In *Growth and constraint in college students: A study of the varieties of psychological development*, edited by J. Katz. H.E.W. proj. no. 5-0799. Stanford, Cal.: Stanford University Institute for the Study of Human Problems, 1967.

Luckmann, T. *The invisible religion: The problem of religion in modern society.* New York: Macmillan, 1967.

Ludwig, E. C., and Eichorn, R. L. Age and disillusionment: A study of value changes associated with aging. *Journal of Gerontology,* 1967, *22,* 59-65.

MacNaughton, W. S. Comparative profiles of emergent value patterns in undergraduate life at Dartmouth: A summary report on selected data from the class of 1965 study of student attitudes. Hanover, N. H.: Dartmouth College, 1966.

Martin, D., and Wrightsman, L. S., Jr. Religion and fears about death: A critical review of research. *Religious Education,* 1964, *59,* 174-76.

Martin, D., and Wrightsman, L. S., Jr. The relationship between religious behavior and concern about death. *Journal of Social Psychology,* 1965, *65,* 317-23.

Marx, T. Religion: Opiate or inspiration of civil rights militancy among Negroes? *American Sociological Review,* 1967, *32,* 64-72.

Maslow, A. *Religions, values, and peak experiences.* New York: Viking, 1964.

Maslow, A. Synanon and eupsychia. *Journal of Humanistic Psychology,* Spring 1967, pp. 28-35.

Masters, R. E. L., and Houston, J. *The varieties of psychedelic experience.* New York: Holt, Rinehart, and Winston, 1966.

Maxey, D. R. Swinging prison priest. *Look,* December 29, 1964, pp. 24-29.

McCann, R. V. The self-image and delinquency: Some implications for religion. *Federal Probation,* 1956, *20,* 14-23.

McCleery, R. H. Authoritarianism and the belief system of incorrigibles. In *The Prison,* edited by D. R. Cressey. New York: Holt, Rinehart, and Winston, 1961.

McConahay, J. B., Jr., and Hough, J. C., Jr. Love and guilt oriented dimensions of religious belief. Paper read at the annual meeting of the Society for the Scientific Study of Religion, Boston, 1969.

McCord, J., and McCord, W. A follow-up report on the Cambridge-Somerville youth study. *The Annals of the American Academy of Political and Social Science,* 1959, *332,* 89-96.

McGreevey, M. V. The aged Catholics in two cities: A comparative analysis of social factors and the theory of disengagement. (Doctoral dissertation, University of Notre Dame.) *Dissertation Abstracts,* 1966, *27* (4A), 1122.

McMahon, J. F. The work of the Volunteers of America in the field of corrections. *American Journal of Correction,* 1963, *25,* 24-29.

Middendorf, W. The criminality of religious sects. *Acta Criminologiae et Medicinae Legalis Japonica*, 1965, *31*, 1-8.

Miller, E. O. Nonacademic changes in college students. *Educational Record*, 1959, *40*, 118-22.

Mintz, E. Time-extended marathon groups. *Psychotherapy*, 1967, *4* (2), 65-70.

Mitchell, P. H. An evaluation of the relationships of values to sociometric choice. Doctoral dissertation, University of Michigan, 1951.

Moberg, D. O. Church membership and personal adjustment in old age. *Journal of Gerontology*, 1953, *8*, 207-11. (a)

Moberg, D. O. Religion and personal adjustment in old age: A study of some aspects of the Christian religion in relation to personal adjustment of the aged in institutions. *Religious Education*, 1953, *48*, 184-85. (b)

Moberg, D. O. Religious activities and personal adjustment in old age. *Journal of Social Psychology*, 1956, *43*, 261-68.

Moberg, D. O. The integration of older members in the church congregation. In *Older people and their social world: The subculture of aging*, edited by A. M. Rose and W. A. Peterson. Philadelphia: Davis, 1965. (a)

Moberg, D. O. Religion in old age. *Geriatrics*, 1965, *20*, 977-82. (b)

Moberg, D. O. Religiosity and old age. *Gerontologist*, 1965, *5*, 78-87. (c)

Moberg, D. O., and Taves, M. J. Church participation and adjustment in old age. In *Older people and their social world: The subculture of the aging*, edited by A. M. Rose and W. A. Peterson. Philadelphia: Davis, 1965.

Monaghan, R. R. Three faces of the true believer: Motivations for attending a fundamentalist church. *Journal for the Scientific Study of Religion*, 1967, *6*, 236-45.

Moreton, F. E. Attitudes to religion among adolescents and adults. *British Journal of Educational Psychology*, 1944, *14*, 68-79.

Morgenstern, J.; Gussow, M.; Woodward, K. L.; and Russin, J. M. Campus '65: The college generation looks at itself and the world around it. *Time*, March 22, 1965, pp. 43-63.

Morris, A. *What's new in the work of the church and the chaplain in correctional institutions?* Boston: United Prison Association of Massachusetts, 1961.

Mowrer, O. H. Is the small-group movement a religious revolution? *Voices*, 1971, *7*, 17ff.

Murray, H. A. *Thematic apperception test*. Cambridge: Harvard University, 1943.

Myers, C. *Light the dark streets*. Greenwich, Conn.: Seabury, 1957.

National Training Laboratories. Objectives of human relations training. Washington, D.C.: National Training Laboratories, 1968.

Nelson, E. N. P. Patterns of religious attitude shifts from college to fourteen years later. *Psychological Monographs*, 1956, *70* (No. 17). Whole no. 424.

Newcomb, T. M. *The acquaintance process*. New York: Holt, 1961.

Newcomb, T. M., Koenig, K. E., Flacks, R., and Warwick, D. P. *Persistence and change: Bennington College and its students after twenty-five years*. New York: Wiley, 1967.

Newstead, R. Advice to one who meets in class. New York: Lane and Sanford, 1843.

Nunnally, J. *Psychometric theory*. New York: McGraw-Hill, 1967.

Nussey, J. B. Crime: A concern of the church. *Concern*, 1963, *5*, 13.

Oden, T. C. *Kerygma and counseling*. Philadelphia: Westminster, 1966.

Oden, T. C. *Contemporary theology and psychotherapy*. Philadelphia: Westminster, 1967.

Oden, T. C. *The structure of awareness*. Nashville: Abingdon, 1969.

Orbach, H. L. Aging and religion. *Geriatrics*, 1961, *16*, 530-40.

O'Reilly, C. T. Religious practice and personal adjustments of older people. *Sociology and Social Research*, 1957, *43*, 119-21.

Ornstein, R. E. *The psychology of consciousness*. San Francisco: Freeman, 1972.

Ornstein, R. E. Right and left thinking. *Psychology Today*, May 1973, pp. 86-92.

Owens, C. M. The mystical experience: Facts and values. In *The highest state of consciousness*, edited by J. White. Garden City, N.Y.: Doubleday, Anchor Books, 1972.

Pahnke, W. N. Drugs and mysticism: An analysis of the relationship between psychedelic drugs and mystical consciousness. Doctoral dissertation, Harvard University, 1963.

Pahnke, W. N. Drugs and mysticism. *International Journal of Parapsychology*, 1966, *8*, 295-315.

Pahnke, W. N., and Richards, W. A. Implications of LSD and experimental mysticism, *Journal of Religion and Health*, 1966, *5*, 175-208.

Pan, J. S. Personal adjustments of old people: A study of old people in Protestant church homes for the aged. *Sociology and Social Research*, 1950, *34*, 3-11.

Perls, F. *Gestalt therapy verbatim*. Lafayette, Cal.: Real People, 1969.

Perls, F., Hefferline, R., and Goodman, P. *Gestalt therapy*. New York:

Dell, 1951.

Peterson, D. Scope and generality of verbally defined personality factors. *Psychological Review*, 1965, 72, 48-59.

Pittard, B. B., and Payne, R. Religious factors in the situations of misdemeanant offenders, four metropolitan counties, 1965-67. Paper presented at the annual meeting of the Religious Research Association, Chicago, 1970.

Plant, W. T. Personality changes associated with a college education. H.E.W. Coop. Res. Branch proj. no. 348. San Jose, Cal.: San Jose State College Press, 1962.

Plant, W. T. Longitudinal changes in intolerance and authoritarianism for subjects differing in amount of college education over four years. *Genetic Psychology Monographs*, 1965, 72, 247-87.

Plant, W. T., and Telford, G. W. Changes in personality for groups completing different amount of college over two years. *Genetic Psychology Monographs*, 1966, 74, 3-36.

Poblete, R., and O'Dea, T. F. Anomie and the quest for community: The formation of sects among the Puerto Ricans in New York. *American Catholic Sociological Review*, 1960, 21, 18-36.

Prince, R., and Savage, C. Mystical states and the concept of regression. In *The highest state of consciousness*, edited by J. White. Garden City, N.Y.: Doubleday, Anchor Books, 1972.

Putney, S., and Middleton, R. Rebellion, conformity and parental religious ideologies. *Sociometry*, 1961, 24, 125-35.

Ramshaw, W. C. Religious participation and the fact of religious ideology on a resident and a nonresident college campus: An exploratory study. Doctoral dissertation, University of Illinois, 1966.

Rapaport, D. The autonomy of the ego. *Bulletin of the Menninger Clinic*, 1951, 15, 113-23.

Rector, M. G. Bridge to the community. *Concern*, 1966, 8, 4-5.

Regimbal, J-P. Pastorale et criminologie. *Bulletin, Society de Criminologie du Quebec*, 1964, 31, 19-27.

Reifsnyder, W. E., and Campbell, E. I. *Religious attitudes of male neuropsychiatric patients: II. Comparison of responses of patients and non-patients. Journal of Pastoral Care*, 1960, 14, 150-59.

Reilly, M. St. A., Comins, W. D., and Stefic, E. G. The complementarity of personality needs in friendship choice. *Journal of Abnormal and Social Psychology*, 1960, 61, 292-94.

Religious News Service. Delinquency in the churches. *City Church*, 1957, 8, 15.

Remmers, H. H., and Radler, D. H. *The American teenager*. New

York: Bobbs-Merrill, 1957.

Riley, M. W., and Foner, A. *Aging and society*. New York: Russell Sage Foundation, 1968. Vol. 1, *An inventory of research findings*.

Roberts, G. L. The religious attitudes and backgrounds of one hundred and fifty Protestant juvenile delinquents. Doctoral dissertation, University of Pittsburgh, 1953.

Rogers, C. R. *Carl Rogers on encounter groups*. New York: Harper and Row, 1970.

Rokeach, M. *The open and closed mind*. New York: Basic Books, 1960.

Rosen, B. C. *Adolescence and religion: The Jewish teenager in American society*. Cambridge, Mass.: Schenkman, 1965.

Ross, M. G. *Religious beliefs of youth*. New York: Association Press, 1950.

Rosser, L. *Class meetings*. Richmond, Va.: The author, 1855.

Ruitenbeek, H. M. *The new group therapies*. New York: Avon, 1970.

Sargant, W. *Battle for the mind*. London: Pan Books, 1957.

Schafer, R. The loving and beloved superego in Freud's structural theory. *The Psychoanalytic Study of the Child*, 1960, *15*, 163-88.

Schafer, R. Introduction to Lederer's monograph. *Psychological Issues*, 1964, *4* (3). Monograph no. 15.

Schneider, K. A. Selected correlates of religious involvement and their implications for teaching scientific materials. Master's thesis, University of Georgia, 1966.

Schutz, W. C. *Joy*. New York: Grove, 1967.

Schutz, W. C. *Here comes everybody*. New York: Harper and Row, 1971.

Scott, W. A. *Values and organizations: A study of fraternities and sororities*. Chicago: Rand McNally, 1965.

Seashore, C. What is sensitivity training? *NTL Institute News and Reports*, April, 1968.

Selznick, G. J., and Steinberg, S. *The tenacity of prejudice*. New York: Harper and Row, 1969.

Semmes, J. Hemispheric specialization: A possible clue to mechanism. *Neuropsychologia*, 1968, *6*, 11-16.

Shapiro, D. A perceptual understanding of color response. In *Rorschach psychology*, edited by Maria A. Rickers-Ovsiankina. New York: Wiley, 1960.

Shaw, M., and Wright, J. *Scales for the measurement of attitudes*. New York: McGraw-Hill, 1967.

Sherwood, J. N., Stolaroff, M. J., and Harman, W. W. The psychedelic experience—a new concept in psychotherapy. *Journal of Neuro-psychiatry*, 1962, *4*, 69-80.

Siegman, A. W. A cross-cultural investigation of the relationship between religiosity, ethnic prejudice and authoritarianism. *Psychological Reports*, 1962, *11*, 419-24.

Sinclair, G., Jr. The religious attitudes of forty institutionalized Protestant girls with implications for Christian education: A comparative study. Valley Forge, Pa.: American Baptist Convention, 1964.

Skager, R., Holland, J. L., and Braskamp, L. A. Changes in self-ratings and life goals among students at colleges with different characteristics. *ACT Research Reports*. No. 14. Iowa City: American College Testing Program, 1966.

Smith, P. M. Organized religion and criminal behavior. *Sociology and Social Research*, 1949, *33*, 262-67.

Smith, P. M. The role of the church in delinquency prevention. *Sociology and Social Research*, 1951, *35*, 183-90.

Spady, W. G., Jr. Peer integration and academic success. Doctoral dissertation, University of Chicago, 1967.

Sperry, R. W. The great cerebral commissure. *Scientific American*, July 1964, pp. 42-52.

Spilka, B., Armatas, P., and Nussbaum, J. The concept of God: A factor analytic approach. *Review of Religious Research*, 1964, *6*, 28-36.

Spoerl, D. T. The values of the post-war college student. *Journal of Social Psychology*, 1952, *35*, 217-22.

Srole, L.; Langer, T. S.; Michael, S. T.; Opler, M. K.; and Rennie, T. A. C. *Mental health in the metropolis: The midtown Manhattan study*. Vol. 1. New York: McGraw-Hill, 1962.

Stace, W. T. *Mysticism and philosophy*. Philadelphia: Lippincott, 1960.

Starbuck, E. D. *The psychology of religion*. London: Walter Scott, 1899.

Stark, R. Age and faith: A changing outlook or an old process? *Sociological Analysis*, 1968, *29*, 1-10.

Stark, R. Psychopathology and religious commitment. *Review of Religious Research*, 1971, *12*, 165-76.

Stark, R., and Glock, C. *American piety: The nature of religious commitment*. Berkeley and Los Angeles: University of California Press, 1968.

Stere, P. J. The Lutheran church and the needs of the aged: A survey of the attitudes of members of the Susquehanna region, Central Pennsylvania Synod. Williamsport, Pa.: Lycoming College Dept. of Sociology and Anthropology, 1966.

Stewart, L. H. Change in personality test scores during college. *Journal of Counseling Psychology*, 1964, *11*, 211-30.

Strickland, B. R., and Shaffer, S. I-E, I-E, & F. *Journal for the Scientific Study of Religion*, 1971, *10*, 366-69.

Strommen, M. P., ed. *Research on religious development: A comprehensive handbook*. New York: Hawthorne, 1971.

Strunk, O., Jr., ed. *Readings in the psychology of religion*. Nashville: Abingdon, 1959.

Suzuki, D. T. *Zen and Japanese culture*. London: Routledge and Kegan Paul, 1959.

Tapp, J. An examination of hypotheses concerning the motivation components of attitude. Master's thesis, University of Illinois, 1957.

Tart, Charles T., ed. *Transpersonal psychologies*. New York: Harper and Row, 1975.

Telford, C. W., and Plant, W. T. The psychological impact of the public two year college on certain non-intellectual functions. H.E.W. Coop. Res. Branch proj. no. SAE 8646. San Jose, Cal.: San Jose State College Press, 1963.

Templar, D. I., and Dotson, E. Religious correlates of death anxiety. *Psychological Reports*, 1970, *26*, 895-97.

Thompson, R. W. Value changes among Macalester College students: 1947 to 1951. Master's thesis, University of Chicago, 1960.

Thurstone, L. L., and Chave, E. J. *The measurement of attitude*. Chicago: University of Chicago Press, 1929.

Tisdale, J. R. Value patterns in three midwest colleges. *Proceedings of the Iowa Academy of Science*, 1965, *72*, 389-95.

Tisdale, J. R. Selected correlates of extrinsic religious values. *Review of Religious Research*, 1966, *7*, 78-84.

Tisdale, J. R. Checking inter-judge reliability in the method of characteristic differences. *Union College Character Research Project Report*. No. D-67-46. Schenectady, N.Y.: Union College Character Research Project, 1967. (a)

Tisdale, J. R. Decision-making skills reflected in Wayland examination questions. *Union College Character Research Project Report*. No. D-67-9. Schenectady, N.Y.: Union College Character Research Project, 1967. (b)

Tisdale, J. R. The selection of college majors. *The Journal of Educational Research*, 1967, *60*, 90-91. (c)

Tisdale, J. R. Pastoral counseling, counseling, and research. *Journal of*

Pastoral Care, 1967, *21*, 1-7. (d)

Tisdale, J. R. Client religious responses. *Pastoral Institute of the Lehigh Valley Research Report*. No. 2. Bethlehem, Pa.: Pastoral Institute of the Lehigh Valley, 1970.

Trent, J. W. The development of intellectual disposition within Catholic colleges. Doctoral dissertation, University of California, Berkeley, 1964.

Trent, J. W. *Catholics in college: Religious commitment and the intellectual life*. Chicago: University of Chicago Press, 1967.

Trent, J. W., and Medsker, I. L. *Beyond high school: A psychological study of 10,000 high school graduates*. San Francisco: Jossey-Bass, 1968.

Twomey, A. E. A study of values of a select group of undergraduate students. Doctoral dissertation, Colorado State College, 1962.

Tyler, F. T. A four-year study of personality traits and values of a group of National Merit Scholars and Certificate of Merit recipients. Berkeley: University of California Center for the Study of Higher Education, 1963.

Underhill, Evelyn. *Mysticism*. 1911. Rev. ed. New York: Dutton, 1930.

Vanecko, J. J. Religious behavior and prejudice: Some dimensions and specifications of the relationship. *Review of Religious Research*, 1966, *8*, 27-37.

Van Etten, H. Prisons and prisoners. In *The Quaker approach*, edited by John Kavanaugh. New York: Putnam's, 1953.

von Senden, M. *Space and sight*. Glencoe, Ill.: Free Press, 1960.

Warren, J. R., and Heist, P. A. Personality attributes of gifted college students. *Science*, 1960, *132*, 330-37.

Wattenburg, W. W. Church attendance and juvenile misconduct. *Sociology and Social Research*, 1950, *34*, 195-202.

Watts, A. *Psychotherapy East and West*. New York: Pantheon, 1961.

Webb, R., and Webb, M. *The churches and juvenile delinquency*. New York: Association Press, 1957. (a)

Webb, R., and Webb, M. How churches can help in the prevention and treatment of juvenile delinquency. *Federal Probation*, 1957, *21*, 22-25. (b)

Webster, H. Changes in attitudes during college. *Journal of Educational Psychology*, 1958, *49*, 109-17.

Webster, H., Freedman, M. B., and Heist, P. Personality changes in college students. In *The American college: A psychological and social interpretation of the higher learning*, edited by N. Sanford.

New York: Wiley, 1962.

Werner, H. *Comparative psychology of mental development*. New York: International Universities, 1957.

Wesley, C. All praise to our redeeming Lord. In *The Methodist Hymnal*. Nashville: Methodist Publishing House, 1964.

Wesley, J. *The works of John Wesley*. Vol. 5. Edited by J. Emery. New York: Lance and Scott, 1850.

Wesley, J. *The letters of the Rev. John Wesley*. 8 vols. Edited by J. Telford. London: Epworth, 1931.

Wesley, J. *Journal*. 8 vols. Edited by N. Curnock. London: Epworth, 1938.

Wesley, J. Rules of the bands. In *John Wesley*, edited by A. Outler. New York: Oxford, 1967.

West, J. V. Characteristics and changes in the 1961 class, Baylor University. In *Design and methodology in institutional research: Proceedings of the Fifth Annual National Institutional Research Forum*, edited by C. H. Bagley. Pullman, Wash.: Washington State University Office of Institutional Research, 1965

West, S. G. The crisis in correctional chaplaincy. *Canadian Journal of Corrections*, 1968, *10*, 327-31.

Whitam, F. L. Subdimensions of religiosity and race prejudice. *Review of Religious Research*, 1962, *3*, 166-74.

Wilensky, H. L. Life cycle, work situation, and participation in formal associations. In *Aging and leisure*, edited by R. W. Kleemeier. New York: Oxford University Press, 1961.

Williams, R. L., and Cole, S. Religiosity, generalized anxiety, and apprehension concerning death. *Journal of Social Psychology*, 1968, *75*, 111-18.

Wilson, W. C. Extrinsic religious values and prejudice. *Journal of Abnormal and Social Psychology*, 1960, *60*, 286-88.

Wingrove, C. R., and Alston, J. P. Age, aging, and church attendance. *Gerontologist*, 1971, *11*, 356-58.

Yinger, J. M. *The scientific study of religion*. New York: Macmillan, 1970.

Young, R. K., Dustin, D. S., and Holtzman, W. H. Change in attitude toward religion in a Southern university. *Psychological Reports*, 1966, *18*, 39-46.

Zinn, E. He begged that gang violence end with his death. *Federal Probation*, 1959, *23*, 24-30.

Index